SOUND RECORDING ADVICE

An instruction and reference manual
that demystifies the
home recording studio experience

John J. Volanski

Second Edition

Pacific Beach Publishing San Diego, California

SOUND RECORDING ADVICE
An instruction and reference manual
that demystifies the
home recording studio experience
John J. Volanski

Published by:
Pacific Beach Publishing
Post Office Box 90471
San Diego, CA 92169 USA
http://www.soundrecordingadvice.com
soundadvice@johnvolanski.com: *Email me for updates!*

ISBN, print ed.   0-972138-0-7
1st Printing 2003; 2nd Printing 2006
Printed in the United States of America

Library of Congress Cataloging-in-Publication Data
Volanski, John J.
Sound Recording Advice: An instruction and reference
 manual that demystifies the home recording studio
experience/John J. Volanski
—   2nd edition
Includes bibliographical references and index.
1. Sound. 2. Recording. 3. Audio. 4. Home Studio.
5. Project Studio 6. Music. 7.Acoustics 8. Mixing
9. Microphone 10. Recorders 11. MIDI 12. Miking
Instruments 13. Tape Deck 14. Analog 15. Digital
ISBN 0-9721383-0-7
LCCN 2002107138

Dedicated to my lovely wife Christie

Contents

ABOUT THE AUTHOR

John Volanski initially became interested in recording audio back in the 1960s when his father first purchased a 4-track reel/reel recorder with the sound-on-sound feature. Since that time, audio engineering and sound recording have always been a part of his personal and professional pursuits.

John is an electrical and audio engineer who has operated his own home recording studio for over 20 years. The text in this book gives his unique and simplified perspectives on the important aspects of home studio recording. He also enjoys writing, and has written articles for *Electronic Musician* magazine and *Avionics* magazine, along with other submissions to *AfterTouch* and *Keyboard* magazines. John has a MBA from National University and a BSEE from Ohio State University.

In his professional life as an electrical engineer, John has over 23 years of engineering design and management experience with successful product development of avionics simulator systems as well as work with Virtual Reality and systems using audio and video. He has held engineering design and engineering management jobs at General Dynamics, Ball Systems Engineering, and Cubic Defense Systems.

At GreyStone Technologies, John won a patent for his work on a motion based Virtual Reality machine.

As Senior Engineering Manager at the Video Systems Division of Sensormatic, John had the overall design and development responsibility for all embedded systems security and surveillance products, including the Integra DVDRAM Digital Time Lapse Video Recorder (which won the SIA Product of the Year award for CCTV for 2000).

As VP Engineering at Excelsus Technologies, John helped win the SIA New Product Showcase 2001 Product Achievement Award for False Alarm Reduction.

John's future plans include updating this book as more cool gear becomes available and pursuing his interests in audio engineering, electrical engineering and music.

PREFACE- A NOTE TO THE READER

Home recording studios have never been more popular than they are today. The prices on recording equipment have come way down into the realm of affordability, while the quality of audio at these price points has improved drastically. If you are interested in recording or making music, the time has never been better to establish a home recording studio.

I have derived much joy and satisfaction from my own home studio, even from its humble beginnings as a single synthesizer, an old 4-channel reel/reel tape deck and a cassette deck. My own home studio has been through a constant metamorphosis since the beginning. I have documented in this book many of the lessons I learned from my own home studio experiences.

Most of the material presented in this book is mainly applicable to home studios and project studios, but some of it can also be helpful to the musician on the road. Details will be somewhat light on the construction of circuits, such as soldering, mounting components, identifying component values, etc. If you are handy with a soldering iron and electrical/mechanical kit building, you might want to try some of the simple modifications or useful little devices detailed in the book. I certainly do not recommend hacking into your favorite piece of studio equipment if you do not know what you are doing!

There is not enough room in this or any one book to adequately discuss all of the areas and topics concerning sound recording and audio engineering. I highly recommend you seek other sources for additional or supplemental material on these subjects. Many of those sources are identified in this book. Also, you will actually need to read the owner's manuals for the equipment you have in your studio. No general book on recording can be a substitute for reading the detailed information contained in those owner's manuals.

John J. Volanski

ACKNOWLEDGMENTS

Writing a book requires quite a bit of time and effort. If you decide to write a book, take your estimate of the time required and multiply it times two. After you get that number, stare at it for a while and become comfortable with it. Now multiply that number again by two, and you will start to get close to how much time it really takes to write a book! In addition, it requires quite a few people to help you, because you certainly can't do it alone.

I would like to call to your attention the individuals who have made very important contributions to this book. Without the help and influence from these people, this book would not exist.

First of all, I would like to thank all of the teachers who have instructed me throughout the years. They are truly unsung heroes in America. As far as this book is concerned, two teachers really stand out. Dr. Robert Lackey of The Ohio State University provided much-welcomed audio engineering instruction. Also, many thanks to David W. Shaner who taught me how to right, er, write (under mutual duress, of course).

For this book, proofreading was provided by fellow engineer Kirk Gramcko, Theresa Freese (Tech Writer) and also by my wife Christie. Dave MacCormack provided technical advice on the quieting of computer systems. Pat Bockstahler of Future Graphx provided book layout advice and cover art. Thanks Pat! Very helpful publishing advice was provided by Larry Hagerty and Dan Poynter.

Sincere thanks to my parents Rita L. and John L. Volanski who have always given me positive encouragement and love since Day One. And many thanks to my father for originally piquing my interest in recording many years ago.

And immeasurable thanks to my precious wife Christie, who provided much love and support during the writing of this book. She is truly my better half.

Wherever possible, I have attempted to cite in this text all of the authorities and sources that I referenced in the creation of this book. Those references are at the end of each section.

I am very grateful to all of these excellent people for their direct or indirect contribution to this work.

WARNING- DISCLAIMER

This book has been written to provide information on the various elements of and the techniques used in a home studio or project studio. The author and Pacific Beach Publishing make no claims regarding the rendering of legal or accounting advice, service or assistance in connection with any home studio, project studio, or any other studio. If legal or accounting advice, service or assistance is required, then a professional competent in these areas should be sought.

The advice the author gives in this book has worked for <u>him</u>. If <u>you</u> buy a recommended item and end up not liking it, or you make a modification to your equipment that goes awry, the author takes no responsibility in any way (financially or otherwise) for the problem, nor will he replace or fix your equipment for you. Also, the landscape in cyberspace is constantly changing. The author has tried to give you up to the minute information in this book, but manufacturers, products and web sites constantly disappear to be replaced by new ones, and he has absolutely no control over that. So, if you find that a manufacturer or a web site he mentions in this book no longer exists, then that's just the way it is in today's cyberspace. The author and Pacific Beach Publishing shall have neither liability nor responsibility to any person or entity with respect to any loss or damage caused, or alleged to have been caused, directly or indirectly, by the information contained in this book.

The author would be writing here forever if he tried to cover <u>all</u> the topics concerning audio engineering, home studios, acoustics, power, grounding, synchronization, digital audio, analog audio, networking, noise, electronics, studio furniture, and the myriad other subjects that come into play when recording audio. This text is designed to be used in conjunction with other texts available to the reader. The author lists some of those texts in this book as additional references you can use.

Even though the author covers most all areas of importance to home recording, you should not expect to become rich and/or famous by following the advice in this book. This book does not cover marketing and selling the material you record. The book was written to inform and entertain you.

Every effort has been made to make the text, pictures and illustrations in this book free from error. However, errors and mistakes do occasionally show up, so use the information contained in this book only as a general guide to home and project studio recording. This book was written during 2002, so the information and references contained herein are only current up to that date.

If you do not wish to be bound by the above disclaimers, you may return this book in good shape to the publisher for a full refund.

INTRODUCTION

Over the last 25 years, I have devoted quite a bit of time and energy to assembling a home recording studio. In the course of building up my home studio and through my electrical engineering background, I've experienced a number of trials and tribulations that I can share with you to save you some time, money, headaches, or quite possibly all three. Much of the advice that I give in this book is based on various items that I have implemented in my own home studio. Some of the information is very simplified electrical or audio theory, and some of the information is just ideas and recommendations that you can try in your own studio. I realize that the major function of a home or project studio is to actually record audio, and it seems that most of the people who are involved with setting up their own home studios want to do exactly that, instead of wading through reams of information on audio theory and technical jargon. **In this book, I have made an effort to distill out all the peripheral information and just include the information that will allow a person to set up his or her own home studio to achieve the best results for the least amount of money.** In general, I will give recommendations for various levels of budgets starting out with "financially embarrassed" (and higher, in case you happen to win the lottery along the way), but the major emphasis in this text will be on the low-cost, do-it-yourself approach.

Most of the ideas here are targeted for people who too often find themselves at the short end of the budgetary stick. So, if you have a 480-channel Neve console and a vast array of digital multi-track recorders synced together, then this text is probably not going to help you very much. I'm not going to discuss how to demagnetize tape heads or give tips on analog tape deck maintenance, because there is already quite a bit of information available on those topics (and I will show you where to get this information for free on the Internet), but I am going to discuss some of the less obvious aspects of implementing a studio. I will focus on some timesavers and make some recommendations regarding inexpensive but effective equipment you can purchase. I will also recommend some equipment that is not so inexpensive, in case you have the budget to afford it. I will be covering such items as audio mixing and recording, studio layout and equipment, modifying your equipment and other miscellaneous tips. My belief is that the person intending to set up a home studio these days is more interested in focusing on making and recording music than becoming wrapped up in a mess of technical gibberish ("What does 128x Delta-Sigma sampling really mean, and how does that affect me?").

This book is organized into 5 main parts. Part 1 (Electronic Studio Equipment) discusses all of the various equipment and recording formats you might encounter in the home studio. Part 1 also discusses equipment I recommend to buy, recommended complete recording systems at various price points, and how to buy new or used equipment. Part 2 (Studio Layout and Furniture) discusses how acoustics affect sound in your studio, what furniture you can use to support the equipment in your studio, and how to remove noise from your studio and your recordings. Part 3 (Modifying Your Equipment) gives some simple ideas for adding to the functionality of the equipment you already have and building some simple but useful recording tools of your own. Part 4 (Capturing Sound Recordings) gives a mini-primer on the nature of sound and gives detailed instruction on the whole recording process from setting up microphones to mastering the final tracks. Part 5 (Tools, Advice and Miscellaneous) gives advice on tools and troubleshooting techniques, home studio security and insurance, plus over 25 other valuable tips relating to home studio operation.

I have made an attempt to simplify things and keep the traditional and technical audio and electrical engineering concepts out of this book; there are plenty of books out there dealing with the technical issues regarding home and project studios. Unfortunately, there really is no way to avoid all of those technical concepts entirely; some of the concepts are ones you really need to know. Also, I believe you will find that no one book covers it all, and I have not seen any books cover the inexpensive approach to home studio recording as this book does. If you need more information on some of the more traditional and technical issues associated with studios and recording audio than what is presented in this book, then I suggest that you buy some of these other books or check them out of your local library:

- Eargle, John, *Sound Recording*, Van Nostrand Reinhold Company, 1976. Some of the information in this book is dated, such as the information on cutting records, but most of the rest of the information presented is excellent. It is the textbook that Dr. Robert Lackey used at Ohio State University to supplement his audio engineering courses. Much of this book is technical.
- Anderton, Craig and Keating, Carol, *Digital Home Recording - Tips, Techniques, and Tools for Home Studio Production.* This book deals mainly with digital recording for the home studio. It is a distillation of the information from various magazine articles. Find it at Amazon.com.
- Anderton, Craig, *Craig Anderton's Home Recording for Musicians.* This is a good companion book to the above book, and functions as a basic tutorial for those new to home recording. Find it at Amazon.com.
- Newell, Philip, *Project Studios: A More Professional Approach.* This book covers many technical aspects of project studios. Find it at Amazon.com.
- Gibson, Bill, *Audiopro Home Recording Course: A Comprehensive Multimedia Audio Recording Text,* Mix Bookshelf, 1998. This is a good basic book for beginning or perhaps intermediate studio owners. It is a bit expensive ($42), but it comes with a couple of CDs that give audible examples of basic studio concepts. Find it at Amazon.com.
- Huber, David Miles, and Runstein, Robert E., *Modern Recording Techniques*, Focal Press, 2001. This book is a good overall treatise on recording. Probably best for beginners and intermediate. Find it at Amazon.com.
- Everest, F. Alton, *Acoustic Techniques for Home and Studio*, TAB Books, 1984. This book also is mostly a

technical dissertation on the audio engineering aspects of recording audio and building a studio.

- Bartlett, Bruce, *Practical Recording Techniques*, Focal Press, 2001. Gives info on how to set up an affordable home studio and how to make quality recordings. $35.
- Everest, F. Alton, and Shea, Mike, *How to Build a Small Budget Recording Studio from Scratch*, TAB Books, 1988. This book not only details the low-budget home studio, it also presents design approaches for radio station studios, video studios that also deal with audio, and film and video screening rooms. The book actually presents 12 studio designs.
- Kefauver, Alan P., *The Audio Recording Handbook*, A-R Editions, Inc., 2001. Good if you want to get more into the technical issues. Expensive at $55.

Finally, if you aren't an electronics hobbyist who has prior experience building electronic projects, or if you're shaky on electronics in general, you might want to pick up Craig Anderton's book *Electronic Projects For Musicians* (published by Amsco). You can buy this book at http://www.paia.com/epfm.htm.

PART ONE: ELECTRONIC STUDIO EQUIPMENT

ELEMENTS OF A HOME STUDIO

What defines a home studio? How do you know when you finally have configured a home studio? Something as simple as a microphone and a cassette deck could be defined as a home studio, since you are at home capturing some sort of audio performance to a recording medium for later playback. However, a simple home studio such as that would give very limited flexibility indeed.

Let's define a home studio as a dedicated space within your home where you can capture the performances of multiple instruments or vocalists (either all of them simultaneously or individually at discrete instances in time) to some sort of recording medium, manipulate the live or recorded sound in some fashion in either the time domain or the frequency domain (I'll explain this shortly), combine them together in some relative fashion to achieve a desired effect, and then transfer the final result to some other medium for later playback. We can also define a project studio as simply a home studio that is used for and possibly by *others* to achieve the same results as defined above. Let's dissect this paragraph one element at a time.

The Dedicated Space:

At best, this might be a spare bedroom, the garage, the basement (if you are lucky enough to have one), the attic, or maybe even a small shed or building out behind your house. At worst, the "dedicated space" might be a section of your living room or family room (i.e., look at the inside cover of Todd Rundgren's *Something/Anything* album). If you share a living space with others, this arrangement of using the living room as your studio space generally does not work amicably for very long. The idea is to get a space that can be dedicated and arranged to support the particular requirements of recording audio.

Capturing Performances:

In order to capture performances, several critical items must be present. First, you will need some musicians or "the talent." The people that you record may be playing traditional acoustic instruments, singing, and/or possibly playing electronic, amplified instruments. Some electrical instruments can be connected directly to the equipment in your studio while others, along with the acoustic instruments and the vocalists, will need to be recorded using microphones. Microphones are simply the reverse of speakers. They convert acoustic sound energy into an electrical signal that can be recorded. The performances you capture might consist of a group or ensemble of players and singers, all playing at the same time. Obviously, this would require multiple microphones in order to capture each individual performer's audio and retain the ability to exercise some control over how it is recorded and processed downstream. Or, the performance you capture might just be you singing and playing different instruments one at a time to build up a complete musical composition.

The Recording Medium:

The performances you capture have to be recorded onto something, and that something is the recording medium. Currently, there are many options and formats for recording audio. Some of the options use magnetic media such as analog tapes (reel-to-reel, cassette), digital tapes (digital audio tape (DAT), PCM digital data on video tape) or computer hard disk drive platters and removable disks (Zip, etc.). Other newer options use optical disks such as the CD (Compact Disc), DVD (Digital Versatile Disk) and MD (MiniDisc) formats. These options will be discussed in more detail later in the book.

Manipulating the Live or Recorded Sound:

Rarely is a sound recorded directly to a recording

medium and then played back without some sort of manipulation en route. There are several ways that a sound can be manipulated. It could have its time domain characteristics changed in some way. This is generally achieved when all or part of the sound is delayed in time. Some of the effects achieved in this way are echo, reverb, flanging, chorusing, phase shifting, detuning, pitch shifting, and harmonizing. Echo is a copy of the sound that arrives at a later time. There might be just one echo from a delay line, or there could be multiple discrete repeats. Reverb is a continuum of echoes that all blend together and die out over time. It is the effect you hear after a single handclap in a large auditorium. Flanging is a strange effect first discovered when playing back two reels of tape containing the same audio and then delaying one of the tape players slightly by pushing on the flange of the tape reel. It gives a soaring inside-out type of effect. Chorusing is an effect that makes one sound be perceived as two or more similar sounds. Phase shifting is an electronic effect where different bands of frequencies are shifted in time relative to each other, and it gives a motion or swooshing effect to the sound. Detuning is a similar effect to chorusing, where a slightly detuned version of the sound is added back to itself to give a fattening or thickening effect to the sound. Pitch Shifting or Harmonizing is a more radical effect than detuning. The actual pitch of the sound can be changed up or down by an octave or more. Harmonizers can provide multiple outputs, each with a different pitch that is harmonically related to the original pitch.

In addition to time-based effects, a sound can have its frequency characteristics changed in some way. Equalization, filtering, distortion/fuzz, noise reduction and excitation are examples of frequency manipulation. Equalization is the boosting or cutting of different frequencies within a sound to achieve a desired effect (e.g., to make a voice sound as if it were being heard over a telephone). Equalizers can come in any one of several different types including graphic, shelving, parametric, and semi-parametric. I discuss these equalizer types in more detail later. Filtering covers a broad range of effects which can remove high frequencies (low pass filtering - LPF), remove low frequencies (high pass filtering - HPF), remove just a band of certain frequencies (notch filtering), or remove from a sound all frequencies except for a band of certain frequencies (band pass filtering - BPF). Distortion and fuzz effects have been popularized by electric guitarists for decades. This effect changes the shape of the waveform of the signal (and therefore its frequency content), usually by chopping off the peaks and adding various harmonics. Noise reduction changes the frequency content of the sound by removing or reducing in amplitude certain bands of frequencies within the sound in the hopes of also removing offending hiss, buzz, clicks, pops and other annoyances that creep into recorded sound. Exciters are used to add a spectral enhancement to the sound. They can make the sound appear to be brighter, clearer and more harmonically rich. Exciters are also called enhancers.

Finally, the sound can have its amplitude manipulated in some way. The volume control on a mixer or preamp is the most obvious example of this, but effects such as compression, expansion, limiting, panning, and noise gating are also examples of amplitude manipulation. Compression is an effect that allows a sound's amplitude to only increase at a certain ratio based upon the original amplitude of the sound. For example, with 2:1 compression applied to an input signal, the output signal will increase only 1 dB (deciBel) for every 2 dB increase in the input signal. This helps to even out the dynamics of a sound, such as when a vocalist moves toward and away from a microphone or when a bass player plays with an uneven dynamic style. An expander performs just the opposite function of the compressor. For example, with 1:2 expansion applied to an input signal, the output signal will increase 2 dB for every 1 dB increase in the input signal. This helps add punch to a sound that has a limited dynamic range. Limiting is a more severe form of compression where the output signal is limited to a certain amplitude, regardless of how high the input signal amplitude becomes. Panning is the placement of a sound in the stereo panorama (i.e., left, right or center) by manipulating the relative amplitude of the sound in each channel. Noise gates cut off the audio signal when the amplitude falls below a certain preset level. This helps remove noise from the recording during quiet passages.

In my opinion, the first outboard boxes you should buy for your studio are a decent reverb, a stereo compressor and a stereo noise gate (in that order).

Combining Sounds Together:

Once all of these separate sounds are recorded to a medium with suitable processing and manipulation, they will need to be combined together onto another recording medium, so that other people will be able to listen to them and so that you can store them in their final mixed-down state. This function of combining the different sounds together is generally accomplished by a piece of equipment called the mixer (also known as a mixing console or a console). The mixer contains many little amplifiers inside, and each amplifier has its own volume control (also known as a potentiometer or a pot) and pan control that allows the sound engineer (that's you) to adjust the relative amplitudes and placements of the signals so that the final combination of the signals results in some desired output. This final combination of signals is then sent out of the mixer's main output to another recording medium to preserve that particular performance mix.

Any good audio mixer will allow a portion of the signal in each channel to be sent to one or more internal buses. These internal buses are usually called aux (short for auxilliary) buses to distinguish them from the mixer's main output buses. These portions of signals acquired from each channel of the mixer are called "sends", because they are picked off the main signal and sent somewhere. If they are picked off before the main volume control for that mixer channel, then they are called pre-sends. If they are picked off after the main volume control for that mixer channel, then they are called post-sends. There are two main reasons for having sends on a mixer. The first reason is to create a separate and unique mix (also called a cue mix) of sounds for any musicians who might be monitoring through headphones. These sends are almost like having another whole mixer at your disposal. The second most popular use for the sends is to send portions of the audio signal out to external effects processors to further manipulate the characteristics of the sound. For example, echo or reverb can be added to the signal sends and then mixed back into the main mix on the mixer. These processed (or effected) signals return to the mixer through a different bus structure called (appropriately enough) the return bus or just the returns. The returns also have their own volume controls, so that just the right amplitude of effected sound can be added to the overall mix. In this manner, the listening experience of a complete sound stage can be recreated at the mixer output that contains all of the different instruments, the processing on their sound, the relative placement and amplitude across the panorama, and the required ambiance effects such as echo and reverb to give the mix a natural reverberant space.

The Final Result:

When all of the songs have been recorded and mixed down to stereo, they will need to be combined into one cohesive unit. This process is called mastering. Generally, mastering assures that all of the songs in the group hang together with a similar volume level, equalization level, and amount of compression. Mastering is also involved with the order in which the songs appear, the amount of silence between them and other aspects of recording finalization.

More about Project Studios:

I have used a simple definition of a project studio in this book (a home studio that is used for and possibly by *others* to capture audio performances), but there are more ramifications when you affix the moniker 'project' in front of studio. Your home's location may not be zoned for commercial business use, so neighbors might complain when they see a steady stream of people filing in and out of your house. And, they might be able to *hear* those people (pounding drums and bass, ripping guitars, screaming synthesizers, wailing vocals) in addition to seeing them, which might not help matters! If you work strictly solo in your project studio, then this probably isn't going to be a problem. Also, project studio owners need to be more involved in and aware of tax implications, depreciation of assets, insurance against loss, financial accounting and invoices, equipment maintenance, the physical appearance of the studio, and a host of other issues.

References:
Cosola, Mary, "Get Serious", *Electronic Musician*, Nov 1995, pp102-108.)

OK, I WANT TO RECORD MUSIC, NOW WHAT?

Everyone has to start somewhere, right? If one were to plan a path to purchase equipment with the intent to record music or some other audio performance at home, what should be purchased first? What if the budget allocated for equipment is limited (and whose budget *isn't* limited?) What if the space allocated for the home studio is relatively small? There are a series of questions you might want to ask yourself to help define what it is you really require in your home studio. You really need to come to grips with how big of an undertaking this is going to be for you. Are you going to start out small, or given a reasonably large budget and appropriate resources, jump into the deep end with a full-up home recording studio?

What is the main reason you want to have a home studio? Is the home studio going to be a place to house all of the items of a personal music hobby? Or, is the home studio going to be used as a business venture for you, perhaps to allow your band to record demos and final masters? Will you rent it out to others? Will it be used both for personal hobby and business purposes? Is there some specific output you want from the studio? Do you already own some of equipment that can be used in this home studio?

Probably one of the most important things to ask yourself is, "What kind of stuff am I going to record?" The answers may dictate the path you end up taking to buying equipment for and configuring your home studio. Will you mainly be recording yourself, laying down track after track of synchronized audio to build larger compositions? Will you be using acoustic instruments (including voice), electrical instruments, MIDI Instruments, or all three types? Will you be recording with others? Or will you just be recording others (solo artists or whole bands at one time)? Will you occasionally be taking the equipment out of the studio to record "on the road"?

If you are going to be recording mainly bands in a converted garage or other large room, you may want to consider buying a used multi-channel analog recorder and a used analog mixer (I will give you sources to find them later in this book), and set up an acoustic space that lends itself to this kind of recording. The new wave of digital recording equipment has relegated once-expensive pro and semi-pro analog gear to the inexpensive used marketplace. You can get some excellent equipment that is usually built to a higher quality standard (i.e., bulletproof) than today's high volume, low cost digital equipment. Of course, there is the down side that this older equipment will require ongoing maintenance and repair. Buying a used multi-track analog recorder and used modules out of a semi-pro mixer is the way I started out on the road to configuring a home studio many years ago. It can still be a valid approach even today.

If you are going to be recording mainly yourself in your own home, you might want to configure a multi-track home studio in one of your spare bedrooms. A couple of decades ago, I wrote an article for *Electronic Musician* magazine entitled "Mapping Your Way Through MIDI Multi-Tracking" (See the June 1988, Vol.4, No.6 Issue). If you can find this article, then I recommend that you refer to it, because much of the information in it is still valid. In that article, I outlined a 7-step approach to planning, configuring and upgrading a MIDI-based recording studio for the home. (Don't know what MIDI is? Then see the next topic in this section.) I would include the article here, but legally I am unable to. You can order back issues of *Electronic Musician* magazine online here: http://images.industryclick.com/files/33/backissues85-90.html. This article outlines some basic approaches from a simple synthesizer playing into a stereo recorder to much more elaborate schemes. However, when I wrote the article, I did not include a computer in any of the schemes. The computer has now become a very flexible piece of equipment for recording studios. It is not a mandatory piece by any means, but it does perform some tasks exceptionally well.

If you are unclear on the definition of multi-tracking, it can be defined as the process of recording single tracks one at a time to construct a multi-instrument composition. This can only be successfully accomplished if all of the separate tracks can be monitored in real time as new additional tracks are added, AND if all of the recorded tracks can be played back in perfect synchronization upon mixdown to a finished master. Part of the process can be to mix tracks together and "bounce" them down to just one or two tracks, thus freeing up the other tracks for additional recording, mixing and bouncing. With this approach, a single talented musician (or even an untalented one, I suppose) could play all of the instruments and record each instrument one track at a time to build up a large orchestration.

You will need to make a decision on how you want to proceed with your studio: record onto standalone recorders (such as reel-to-reel, cassette, and digital multi-tracks) or record onto a digital disk on your computer. There are a whole list of pros and cons to each approach. Computer recording is nice, because you can digitally edit your recordings (MIDI and audio) and manipulate data in the digital domain, which doesn't add any additional noise to your recordings. Actually, all of the various functions of a home studio (synthesizing and sampling audio, recording, editing, adding effects, mixing, mastering, etc.) could be contained within one computer, given a computer that is capable enough to handle it. You can even use your computer online to download sound samples from various web sites, share compressed audio recordings (such as MP3s) with other musicians and print out inserts for your latest CD or cassette. However, the down side is that some people are put off by computers. You have to own a fairly capable computer to perform audio digitization (converting audio from an analog sound into digital bits of information) and recording. Additionally, if your computer goes down, your studio is *really* dead in the water (and you can count on the fact that all computers go down at some point)!

Recording onto standalone recorders (the old traditional method) allows you to buy low-cost, used equipment to populate your studio at the beginning, avoids the technical challenge of keeping a computer operating in peak shape, and is usually fairly simple to accomplish. There is no single point of failure, so if one piece quits working, then you may still be able to accomplish other things in the studio. Some non-computer standalone digital recorders include microphone preamp inputs, a mixer, equalization, effects such as reverb and echo, recording to an internal digital disk, and the capability of burning your own CD on an internal CD-R drive— everything you need from start to finish! However, editing on standalone recorders (even the new digital multi-tracks in some cases) is nowhere near as easy as editing on a large computer CRT screen. An analogy of the difference is correcting mistakes on a manually typewritten document versus correcting mistakes on a word processing computer application— a couple of keystrokes, and the computer editing quickly dispatches most errors.

If you are only going to record acoustic (via a microphone) or electrical analog (e.g., an electric guitar or bass) audio, you can easily do the whole thing without involving computers at all. If you are going to include MIDI instruments in your recordings, then you might want to include a computer in the scheme to function as a sequencer (see below), although it is certainly not mandatory.

One flexible option that a computer offers is the ability to use "plug-ins". Plug-ins are additional software applications that integrate into the recording software application on the computer and provide increased functionality such as modeled analog synthesizers, compressors, expanders, noise reduction, echo, vocoders, enhancers, reverb, delay, equalization, you name it. Of course, you will need a fair amount of processor power to drive all of these additional software applications.

With current technology, you can develop a hybrid home studio that makes use of computers, MIDI, microphones, standalone recorders, outboard mixers and processors. If you are going to deal extensively with MIDI recording in your home studio, then one thing that is handy is a sequencer. A sequencer can be a program running on a computer (even low-end computers can generally handle the relatively modest processor requirements of a software sequencer running by itself), or a sequencer can be a standalone piece of hardware equipment. The sequencer allows you to digitally record all the data associated with a digital MIDI performance (and only MIDI, not anything recorded with microphones). The reason this is powerful is that you are just recording the performance (which notes were hit, how long and hard they were hit, etc.) and not the actual audio. You can go back later to the recorded sequence and fix a flubbed note, change the synthesizer sound or sampler sound you were going to use, transpose notes, or even change the tempo of the whole song. Recording the MIDI sequence is different than recording actual audio, because once you record audio, it is tough to change it very drastically. In a hybrid studio with a sequencer running on a computer to record MIDI instruments and one or more separate standalone recorders to record analog audio, you are immediately going to be faced with the problem of synchronization. How can the computer be synchronized with the standalone recorders?

That's a good question, and it entirely depends on which standalone recorder(s) you are using in your home studio. If the standalone recorder does not have the capability to adjust its speed or timing based on some sort of timing code that it receives (most affordable cassette decks or reel-to-reels do not have this capability, but many digital multi-tracks do), then the computer will have to be synchronized somehow to the standalone recorder (i.e., the standalone recorder is the master, and the computer sequencer is the slave). This is achieved by a process called "striping" (i.e., recording) synchronizing time code onto the tape of the standalone recorder. (Obviously, this is a process that is mainly used on a standalone multi-track recorder.) Basically, a time code such as SMPTE (Society of Motion Picture and Television Engineers) time code is recorded onto one track of the standalone multi-track recorder (this is also called a longitudinal time code, because it is recorded longitudinally along the tape as time progresses). Then upon playback of the tape, that track with the sync code is routed to the sequencer, and the sequencer can then keep in synchronization with the audio material that has been recorded onto the other tracks of the standalone multi-track recorder. If your standalone recorder has the capability to adjust its timing to an incoming synchronization time code or to "chase" the code and sync up to it, then either the standalone recorder or the computer sequencer can be the master or the slave. Other types of time code for synchronization are VITC (Vertical Interval Time Code), a time code that is used for synchronizing video media and is carried over a video cable, and MTC (MIDI Time Code), a time code that is carried over a MIDI cable.

In my own home studio, I have elected to take the hybrid approach. I have a combination of two standalone digital hard disk recorders, an analog 8-track tape recorder, and a Mac computer that can record virtual MIDI tracks and digital audio. All of these recorders are synced together with MIDI Time Code. This allows me the best possible advantages of all formats. However, it has taken quite a bit of time and money to get to this point. I certainly didn't arrive at this position on Day One right out of the starting gate. I started with a 4-channel reel-to-reel deck, a 2-channel reel-to-reel deck and a single monophonic Korg synthesizer!

So what is your decision on how to proceed with your home studio? If you go the pure computer route, you will pay between $800 and $1800 (early 2002) for a capable PC-type of computer running some sort of Windows operating system on it. Plus, expect to pay another $500 to $700 or so for the hardware interfaces that allow you to get audio in and out of the computer and the software that allows you to record and edit MIDI data and audio signals. This doesn't include cables, microphones and all the other incidentals required in the studio. (You can most likely beat these prices on the used market if you look around. If you buy a used PC computer, you should get at least a 200MHz Pentium II machine. Of course, the faster the processor, the faster and bigger the hard drive and the more RAM memory in the computer, the better the system performance is going to be for audio recording.) This will give you a spiffy digital recording and editing system, plus the capability to burn your final mix onto a CD-R or CD-RW disk, which is fairly decent for $1300 to $2500.

If you elect to go with the non-computer route, you can buy a low-end multi-track cassette deck for as little as $99 (street price for a new Tascam PortaMF-P01 4-track). Of course, there is no way that the sound on this cassette 4-tracker is going to compare with even the $1300 computer system above, due to high levels of noise, tape wow and flutter, low dynamic range and other nasty cassette effects. (To be fair, you could buy a lower performance, lower cost used computer with a basic sound card for several hundred dollars and perform recording with it, but the capability of such a device will be limited, in my opinion.) However, for approximately the same $1300, you could purchase an all-in-one standalone home recording solution, such as the Fostex VF-160 16-track Digital Multi-track Recorder with internal CD burner, and achieve excellent digital recording quality, just like on the $1300 computer system above.

So, in the end, it really does come down to a budget decision: if you want to record music at home and all you have is $99 (which is fairly distant from $1300), then the decision is a pretty simple one, isn't it? ~~Steal the money and buy the computer.~~ I mean, of course, buy the little 4-tracker and see how creative you can be. Remember, The Beatles made Sgt. Pepper's on a 4-track recorder!! (Yeah, I know, they also had Sir George Martin.) Later in this book, I give some recommended studio systems at various budget levels to help people who are just starting out.

References:
Rona, Jeff, O'Donnell, Bob, Hall, Gary, "Studio, Sweet Studio", *Electronic Musician*, Sept. 1990, p.35

RECORDING FORMATS FOR THE HOME STUDIO

There are now quite a few competing recording formats for the home studio. I will run down the most popular of them here so that you can understand what they are and how they differ.

Reel-to-Reel:
The reel-to-reel (R/R) recorder has been around for decades, and there are many different types of R/R recorders. Historically, the use of R/R recorders was the only way professional, commercial recordings were accomplished. Basically, the R/R deck is a large and heavy machine which records onto open reels of tape at tape speeds from $1^7/8$ IPS (inches per second) to 30 IPS. You can get R/R recorders with 2, 4, 8, 16 or 32 side-by-side tracks that use tapes of 1/4", 1/2", 1" and 2" thickness. In general, the faster the tape speed and the wider the tape, the better will be the audio recording quality of the tape. The bad news is that many R/R manufacturers no longer make many of these types of units; digital recorders have supplanted them. The good news is that there are many, many R/R recorders available on the used market. You can buy some of the professional and semi-professional units for a small fraction of their original cost. Some of these units have been removed from professional recording studios. If you do buy a used R/R recorder, be aware that it is going to require ongoing maintenance on your part, and that 1/2", 1" and 2" tapes can get expensive. On the other hand, most of these recorders are built like Sherman Tanks, and they should give years of additional service if maintained properly.

Cassette:
The cassette format has been around for about 30 years. In that time it has undergone many changes, and I am still amazed at the level of performance that some of today's decks can achieve. Most cassette decks use 1/8" tape with a tape speed of $1^7/8$ IPS, although some decks use $3^3/4$ IPS to achieve a better frequency response. You

can get cassette recorders with 2, 3, 4, and 8 side-by-side tracks. This recording format does have some attractive features such as low price, portability, compactness, low-cost media, and universal format acceptance (at least for the 2-channel, 4-track version). The main problems with this format are high levels of noise, tape wow and flutter, low dynamic range, plus the inability to perform any meaningful editing once the audio is recorded onto that little tape. Even adding the magic of dbx or Dolby noise reduction does not get rid of all the broadband noise.

MiniDisc:

This is a relatively new format (originally developed by Sony Corporation) that uses a small 2.5" magneto-optical disk for recording compressed digital audio data. What does that mean? It means that Sony has developed a recording format that takes normal analog audio, digitizes it into digital data, runs it through a digital encoding algorithm to compress that data to about 1/5 its original size, and then writes that data onto a tiny disk using a laser beam (similar to, but not exactly like, a CD). The MiniDisc (MD) recorder is then able to play back the audio by reversing the process and reading a reflected laser beam off of the digital 'ones' and 'zeros' on the little disk. This format is very compact, and you can get stereo MD recorders as small as 3.5" x 3" and less than 1" thick!

The MD format also has some other nice features, such as easy digital editing, the ability to erase any track on the disk at any time, the ability to lock the disk to any further modifications, high portability, relatively low cost (I've seen the Yamaha MD8 8-Track MiniDisc Recorder for under $700 street price), and the ability to perform optical S/PDIF (which stands for Sony/Philips Digital InterFace) transfers from another deck (such as from a CD player). You can get MD recorders with 2, 4 and 8 track capability, and all of them use the same type of media.

Unfortunately, the MD format also has some drawbacks. The process of reducing the data to 20% of its original size is called lossy compression. The lossy part is the bad news, because once that 80% of data is thrown out, it can never be recovered and transformed back into 100% of data again. Sony has developed an algorithm that analyzes the original analog audio and detects what frequencies will be masked by other frequencies (and therefore not able to be heard by the normal human ear); the algorithm then deletes the information associated with these masked frequencies. This is how the data reduction is accomplished.

Of course, the audio purists will have none of this, due to the fact that the audio end product is not the same as the original. I don't think I would use one of these units as my multi-track studio recorder, but I do think this is a fairly slick format. Sony has done an excellent job with their compression scheme, and the compressed audio sounds very close to the original uncompressed audio. I have a stereo MD recorder that I use to copy CDs (the MD can hold either 74 minutes or 80 minutes of audio just like a CD-R) and other recordings I do in the studio, and then I take the MD jogging with me. I much prefer this to jogging with cassettes.

This is probably a good time to mention SCMS (pronounced SCUMS, and it's pretty much just what it sounds like). SCMS is an acronym for Serial Copy Management System. This system is built into all MD recorders and all consumer CD-R and CD-RW recorders. SCMS is a digital flag in the recorded data that limits dubbing via the MD digital interface to just one generation (i.e., you can't make a copy of a copy). This was done to prevent copyright problems on commercial recordings. However, for the MD format, it is a ridiculous limitation, in my opinion. The MD is a lossy format as I mentioned above, so it does not record an exact version (digitally or sonically) of a 16-bit, 44.1kHz CD recording. Plus, it doesn't matter if you are copying a commercial CD or your own recording from your own studio, you get only one generation. For this reason alone, I would stay away from the MD format as the main recording deck in a home studio.

DAT:

DAT is an acronym for Digital Audio Tape. The

DAT recorder shares its roots with the VCR. They both use a quickly rotating recording head to impart information onto a slowly moving magnetic tape. In the case of DAT, the information written to the tape can be played back as linear 16-bit PCM (Pulse Code Modulation, a scheme for ordering digital bits). In this regard, DAT tape has the same audio performance as a CD. You can only get DAT recorders in 2-channel versions, so they won't work as multi-track recorders. They do, however, make excellent mastering decks (i.e., they are used to record the 2-track stereo master resulting from the mixdown of multiple tracks on one or more multi-track recorders), and you can buy a portable DAT deck if you want to perform 2-track recording in the field or on the road. On the negative side, DAT tapes are magnetic tapes, so they can oxidize (an undesirable process where the magnetic particles flake off of the tape), and they can be easily erased by stray magnetic fields. Additionally, some DAT decks have SCMS incorporated, which will limit digital copying abilities.

As a subset of the DAT category, there are some PCM recorders available on the used market. Sony made a PCM Adapter (called the F1) that allowed you to make digital PCM recordings with a VCR, essentially mating the outboard A/D and D/A circuitry to the VCR. Later, they combined both of these units into one chassis. Toshiba made a very nice combination PCM recorder like this called the DX-900. It functioned as a stereo VHS video recorder, but with the push of a button, it transformed into a stereo PCM digital audio recorder (using VHS tapes instead of DAT tapes, of course). I still have one in my studio, though I don't use it for mastering any more since CD-R came along. Any of these used PCM decks can function as a good mastering recorder in the home studio, but you may have format compatibility problems in other studios, unless you take your deck with you!

CD-R and CD-RW:

Recordable Compact Discs come in two flavors now, CD-R and CD-RW. CD-R decks use a scheme where normal analog audio is digitized into digital data, and then written onto an optical disk using a laser beam. When the disk is totally recorded, then a secondary operation "finalizes" the disk by writing a table of contents directory to index the tracks on the disk. Note that before the disk is finalized, it can't be played on a conventional CD player, only on a CD-R or CD-RW deck. Once the CD-R disk is finalized, then it can't be used to record data again.

CD-RW (where RW means rewritable) uses a similar approach, but different materials in the layers that make up the disk allow tracks to be recorded, (the last track or all tracks to be) erased and then subsequently re-recorded thousands of times. CD-RW disks have the additional limitation that they will not play on most consumer CD players or DVD players. Both formats will play on a computer CD burner drive that is CD-R and CD-RW compatible.

Both formats yield uncompressed 16-bit linear PCM data that is virtually indistinguishable from the original analog audio. They do sound good! This is what I now use for mastering in my studio. You can get blank CD-R disks for less than 20 cents each now (in spindles of 50). CD-RW disks are now down around $3 each or less.

Multi-track Digital Recorders:
You can get standalone multi-track digital recorders in one of two flavors. One type uses a tape (these are known as Modular Digital Multi-tracks or MDMs), and the other type uses a computer-type internal hard disk drive (these are known as Modular Hard Disk Multi-tracks – MHDMs or Modular Hard Disk Recorders – MHDRs). Of the types that use tape, Alesis (S-VHS tape), Tascam (Hi-8 tape) and Sony (Hi-8 tape) seem to have the most offerings. These MDMs can record multiple tracks with the same clarity as CDs. The only drawback really is that you are shuttling tape back and forth. The MHDMs on the other hand use a hard disk drive to record the digitized data. There are many subtypes of recorders within the MHDM genre (4, 8, 16, and 24 track, some with A/D and D/A converters, some without, some with onboard mix-

ers, some without, etc.). But, basically, they all have the capability to record CD quality recordings on each track. All of them also can be synchronized together with MTC (MIDI Time Code), MIDI Clock (usually with a mechanism called Song Position Pointer which keeps track of where you are within the song), and/or SMPTE (Society of Motion Picture and Television Engineers) time synchronization code).

The capability to synchronize multiple recorders so that they all march to the same beat is extremely powerful. In my home studio, I synchronize 3 different 8-track recorders (for 24 tracks total) to the software sequencer running on my Mac computer (for an unlimited number of "virtual" tracks). The simplest synchronization method is to use a converter box such as the JL Cooper PPS-2 to convert back and forth from MIDI Time Code (a digital signal used by sequencers and computers) to SMPTE Time Code (an audio signal used on the tape deck). In this manner, I can build up huge orchestrations one track at a time by myself. With the standalone 8-track recorders, I can record conventional instruments and vocals, plus I can record non-MIDI electronic instruments (such as my old Minimoog and ARP Odyssey synthesizers). The prices on these digital recorders continue to fall. Given the choice among multi-track cassette decks, multi-track reel/reel decks and multi-track digital decks, I would opt for the multi-track digital decks due to the superior sound quality and editing features they have. Of course, you can only buy what you can afford. Bummer, right?

There are some other strong points regarding multi-track digital recorders. They have an onboard operating system and software which is specifically designed for only recording and mixing audio, unlike a PC or Mac computer which can do countless other tasks. This makes the multi-track digital recorder generally a more stable recording platform than the computer. (Believe me, having your computer crash in the middle of recording a track is really no fun at all.) The multi-track digital recorder may not have the depth and width of audio editing tools available on a computer system, but the tools that are available are usually quicker to learn and easier to use. Building a computer platform to use as a digital recording tool can be a frustrating experience with myriad hardware and software incompatibilities, but most standalone multi-track digital recorders have everything totally integrated as a system, so incompatibilities are generally not a problem.

Another powerful tool shared among most multi-track digital recorders is the concept of virtual tracks. For each track that can be played back simultaneously, the recorder may allow you to record 1, 2, or more additional tracks (or "takes"). You can then choose the best takes for the final tracks to be played back upon mixdown. You can even take elements of each virtual track and combine them to get the best of all the virtual tracks (i.e., the first 30 seconds of virtual track 1, the middle part of virtual track 2, and the ending of virtual track 3).

Digital Audio Workstations:

The Digital Audio Workstation (DAW) is a fancy name for a computer with some sort of audio card in it and some application software hosted on it. The audio card performs the function of getting signals (analog, digital, MIDI, or other types) into and out of the computer. The application software that runs on the computer can be a software sequencer, a software recorder, a librarian program or all those and more rolled into one.

Depending on the capabilities of the audio card, the DAW should be able to record one or more tracks simultaneously with CD sound quality (16-bits at 44.1kHz). In fact, a higher performance standard is now emerging that records and plays digitized data at 24-bit resolution with a 96kHz sampling rate. The higher the number of bits used in digitizing the data, the greater the number of discrete levels available to define the waveform being converted from the analog domain to the digital domain. For example, 16 bits of resolution gives 65,536 discrete levels to define the amplitude of the analog signal (calculated by taking 2 to the 16th power). However, 24 bits of resolution gives over 16 million discrete levels to define the waveform amplitude, which is much higher resolution. The sampling rate refers to how many times each second the waveform "picture" is taken to determine the amplitude of the waveform at any point in time. So, at a 44.1kHz sampling rate, the amplitude is determined 44,100 times each second, while at a 96kHz sampling rate, the amplitude is determined 96,000 times per second.

As you can see, a DAW that has 24/96 capabilities can much more accurately define an analog waveform than a DAW that has 16/44.1 capability. MDMs and MDHRs also have now come on the market with 24/96 recording and playback capabilities.

One big plus with DAWs is the ability to use different plug-in software modules to enhance the functionality of the system. There is no hardware involved; all of the signal processing takes place in the computer in the digital domain. You can buy plug-in software modules that give you all sorts of unique reverb environments, software synthesizers, powerful noise reduction systems, and more. Adding these types of enhancements in the analog hardware world would cost much more money and add interconnection headaches.

Another big plus with recording to a hard disk drive in a DAW is the concept of pointer-based editing. Pointer-based editing is what separates a hard disk recorder from either an analog or digital tape-based recorder. For example, when you record an audio signal on a tape, and then go back to edit that recording somehow, you are erasing that signal from the tape. It is gone forever. In a hard disk system, editing can be non-destructive. You merely tell the computer not to play a certain section of the audio; you don't permanently erase that section of audio. That way, you have quite a bit of flexibility to go back and change (or undo) your edit if you don't like it later on. Pointer-based editing is a powerful concept, and once you experience it, it is hard to go back to splicing analog tape.

Be aware that when you put your whole studio into your computer though, you may be pushing the limits of today's technology. Even in a multi-processor high speed computer, it is asking quite a bit for the processor to handle, analog/digital conversion, effects processing, mixing, recording some tracks while playing back others, digital/analog conversion, handling MIDI inputs and outputs, executing the tasks in various plug-in modules in real-time, and performing other necessary background tasks all virtually at the same time! You may want to (or have to) allocate certain critical functions to dedicated outboard hardware equipment. Detrimental latency effects (i.e., the delay in how long it takes all required elements in a certain scenario to be processed and transmitted by the processor) can result from an overloaded computer. This will show up as late or completely missing timing cues during recording or playback of the audio (and/or video). On my Mac, I can always tell when the desktop needs to be rebuilt, because the sequencer will start missing notes during playback.

So, which comes first, the DAW computer or the software applications that run on it? If you already have a fast, powerful computer (Mac or PC variety), then obviously that is what comes first. If you have not purchased a computer yet, or you have a wimpy computer that can't support audio recording demands, then you may want to choose the software application first. Go get some demos of the various software applications at your local music equipment retailer (or at a friend's house). Some applications can run on both the Mac and the PC, but others only run on one or the other platform. Also, consider what platforms and software applications your friends have (for sharing files and for technical advice), and make the decision that best suits your needs.

If you are going to choose the DAW option as the basis of your studio, you really need to have at least some technical savvy. Trying to get a computer to work with a bunch of different software programs, internal PC boards, and various outboard hardware interface units can be overwhelming for the beginner. Unless you know your way around this arena or have friends that are willing to spend the time to help you get your system up and running, you may want to look at one of the other options for recording multiple tracks of audio.

DAW Plug-Ins:

One of the powerful aspects of owning a computer-based DAW is the ability to use off the shelf software plug-ins. Plug-ins are basically additional software applications that add functionality to your studio computer. There are some excellent plug-ins available now for both PCs and Macs. Some of the functions available include compressor, de-esser, delay, EQ, expander, noise gate, chorus, noise reduction of many types, pitch shifting, filtering, flanging, stereo imaging, 3D spatialization, reverb, tube emulation, time stretching, synthesis, sampling, and even intonation-correction.

Unfortunately, there are many different format types of plug-ins, and you need to know which plug-ins your computer and host application software are compatible with to avoid disappointment. Some plug-ins execute on (run on) the computer's processor (called native plug-ins), and other plug-ins run on a separate hardware processor board plugged into the computer. You will need to purchase this additional hardware in the latter case.

The Mac has a suite of software plug-ins available that do not run in real time. These plug-ins use the Mac's processor to perform the required modifications to the audio off-line (i.e., in non-real time). After the operation is done, you can monitor the results. The Mac also has a suite of plug-ins that can run in real time as you are mixing or recording the audio. Most of these plug-ins adhere to proprietary formats that only work with their own host application programs. The different formats on the Mac (as defined by the host programs available) are Adobe Premiere, SoundMaker, Bias, Sound Designer II, Digidesign Real Time Audio Suite (RTAS), Emagic, Digidesign TDM, MOTU Audio System, and Steinberg VST. Would you like me to make the decision easy for you? If you select Digidesign's TDM format using Pro Tools (or Pro Tools LE) as the host program, you can't go too far wrong.

The PC also has host programs available with their own formats, and some of them are compatible with the formats available on the Mac. The plug-in formats on the PC (as again defined by the host programs available) are

Microsoft DirectX, Creamware, Emagic, Steinberg VST, Digidesign Real Time Audio Suite (RTAS), and Digidesign TDM, Cakewalk CFX, MOTU MAS. VST and DirectX appear to be the most popular formats on the PC.

What's Next?

Back in the mid-1990s, I worked on the design and development of one of the first time lapse video recorders using DVDRAM as the recording media. DVDRAM is a format using DVD disks that can be re-written thousands of times. During that project, I always thought that DVDRAM would make a great audio recording medium. Given the popularity of the standalone hardware digital multi-track recorders these days, recorders based on DVDRAM should be right around the corner. (As I edit this text just before publishing, I see that Fostex has just come out with the DV40 DVDRAM Master Recorder.)

With the new 24-track hard disk-based multi-tracks cracking the $2000 barrier, look for further price drops on these awesome machines. Hard disk drive technology keeps enabling higher recording rates and longer recording times at lower and lower price points. We are seeing 150GB drives now, and they should keep going up in recording capacity. We should also see the solid state memory capacities increase, which will be great for small portable digital recorders.

There are many R&D (research and development) efforts underway right now to improve the density of recording media. One promising technology is Blu-Ray. Blu-Ray uses a blue laser to record and playback phase-change data on a 12 cm optical disk. The first Blu-Ray disks we will see should be able to hold 27GB of digital computer data, 13 hours of broadcast TV video, or 2 hours High Definition video information. The interesting aspect of Blu-Ray is that nine of the biggest manufacturers have already embraced the standard, including Hitachi, Panasonic, Pioneer, Philips, Samsung, Sharp, Sony and Thomson. The planned second generation disks for Blu-Ray should hold 50GB. This new technology should totally swamp the technology roadmap for DVD. Unfortunately, the Blu-Ray machines will not be compatible with the existing laser technology of CDs and DVDs.

References:
Barry Fox, www.newscientist.com, Feb. 20, 2002

POWER FOR YOUR STUDIO

Having dependable and clean power for your studio is very important. At worst, poor power distribution can result in blown or burned out electrical equipment, or even a blown up you. At best, poor power distribution can result in nagging little intermittent problems (drop-outs, buzzes, clicks, undependable equipment operation and other untraceable phantoms) that seem to come and go without reason or logic. Poor power distribution can result in brownouts (low voltage over an extended time period), sags (low voltage over a short time period), surges (a higher voltage increase over a short time period) and spikes (a very high voltage increase over a very short period of time).

Power Distribution to the Studio:

The power that arrives at your house from the power company usually comes in on two hot conductors and one ground conductor. The two hot conductors are nominally 117VAC (volts alternating current) with respect to the ground conductor, and the two hot conductors are also 180 degrees out of phase (meaning that the waveforms on each power line are the mirror images of each other- when one is rising, the other is falling). The reason your house has two hot conductors is so that you can derive 220VAC to 240VAC (from one hot conductor to the other hot conductor: 117 + 117 = 234) to power such appliances as your clothes dryer or your kitchen stove. All of the other lower voltage (110VAC to 120VAC) equipment in your house will run off of just one hot conductor referenced to ground. Most houses in the USA are configured this way.

If you can afford to do it, connecting a dedicated run from your electrical box to your studio is the best approach to starting out with a known good power source. Unless you are an electrician or a construction contractor, I would leave the installation of AC electrical cabling to the professional electrician. It is important that any electrical cabling you put in your house meets the National Electrical Code. If the electrical cabling in your studio shares the load with other equipment in your house, you may find that switching transients (power spikes due to equipment turning on and off) cause audible noise spikes in your recordings. However, there is action you can take to minimize this problem, such as installing power conditioners and other similar equipment. We will discuss these conditioners shortly.

If you do have an electrician update the wiring in your house, there are some actions he or she can take to mitigate power problems. Err on the side of thicker copper wire (i.e., a lower number gauge of wire) when installing long power runs from your electrical box to your studio. If you are going to pay an electrician to do some wiring work for you, see if he can balance your electrical power system between the two 117VAC feeds so that both legs have about the same amount of electrical load on them. Also, see if the electrician can balance out the load so that devices which generate a great deal of electrical noise and hash (any highly reactive devices such as appliances with motors or other electromagnetic devices inside, light dimmers, etc.) are on one leg of 117VAC feed, while your studio and other generally non-reactive devices are on the other 117VAC feed.

The 117VAC power is distributed throughout your house at 2-prong or 3-prong AC receptacles. In a standard 2-prong receptacle, the current is provided by the "hot" wire (the black wire) that attaches to the smaller of the two rectangular slotted receptacles. During the positive part of the power waveform, the current flows out of this conductor, through the electrical equipment connected to that receptacle, and then returns back to the receptacle on the larger of the two rectangular slotted receptacles, which in turn connects to the "neutral" wire (the white wire). During the negative part of the power waveform, the opposite is true. This is the way it is *supposed* to be!

In a 3-prong receptacle, the third (green or bare) wire (it's the one connected to the round hole) is a safety ground. This safety ground generally has no current traveling in it and is provided as a true ground, since the neutral power wire can't be considered a true electrical ground. This green wire travels back to your electrical box and is connected to a grounded copper bus bar, so all of the green safety grounds are connected together for your house at this one location. Again, this is the way it is *supposed* to be! Don't be a bit surprised if you find that your house is wired incorrectly or that just certain outlets are incorrectly wired.

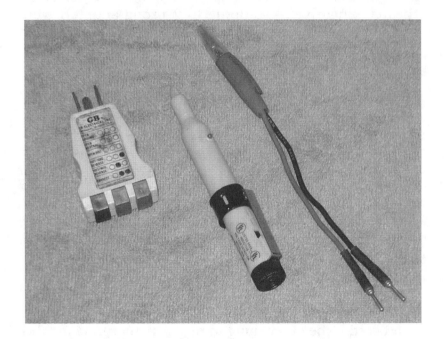

Figure 1: AC Voltage Analysis Tools

One piece of equipment I recommend that you buy is a little AC Outlet Analyzer. You can pick one up at Radio Shack for about $6.00 (P/N 22-101). It plugs into 3-wire outlets and tells you if any fault conditions or incorrectly wired power conductors exist. The AC Outlet Analyzer is shown on the left in Figure 1. The device in the center is an AC Wireless Voltage Sensor (Radio Shack P/N 22-103). It will signal if any conductor has a high level AC voltage running through it, just by holding it near the conductor. This is a very handy little device to own. The device on the right signals an energized AC outlet when it is physically inserted into that outlet.

If you live in an older house, you may find that some or all of the AC receptacles are 2-prong receptacles rather than 3-prong receptacles. This turns out to be a bummer for home studios, since a high percentage of the studio units that don't use wall warts (the big black plastic transformers on the end of a power cord) do use 3-prong plugs. However, before you reach for one of those cheater plugs (i.e., a 3-prong to 2-prong adapter), you should be aware of a couple of facts. First, the cheater plug instructs you to connect the pigtail wire (the safety ground) to the screw on the faceplate of the AC outlet. You need to make sure that this screw actually ends up connecting to earth ground somewhere. In both houses I've owned, these screws did not connect to earth ground. In both houses, the outlet boxes in the wall are plastic, and the outlet boxes are nailed to wooden studs in the wall! Since plastic and wood are not very good conductors, using the cheater plugs in my house achieves nothing, except perhaps to set up an electrical fault condition.

The safest solution to this problem is to get a licensed electrician to run a dedicated safety wire from the ground bus bar in your electrical box to your studio AC receptacles, and then actually convert the receptacles from 2-prong to 3-prong (i.e., buy new receptacles and install them). Yes, it is definitely a hassle, but it is the safest way to proceed. The other thing to realize is that in using the cheater plugs, you may be setting yourself up for a nasty ground loop. (For a discussion of ground loops, see the section on hum and magnetic noise induction later in this book.) When it comes to AC power distribution, it is just better to do it correctly.

In my home studio, all of the AC outlets were of the 2-prong variety when I bought the house. I chose one of the AC outlets on an outside wall to update from 2-prong to 3-prong. I turned off the power to the studio and removed the AC receptacle wall plate. Then I removed the 2-prong AC receptacle. I drilled a hole through the back of the receptacle wall box and through the outside wall of the house to the outside. I then ran an approved green ground wire by itself from the electrical box to that outlet using metal conduit to protect it. I hooked up that new ground wire to the new 3-prong outlet in the studio. Then, one by one, I swapped the black and white AC wires over from the old 2-prong outlet to the new 3-prong outlet. Next, I screwed the new 3-prong outlet into the wall and replaced the receptacle wall plate. When I finished, I used the AC Outlet Analyzer to make sure all the connections were correct. Now I have properly grounded AC power at one central point in my studio.

Power Distribution in the Studio:

Once you get reasonably safe and stable power to your home studio or project studio, you will need to distribute it within your studio. There are now many devices out on the market to help you maintain clean and safe power distribution within your studio.

The lowest cost approach is to use only a stout surge/spike suppressor to protect the equipment downstream. This is a device that sits by idly monitoring the power line for power surges (a higher voltage increase over a short time period) and power spikes (a very high voltage increase over a very short period of time), and when it detects them, it very quickly suppresses or absorbs the increased energy before it can do damage to the equipment connected downstream. The component inside the suppressor that absorbs this energy is called a MOV (Metal Oxide Varistor). Generally, the ability to absorb this increased energy is given by the Joules rating of the suppressor. The higher that rating, the better the suppressor is able to absorb or suppress the energy spikes.

If you are going to use a surge/spike suppressor in your studio, then my recommendation is to use a power conditioner that includes the surge/spike suppressor along with an RFI/EMI interference filter, a circuit breaker, and a switch that applies or removes power to several integral outlet plugs. The RFI/EMI (Radio Frequency Interference/ElectroMagnetic Interference) filter acts a circuit to remove high frequency noise that may be riding on the AC power lines from appliances, motors, radio transmitters, TV transmitters, and other high frequency sources. The circuit breaker is used as an inline protection device that should trip before you trip the circuit breaker out at your house's electrical box. The power switch and switched outlets on the power conditioner provides a convenient point at which to apply power to your whole studio (or at least part of it). Believe me, this is much better than running around pushing twenty power buttons every time you want to power up the studio.

There are several manufacturers of power conditioning equipment on the market now. Some of theses manufacturers are Furman, Samson, Gemini, Juice Goose, Nady and Tripp Lite. Good bets for the home studio are the Juice Goose JG8.0L, the Furman PL-8, the Nady PCL-810, and the Samson PowerBrite power conditioner. All of these units sell for between $100 and $150. These are all essentially similar: rack mountable, 8 switched outlets, RFI/EMI filtering, circuit breaker, and front-mounted lights to illuminate the rack equipment below. Adding a power meter to the power conditioner is a good idea, since it allows you to see what the current situation is with the power feed to your studio. The above manufacturers add a power meter in their Juice Goose JG8.0M, Furman PLPlus, Nady PCL-815, and Samson PowerBrite Pro product offerings. The meter adds $30 to $50 to the above prices, and it allows you to visually monitor the input voltage to your system.

Once you have the power conditioner, you can plug your equipment into the switched outlets on the rear of the unit. You can plug in power strips to those switched outlets also. Avoid daisy-chaining the outlet strips (i.e., plugging one outlet strip into the next one, and then plugging that one into the next one, and the next, etc.). This could eventually compromise your third wire safety ground.

There is just one problem with the MOV suppressor approach, however. Once it detects and absorbs an abnormal amount of energy in a spike or surge, then the MOV is effectively burned out and no longer functions in a protective mode! If you've had a MOV plugged into the AC power mains for a couple of years, chances are good that it isn't doing the job anymore. You can open up the power conditioner and replace the MOVs (if you are handy with a soldering iron). If you elect to do this yourself, you may find that there is one MOV in the conditioner, or you may find three MOVs in there (one between the hot and neutral, one between neutral and ground, and one between hot and ground). You should replace all of them. Radio Shack sells MOVs (P/N 276-568) for about $2.00 each, or you should be able get them at most of the parts supply houses I list later in this book.

So, what can you do to avoid the problem of burned-out MOVs in your power conditioners? Not much really, so pack up all your studio equipment and send it to me immediately. Well, actually there is one good solution to this problem: use a voltage regulator. A voltage regulator is a device that stabilizes all types of voltage fluctuations and provides a nominal voltage value as long as the input voltage is within its operating range. For example, the Furman AR-1215 contains active circuitry which always outputs 117VAC at 15Amps as long as the input voltage is anywhere within a range of 97VAC to131VAC. It does this by continually monitoring the input voltage and then automatically switching the output of an eight-tap toroidal autoformer so that the output voltage always stays in regulation. In this manner, the AR-1215 protects against spikes, surges, sags and brownouts without the problem of blown MOV components.

Several years back, I used the AR-1215 in Virtual Reality (VR) systems I designed for location-based entertainment complexes and video game complexes. By using the AR-1215 in the rack, I always knew I was going to get stable power to the data acquisition system, samplers and power amplifiers in the rack, regardless of what kind of ugly power was supplied to the VR system. The AR-1215 takes the place of the power conditioner unit in your studio, as it has a front panel-mounted power switch, 9 switched/conditioned outlets, and an 11-LED bar graph meter that tells you exactly what the input voltage is at any instant. This is an excellent unit for the home or project studio, if you can afford it (~$450). Furman also makes a 20 Amp version (AR-1220) and a 30 Amp version (AR-1230) of this product. Use only the voltage regulator version that the power feed Ampacity of your studio can safely support (i.e., don't use the 20A voltage regulator with a 15A AC power feed from your electrical panel).

If you are going to take some of your studio equipment on the road to record gigs, I highly recommend that you use a voltage regulator in the equipment rack. It is worth the money.

Sequencing of Power:

Even though I have one main power switch that provides conditioned power to all of the equipment in my racks and on the mixing desk, I still do manual power sequencing on certain units. Power sequencing is the act of turning on certain units one after another in order to avoid a nasty transient that goes through some electrical circuits when they first turn on. I usually apply power to everything except the power amplifier that drives the monitor speakers. After any turn-on power transients have disappeared, then I apply power to the power amp. This protects the power amp from trying to track any huge transients appearing at the input terminals. The power amp I use has its own relay delay circuit for connection of the speakers. This protects the speakers from any transients the power amp itself generates. When I am ready to turn off power to the studio, I always manually turn off the power amp first. Then I turn down any volume controls that have headphones plugged into them. This will protect the headphones later from any turn-on transients in that equipment. Then I remove power from the whole studio.

Power Distribution for the Computer:

The last power-related piece of equipment to discuss is the uninterruptible power supply (UPS). The voltage regulator we just discussed is great for the studio, but it can't provide dependable power if the input voltage drops below 97VAC or disappears altogether. The one component of your studio that can't tolerate this scenario is your computer. If you are in the middle of editing a file or transferring data from one drive to another when the power goes south, your data file might be corrupted (sometimes permanently). To protect against this possibility, it is a good idea to use a UPS to provide power to your computer.

There are two main types of UPS topologies: the "standby" system and the "on-line" system. In the standby topology, a battery is constantly being charged by the input AC line, but it remains in a standby mode until needed. The input AC line is passed through to the output of the UPS until the input power fails. Then the standby battery is switched into the circuit, and the battery's DC voltage is converted from DC to AC by a device called an inverter. In the on-line topology, the battery and inverter are always connected to the output of the UPS. The major concern is this: in the on-line design, the battery charger must have enough capacity to handle the entire output load, while in the standby design, the charger is required only to have enough capacity to charge the battery. As for the computer in your home or project studio, you will mainly be concerned that the UPS has the ability to deliver the power you need for the amount of time you need it (generally, long enough to finish whatever you were doing and shutdown the computer in an orderly manner). Determine what the power requirements are of your computer and critical peripherals (external disk drives, CRT monitor, etc.), give yourself a safety margin (say 20%) above that amount, and then buy a UPS that will provide that amount of power for a reasonable amount of time (10 minutes, 15 minutes, etc.).

References:
Anderton, Craig, "Getting Wired", *Electronic Musician*, April 1990, pp 58-60.
Oppenheimer, Steve, "Power Hitters", *2002 Personal Studio Buyer's Guide*, p. 50, an Electronic Musician magazine supplement.
Travis, Bill, "Paranoid About Data Loss? Choose Your UPS Carefully", *EDN*, September 14, 1995, pp. 131-132.

MICROPHONE PREAMPLIFIERS

There seems to be a large movement towards using line mixers these days, particularly for electronic musicians using multiple keyboard setups in a MIDI environment. At one point, I found myself in this group, using the line level mixer I had put together from surplus Teac mixer modules. Unfortunately, I had lots of applications in which I recorded vocals, acoustic instruments and miked electrical instruments. If you have only a line mixer, or if you have a microphone mixer with noisy inputs, or if you have no mixer at all and you'd like to record using microphones, the following solution may be for you.

As a rule of thumb, the quality of a mixer is generally judged by the sonic capability of its microphone preamplifier section. You can use any of the best microphones available, but if your mixer's microphone preamplifier is only capable of a 60dB signal/noise ratio or a 1% total harmonic distortion figure, you're certainly not going to realize the potential of your microphones or your performance. For a long time, I used the microphone preamp inputs on my stereo open reel and cassette decks. Using this approach, I just couldn't get a clean, clear microphone recording. Their poor transient handling capability resulted in muddy audio, and the lack of any headroom seemed to make everything flat and lifeless. Then I purchased two Symetrix SX202 Dual Mic Preamps.

The SX202 is a super clean two-channel microphone preamplifier with excellent features and specifications. The unit has two low impedance XLR-type inputs that can handle any signal level up to +14dBV. 48 Volt phantom power for condenser microphones is front panel selectable. Channel 1 includes a polarity switch to select phase reversal that can rectify problems such as mis-wired cables or microphone placement cancellations. Outputs are provided for left, right, and combined left + right signals. Balanced and unbalanced outputs are capable of +24dBm and +18dBm maximum, respectively. Let's review some of the SX202's specifications.

Equivalent input noise (EIN) is a preamplifier specification that is a measure of the noise voltage in the device that is attributed to the thermal agitation of its molecular structure (i.e., all those molecules banging around are going to cause electrical noise). All preamps will generate noise merely from the random collisions of molecules regardless of whether an input signal is present or not. Under its normal operating conditions, the SX202 approaches the theoretical limit of equivalent input noise with an EIN of -127dB. If none of this makes sense to you, suffice to say the SX202 may be one of the most noise-free pieces of audio equipment you can put in your home studio for a rock-bottom price. The SX202 also has excellent imaging, since there is only a 10-degree phase shift at 20kHz and an almost immeasurable distortion figure of 0.007%. The unit has a maximum gain of 60dB and a ruler-flat frequency response of 20Hz to 20kHz, +0dB/-1dB.

But these are all just numbers, aren't they? How does the SX202 sound? Great! Unless you have a very expensive state-of-the-art microphone mixing console, you will probably realize an immediate sonic improvement with the SX202. It makes vocals sound crystal clear. For the ultra purist, a simple setup of a high quality condenser microphone feeding the SX202 and being recorded by a digital audio recorder is about as good as you can get with today's technology and still remain in the realm of affordability. As a matter of fact, when I go on the road to record a performance with just a pair of microphones, I use two matched condenser microphones with one of my SX202 preamps and feed that signal directly into a digital CD-R recorder. This setup gives super clean audio upon playback!

Unfortunately, the SX202s are no longer being sold new by Symetrix. You can find them on the used market; reference my section on used equipment web sites. Expect to pay somewhere between $100 and $150. You can check out *Electronic Musician's* June 1997 issue for an excellent shoot out between high-cost and low-cost microphone preamps, including the SX202; however, this *Electronic Musician* article is a bit dated now. Later on in this book, I give some recommendations on which microphone preamplifiers to buy if you can't find the SX202.

Tubes vs. ICs in Amplifiers:

Before we leave the subject of microphone preamps, I want to touch on the issue of vacuum tubes versus integrated circuits (ICs), since many of the newer microphone preamps have some sort of vacuum tube in them. All circuits that perform an amplifying function end up distorting the signal to some degree. It is an unavoidable fact of physics. However, factors such as how the circuit was designed, the types of components used in the circuit and the quality of those components will dictate the amount and type of distortion contributed by that circuit.

In general, the type of distortion created by a vacuum tube circuit is more pleasing to the human ear than the type of distortion created by an IC or transistor circuit. The reason for this involves plenty of electrical theory and physics, but it centers around several factors such as the types of harmonic distortion generated by the amplifier, the onset of that distortion, the linearity of the amplifier circuit, and the amount of negative feedback required to correct distortion and non-linearity. The even harmonics that are predominantly generated in a tube amplifier, even though they are a form of distortion, simply sound less objectionable to the human ear than the odd harmonics predominantly generated by IC or transistor amplifiers. In addition, the even harmonics in tube amplifiers have a gradual onset, as compared to the quick onset of heavy odd harmonic distortion in a transistor or IC amplifier. Additionally, tube amplifier circuits generally require much less negative feedback than IC or transistor amplifiers to obtain linearity. I know this is a lot of electrical engineering jargon, but the increased negative feedback in the transistor or IC amplifiers is one thing that contributes to the "sterile" sound in comparison to tube amplifiers.

With the advent of digital recorders, much lip service has been paid to the "cold, lifeless" digital recording as compared to the "warm, fat" analog recordings. This argument hovers around such topics as digital microphone preamps vs. tube microphone preamps, digital effects processors vs. effects processors with a tube in the circuit, digital hard disk recorders vs. analog R/R recorders, and even the newer digital synthesizers vs. the older analog synthesizers (such as the Moog, ARP and Oberheim analog synthesizers). I have to admit that there is truth to the argument, because it is easy for me to hear the difference in the character of the sound. Nevertheless, you should be aware of the hefty marketing hype surrounding tubes vs. ICs (and also possibly the inflated prices attached to tube equipment).

WHAT IS MIDI?

You may keep hearing the word MIDI, and yet not know what it is. MIDI is an acronym for Musical Instrument Digital Interface. It is a 16-channel protocol that travels over a serial bus and connects to various electronic studio units to allow them to control and communicate with each other. It is electrically similar to RS-232C for computers, if that helps you understand it. This interface has been around since the early 1980s, so it is fairly ubiquitous now. There was a time when interfacing various synthesizers and electronic modules in the studio was a bit of a struggle, especially between the equipment of different manufacturers. However, the original MIDI Specification was written and agreed upon by a consortium of companies, and now most all synthesizers, samplers, digital recorders, effects units and processors contain a MIDI connector. You can even get a MIDI interface for your Mac or PC computer.

Many MIDI units have separate MIDI In, MIDI Out, and MIDI Thru connectors. All MIDI connectors are 5-pin DIN plugs or jacks. The MIDI In jack allows a MIDI signal from some other piece of equipment to control that unit. The MIDI Out connector allows the unit to control or send commands to some other unit. And the MIDI Thru connector just replicates whatever signal the unit received at the MIDI In connector, so that the MIDI units can be connected in a daisy-chained manner. Be aware, however, that just because a unit has one or more MIDI connectors, it doesn't mean that the unit can respond to all MIDI commands and messages. To understand what the unit can and can't do over MIDI, you will need to reference the MIDI Implementation Chart in your owner's manual. This is a standard chart for all MIDI equipment, and it is usually found in the back of the owner's manual. The MIDI Implementation Chart will tell you what types of MIDI commands and information are recognized and transmitted by that particular unit.

I could write a whole separate book about MIDI, but there are some excellent free resources online that you can access that will save me the trouble.

MIDI World (http://www.midiworld.com) is an excellent place to start learning about MIDI. It has a section on MIDI basics that starts from ground zero. It also has many resources for more advanced users, including a copy of the MIDI Spec itself.

The MIDI Farm (http://www.midifarm.com) also has quite a bit of good information, including a forum where you can submit MIDI questions and receive answers.

Harmony Central has a MIDI page at http://www.harmony-central.com/midi. If you are involved in music and you don't know about Harmony Central (www.harmony-central.com), then you need to get yourself to that web site post haste. There is a ton of useful information there for the home studio owner.

CONNECTING EQUIPMENT IN YOUR STUDIO

Audio Patch Bays:

Depending on the number and types of elements in your studio system and how often you find yourself changing the configuration (e.g., "on that bass part, I'll put the compressor before the flanger, but when I record the keyboard, I need a parametric EQ before the digital delay"), you may want to consider getting a patch bay for your system. I know I'd be totally lost and frustrated without the patch bays in my studio.

Basically, a patch bay is a matrix of audio connectors that allows the interconnection of all of the various electronic units at just one accessible location in a studio. It offers increased flexibility in connecting your equipment. The patch bay lets you connect all the important tie points of the system (such as effects inputs and outputs, synthesizer outputs, tape recorder inputs and outputs, mixer inputs, outputs, sends and returns, etc.) to the rear panel of the patch bay. Internally, each rear panel connector is directly fed through to a corresponding front panel connector. Short patch cables are used on the front panel to interconnect each element as desired. This scheme (called the non-normalled patch bay) is depicted in Figure 2. Note that the patch bay shown in the figure is just one of three general types of patch bays.

The three types of patch bays are non-normalled(just discussed) , full-normalled and half-normalled. In a full-normalled patch bay, there are two vertical pairs of jacks (In and Out) on the front and the rear of the patch bay between which the audio is internally routed without requiring a patch cord. If a plug is plugged into either one of the corresponding front panel jacks, then the internally connected rear panel connection is physically interrupted, and the rear panel jack is connected to only the front panel jack (i.e., the signal now follows and flows through the cable plugged into the front of the patch bay). A half-normalled patch bay is similar, but when a front-panel plug is inserted, the rear panel internal connection is still maintained. This allows the signal coming into the rear panel of the half-normalled patch bay to drive two destinations. This is made possible (in most cases) because of the low impedance of most studio signal sources and the high impedance of most studio destinations (or loads). In general, the input circuitry of the second destination is of high enough impedance so that it doesn't load down the source output circuit.

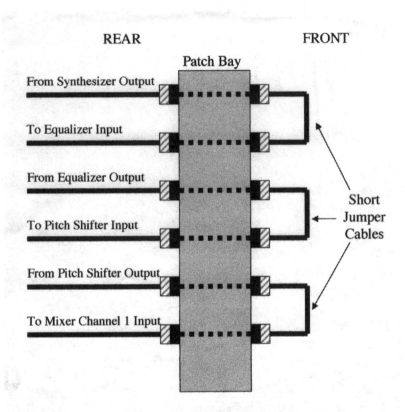

Typical Non-Normaled Patch Bay

Figure 2

Which type of patch bay is best for you? That is entirely up to you! The best way to figure it out is to take a look at the type of inputs and outputs you now have in your studio. Also, what kinds of new equipment are you planning to add in the not too distant future? Now, how do you normally use all of this equipment? Do you normally leave certain units hooked to each other and just occasionally patch other units into the chain? Do you regularly need to drive two destinations with one source? One thing to keep in mind is that the full-normalled and half-normalled patch bays can act like non-normalled patch bays, but the reverse is not true.

Figure 3: Patch Bay in Author's Studio

The patch bay is a real time saver. How much time do you spend crawling around behind your equipment to fumble with cables? Have you ever plugged the output of your drum machine into the output of your equalizer instead of the input because you couldn't see what you were doing behind a piece of equipment? That's the shortest path to distorted audio, no audio, or even worse, a trip to the repair shop for some replacement audio output circuitry. With a patch bay, all connections are right out front and centralized, minimizing the propensity for error.

The patch bay is also an excellent troubleshooting tool. Since all system tie points are located in one place, isolation of a distorted signal or a source of hum is much easier. When a suspected faulty link is identified, you can patch right around it to verify your suspicions. An example of a patch bay in my own home studio is shown in Figure 3 on the previous page.

Finally, the patch bay typically uses a sturdy metal frame construction with the connectors securely anchored to the metal frame. In some cheaper studio equipment, input and output connectors are anchored only to an internal circuit board, so that any substantial bending moment or shear stress imparted to the cable while attaching it or removing it from the connector can snap the connector off of the circuit board. I have done this, and I was hopping mad after I discovered the damage (because it is not easily fixed). The patch bay reduces the likelihood of this happening, since you only connect to the studio equipment once, and all subsequent reconfigurations of cables take place only at the patch bay. Even so, it is a good idea to provide some sort of stress relief on the back of the patch bay to reduce the sheer stress on the rear connectors of the patch bay (there are over 200 cables plugged into the back of my patch bays and that equals quite a bit of weight hanging on the patch bay connectors).

If the patch bay you purchased does not have some sort of integral stress relief system, you can make one yourself and fasten it to the back of your patch bay or rack. The poor man's approach is to get some tie wraps from Radio Shack or Home Depot, wrap a group of patch bay cables with the tie wraps, and then use another tie wrap to suspend that group from above (i.e., fasten the suspending tie wrap to the top of the rack).

At the modest price of about $100 to $130 or so (or

even as low as $48 for the Behringer PX2000 UltraPatch Pro 48-pt Patch Bay), a patch bay is a small investment for saving time and possibly money in the studio. Be careful of used patch bays, however. The patch bay is definitely one product that I would buy new rather than used to avoid oxidation and intermittent signal connection problems. Each non-normalled patch bay generally only has the point where the plugs from the audio cables touch the conductors of the jack to make contact. It is imperative to keep these areas clean and free from oxidation. If you don't, you will have signals dropping out at inopportune times (such as during mixdown), or you will get crackling, intermittent audio.

If your patch bay uses 1/4" jacks and plugs, there is a tool you can buy to clean the jacks and the plugs. Check out the Synersonix Conduct Tool (~$20) at http:// www.musiciansfriend.com. The half-normalled and full-normalled patch bays have additional places where signals make contact— at the points where the jack springs for the tip, ring and sleeve (if it is a 3-conductor patch bay) make the open and closed contact connections. Unfortunately, you may not be able to adequately clean these internal contact points without taking the patch bay apart.

MIDI Patch Bays:

All of the advantages of the audio patch bay also apply to MIDI patch bays. A MIDI patch bay is a central point in the system that controls the routing of all MIDI messages and allows any MIDI source to be connected to one or more MIDI destinations. MIDI patch bays differ from audio patch bays in the respect that MIDI patch bays use only serial digital MIDI signals, while audio patch bays use only analog audio signals.

On most MIDI patch bays, all of the MIDI devices are connected at the rear of the patch bay panel into standard MIDI connectors. Active circuitry inside the patch bay then allows the MIDI signal sources to be routed to any output jack sockets (which may be on the front or rear panel of the unit). Some MIDI patch bays have both full-normalled and half-normalled modes of operation.

MIDI patch bays can offer some internal signal processing to perform changes to MIDI data and MIDI set-ups (e.g., merge MIDI inputs, perform MIDI filtering, transpose notes, perform digital delays, implement program changes, etc.).

Digital Signal Standards:

If your studio is all analog, you may never encounter these kinds of signals. However, for studios containing digital components, there are now several different types of digital interfaces that allow the transfer of digital signals from one piece of equipment to another without converting the signal to analog as an intermediate step.

S/PDIF (Sony/Philips Digital Interface) is a digital audio transfer interface that is found on both consumer and pro equipment. It can transfer digital word data over either a 75Ω coaxial cable (with RCA connectors) or over an optical interface (sometimes called TOSLink.)

AES/EBU (Audio Engineering Society, European Broadcast Union) is predominantly a professional standard for digital audio transfers. It can transfer digital word data of an electrical interface that uses balanced 3-pin XLR-style connectors (the same kind as used on low-impedance microphones). This standard is simply an alternate digital interface standard to the S/PDIF interface. The two standards are not compatible directly; however, you can buy a converter to convert from one standard to another. (If you need to convert among these standards, then check out the Midiman CO3 (~$175). It converts between AES/EBU, S/PDIF Coax and S/PDIF Optical (TOSLink) format digital audio streams. It is an efficient design because the digital source input signal is converted to all three output formats simultaneously.)

Alesis originally developed the ADAT optical interface for interconnecting their ADAT digital multi-track recorders. It is an optical 8-channel interface that transfers digital signals over an optical interface, and has become a de facto standard that appears on many diversified types of studio equipment now (mixers, synthesizers, effects processors, digital format converters, etc.). I use it in my studio to transfer digital signals between my 8 track digital recorder and a separate A/D-D/A converter box. Advantages of this format are that you can transmit digital signals up to about 10 meters without fear of ground loops the signal is all light, and no electrical connections are involved.

The Tascam TDIF 8-channel digital interface is a similar concept to the ADAT optical interface, but the TDIF interface uses electrical connections instead of light. The TDIF interface was originally designed by Tascam to allow interconnection of their DA-88 digital multi-track recorders. Some new digital mixers are now being offered with this standard interface.

USB is the Universal Serial Bus, a digital interface that now appears on most all new Mac and PC computers. It is a plug-and-play interface (i.e., it offers the capability to plug a device into a computer and have the computer automatically recognize that the device is there) that transfers digital data at a speed of up to 12Mb (megabits or millions of bits) per second.

IEEE-1394 (also called FireWire) is another type of digital serial bus that allows up to 63 devices to be interconnected and digital data to be sent back and forth at rates up to 400Mb per second. It was designed originally as a high-speed computer interface to replace some of the older digital signal transfer standards such as SCSI, RS-232C and the Parallel interface.

A special mention is needed for the digital word clock. The digital word clock is a special-purpose digital interface that serves to synchronize all of the various digital units in the studio; however, no digital audio is sent over this interface. If a studio utilizes a digital recorder, digital mixer, digital samplers and synthesizers, digital effects devices, and digital format converters (A/D, D/A), then they all need to be marching to the same internal time clock. If they are not all run from a digital master word clock, then they will most definitely drift apart in time (just like two analog tape decks started at the same time playing the same song on tape). This drifting apart will result in undesirable artifacts such as pops, clicks and garbled audio. If you happen to have several digital units in your studio and intend to perform digital transfers among them, you will want to use a master clock word generator to synchronize them all. In order for this to work properly, each unit must be able to receive the word clock on a connector on its back panel and also be able to function as a word clock slave (as opposed to a word clock master). If certain units can't be operated as word clock slaves, then you will have to do analog audio transfers for that particular unit or find some other way around the synchronization problem.

References: Anderton, Craig, "The All-Digital Studio: Are We There Yet?", *Keyboard*, Dec. 1999, p.48.)

Audio Cables:

Chances are high that you will be using quite a few audio cables in your studio, unless you have some sort of all-in-one integrated recording system. Here is the bottom line on audio cables: don't skimp!

Buying poorly made cables can result in intermittent connections from cheap connectors, induced noise in the signal due to inadequate shielding in the cable, and poor frequency response due to high capacitance and inductance in the cable. High capacitance in the cable will actually act like a low pass filter (filtering out the high frequency signals) when that capacitance combines with the series resistance in the cable. All cables have a certain amount of resistance, capacitance and inductance per foot of cable. The better cables (which are usually the more expensive cables, but not always) are designed and built in such a way to minimize the detrimental effects of impedance on the signal.

Buying cables that have gold connectors, tightly woven braided shields or even double shielding, and oxygen-free signal conductors can all help with signal integrity. One place I have found for high quality audio cables at a low price is Gateway Electronics. Check out their audio cables at http://www.gatewayelex.com/audcable.htm. I use their RCA cables all over my studio. Not only can these cables carry the full audio bandwidth easily, they can also be used to pass baseband video signals into the MHz range! These cables are designed to pass audio and video signals in one direction only, so pay attention to the arrows on the cable jackets. You can buy bulk microphone and instrument cable from Gateway Electronics also, or build your own custom audio cables, if desired.

Another source to check out for low-cost, high-quality audio cables is Parts Express. If you want to buy 1' patch cables for your RCA patch bay, then check out their P/N 249-400 at http://www.partsexpress.com. These cables have a tightly woven copper braided shield to help eliminate induced interference and noise, 24K gold-plated RCA connectors, a pure copper center, and a low capacitance dielectric. At less than $1 each, this is a killer deal.

MONITORING SOUND IN YOUR STUDIO

Unless you have a respectable quantity of dollars to throw at the room acoustics of your studio to flatten, balance and fix any uneven reflections or absorptions, the problem of reference monitors versus the listening environment will be a compromise at best. If you have set up your studio in a room of your house that doubles as a living space, or if you are unwilling to transform the room (by removing square corners, adding angled ceilings and the proper finishing materials, and generally isolating the room from the external environment), then you might experience unsatisfactory audio performance from even an excellent pair of loudspeakers. My studio resides in a 10' x 10' x 8' box, hardly the ideal recording environment when using microphones and loudspeakers. If your studio suffers from these kinds of limitations, you may want to use a pair of close field monitors. This approach does not eliminate all deleterious effects from listening to monitors in a small 10' x 10' box, but it can go a long way towards fairly minimizing those effects.

In general, the close field of a pair of speakers is an area on-axis and equidistant from the pair that is close enough to be unaffected by any extraneous acoustic phenomena that the room may contribute. The close field is also sometimes referred to as the near field. This area may extend from 1.5 to 3 feet from the speakers as shown in Figure 4. In technical terms, the close field is that part of the field where significant departures from the inverse square law are encountered. So, what in the world is the inverse square law? The inverse square law states that each time we double our distance from an acoustic radiator (speaker) in a free field, the sound pressure level (SPL) decreases fourfold, or 6 dB. (We'll touch on a little more audio theory later on in the book, which will explain this in more detail.)

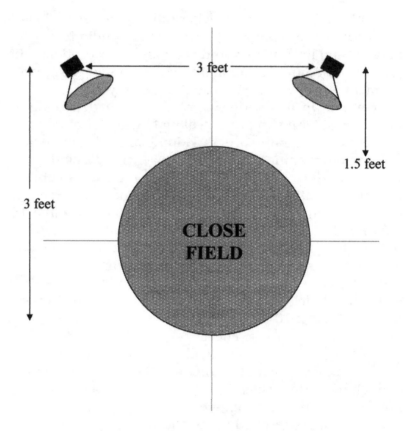

APPROXIMATE CLOSE FIELD AREA

Figure 4

Usually, you don't listen to your speakers in their close field, but you may quite often record with your microphones in their close field, which is a good way to minimize extraneous effects from the room or environment. Have you ever encountered the proximity effect (bass boost) when close miking with a Shure SM-58 microphone? That is the close field effect of the microphone.

The problem is that close field monitors don't always tell the whole story of what is transpiring in a recording, but neither do headphones. Headphones can give poor imaging cues. That's why I use both types of monitoring. If the song sounds good in both of my headphones (Sennheiser HD580s and AKG K280s) and on the monitors, I can feel reasonably sure that I've got the best recording I'm going to get in that situation. I continually bounce back and forth between both methods of monitoring until I've got the mix reasonably dialed in. I also try to monitor the mix in both stereo and in mono. The reason to do this is that certain cancellations may occur when the image is collapsed to mono. If your mix is ever played on a monophonic system later (such as AM radio), portions of the mix may simply disappear! A good way to prevent this is to listen to the mix on a cheap mono speaker and check for cancellations. And finally, I always listen to the recording in my car as a final reference point! I spend more time listening to my car stereo than any other sound source, so I am very familiar with how commercial CDs sound in there. As a final check of your mix, I recommend that you compare how your recordings sound compared to your favorite commercial recordings on a sound system that you know very well. Your mix won't sound exactly the same on every system, but it will take on the sonic character of each system.

A quick comment about headphones: it is generally better to try to mix your audio on a pair of stereo monitors rather than headphones. When you put on a set of headphones, the transducers (i.e., miniature speakers) are pressed right up against your ears. In real life, you rarely have any sound source located in that position. The human ear is calibrated to use the outside of the head and the outer ear as part of the whole hearing system. We get our spatial (localizing) cues from sounds traveling around the head and arriving at the ears at different times. None of this happens with headphones, so all of the sounds seem to be located inside of your head! Sound from one headphone channel never reaches the other ear, which is rarely the case with real life sounds or even with speaker monitors. (Several companies have been experimenting with a technique called crossfeed, which feeds some of each channel over into the other channel, thereby reducing the in-the-head, sound-localization problems common with headphones. You can find out more about this by doing an Internet search on headphone crossfeed.) Also, headphones are not able to convey the low frequency tones that the rest of your body perceives in addition to your eardrums.

However, headphones do have an important role in the studio. I use mine all the time to check for the accuracy of minute details in a mix, things that are difficult to hear accurately from the monitors. I use headphones almost exclusively when I am editing a sample or editing audio on the computer. Headphones are great when you don't want to disturb others in the house with your mixing or practice sessions. They are also indispensable for multi-tracking purposes. Closed-back headphones work best in this instance to prevent bleed from previously recorded tracks into the microphone.

As background information, there are special cases that avoid the standard headphone monitoring problems listed above. These are binaural recording and 3D sound using head-related transfer functions (HRTFs). Binaural sound is accomplished by originally recording the audio with two microphones located inside the ear canals of a dummy head. This allows the timing, frequency and amplitude cues of the sound to remain realistic as perceived in real life. When these binaural recordings are played back through a set of normal headphones, then the realistic cues are transferred directly to the eardrums, and a unique listening experience is perceived. HRTFs are used in Virtual Reality (VR) and 3D sound systems to allow sounds to be perceived in areas other than just between a set of speakers or between a set of headphone transducers. HRTFs are basically algorithmic transfer functions that are determined for each individual person through a painstaking set of audio measurements. The response of that person's ears to sounds located in 3D space is mapped out, and then those algorithms (HRTFs) can be used to steer sounds around the listener's head in a perceived 3D space. Through my research in VR, I have listened to several HRTF systems, and they can be very convincing. In fact, I bought a consumer-level system manufactured by Sennheiser (DSP Pro) that provides some generic HRTFs (you select the one that best fits your hearing) for use with any headphones. It is interesting listening to movies that have been recorded in Surround Sound using that system.

I used a pair of Yamaha NS-044 speakers for many years as my close field studio monitors. These are basically the forerunners of the Yamaha NS-10 speakers, since they share the same woofer and similar cabinetry dimensions. I was looking for a way that I could play my keyboards and synthesizers in real time while monitoring the speakers in the close field, and for a way to mount the speakers so I could sit in the close field and listen to them while I mixed down a recording. Here is one relatively simple solution.

Ultimate Support Systems sells short sections of their tubular support pipe. Using these with a pair of horizontal support arms makes an excellent mounting platform for the monitors. This is shown in the photo in Figure 5. The arms are extremely flexible for positioning the monitors at virtually any attitude. It sure beats mounting the monitors on the wall, since they are now able to move wherever the support stand moves. If the monitors are going to lay down horizontally, then position them such that the tweeters are at the farthest ends from each other. This is to preserve stereo imaging, since most imaging information is in the mid- or high-frequency range, while the bass signals put out by the woofers are essentially omnidirectional (i.e., they radiate in all directions equally).

This configuration has worked well for me with a minimum cash outlay. If you have a pair of Yamaha, Tannoy or similar monitors, try them in this close field arrangement to minimize the disturbing effects of room acoustics.

Note that the best speakers to use for close field monitoring applications are speakers that have closely-spaced drivers on each speaker (simulating a point source). This is so that the phase of each individual driver is as coherent as possible. This will give the clearest and cleanest imaging possible. So, if you have a huge set of stereo speakers, it may be best not to use them for close field monitoring applications.

Figure 5: Monitors on Tubular Support Arms

Speaking of minimum cash outlay, it is not absolutely necessary to drop megabucks on the latest studio monitors and a 10 kiloWatt amplifier to drive them. You may be surprised at how much better even the most mediocre loudspeakers sound when you listen to them in their close field. The bass improves by an order of magnitude over how it sounds out in the middle of a room. Be aware though that reference monitors are specifically designed to have a flat response across the entire audio bandwidth and to be as neutral as possible, while home stereo speakers are generally not so designed. (Here's why: most all compact consumer stereo speakers try to extend the bass response into the bottom octave (below 100Hz) as far as they can. In order to do this, they generally bump up the speaker's response in the low midrange/upper bass region, so that the response curve stretches as far down into the bottom octave as possible. So, with this adjustment to the response curve, these compact speakers (using 4" or 6" woofers) are able to replicate the lower tones, but unfortunately at the expense of coloring the sound.) One set of compact consumer speakers that avoids this bump coloration is the NHT SuperZero. It has no appreciable response below 100Hz, but the rest of the audible spectrum is ruler-flat, transparent and airy. The SuperZero has the detail and clarity to tell you exactly what the audio really sounds like. That's why I use them in my studio with a subwoofer to cover the bottom octave. You can learn more about them at NHT's web site: http://www.nhthifi.com/nht/bedroom/superzerodisplayindex.html). As with most other aspects of the studio, it comes down to the tradeoff of spending money or making do with what you have. Close field monitoring may improve the price/performance ratio of what you already have in your studio or home.

As for the amplifier, what's wrong with using an old stereo amp to drive the close field monitors? You're not going to be able to crank the volume on the close field monitors anyway, or they'll blow your head off, since your ears are only about 2 or 3 feet away from them. For many years, I used a Technics Quadraphonic Receiver that I bought in the mid-70s to drive my close field monitors. It only put out 40 Watts RMS continuous, but that was more than I needed from 2 feet away. If you haven't purchased a monitor system yet, give some thought to a close field approach with a used stereo amp from the classifieds and save yourself some money. Again, many of the decisions you make regarding equipment, processes, and procedures in your home studio come down to a tradeoff between money and performance. Sometimes, though, you can tilt the odds in your favor with a little do-it-yourself (DIY) ingenuity.

References: Petersen, George, "Choosing and Using Near-Field Monitors", *Electronic Musician*, Nov. 1989, p.48.

EQUIPMENT RECOMMENDATIONS

What equipment should you buy for your home studio? The correct answer is you should buy the equipment that sounds best to you, that you are comfortable in operating, and that produces the best results for you. It also helps tremendously if you can afford it!! If you are new to recording, you may not have a clue where to begin. If you ask a salesperson, he or she might point you in the direction of the most items they have in stock or whatever equipment they are trying to move that particular month. I will go out on a limb and make some recommendations on equipment that is cost effective yet yields very good performance. (Everyone has his or her own opinion. And incredibly, opinions differ, but here are mine.)

There is a vast supply of used equipment available to you. Usually, this equipment is perfectly functional, but it has been supplanted in the marketplace by the "next fantastic new thing". New gear lust gets the best of all of us. However, if you are willing to buy used equipment, you can get some great deals that yield excellent equipment and excellent results at relatively low prices. If you have a small budget for your home studio (and it seems that any budget is a small budget, doesn't it?), you are going to want to maximize performance per each dollar spent. The used market is definitely the best way to do this. The used equipment will come with either a short check-out period or perhaps with no warranty/as-is. At the end of this section, I will give you a list of used equipment dealers, and also some web sites you can check out on-line. Note also that many of the new equipment dealers offer some rock bottom prices on new equipment that have been used for in-store demos or that have dents and scratches on them. Generally, these units come with a full (but a possibly shorter duration) manufacturer's warranty. Keep this in mind, as this equipment is sometimes not advertised, and you will have to ask specifically about it.

My recommendation is to spend your serious money on your microphones (if you are intending to do live recording, of course), your mixer (which includes the micro-phone preamplifier), and your audio recorders. This is where the heart of the recording studio lies, and generally, the better the equipment here, the better the overall re-sults obtained. All of the prices I quote here were freely available on the Internet or in sales catalogs. I try to give the actual street prices (wherever possible) that you can expect to pay for this equipment, so that you can more accurately compare apples to apples.

Computer:

If you are going to buy a PC computer for analog signal recording and MIDI sequencing in your home stu-dio (the Digital Audio Workstation described earlier), you will need at least a 200 MHz Pentium II-class machine to achieve any kind of realistic result. There are many fac-tors that determine the performance of a computer for this task, including the hardware that is used in it and the software application(s) that are being run on it. Assuming the 200 MHz Pentium II is the minimum level of machine required, here are some factors that will improve the level of performance of your machine. (Always check to see what the minimum level of machine is required for the software applications that you buy.) A Pentium III or Pentium IV is generally a more capable processor than the Pentium II processor. I personally prefer the Athlon processors over the Pentium processors, but either the Athlon or the Pentium processors will execute Windows-types of appli-cations. The faster the processor speed over 200 MHz, generally the better the audio recording performance of the software application. You will want a disk drive that has at least a 7200 RPM rotational disk speed, so that it can more easily keep up with the seek and access times required for audio reads and writes. The amount of RAM memory definitely affects the performance and execution speeds of your computer and the software running on it. Digitized audio is a notorious memory hog, and digitized video is even worse. Just one minute of stereo 16-bit uncompressed audio eats up about 10 MB of memory. So, the more RAM that the processor can directly access (and the faster the bus to which the memory chips are connected), the better the overall performance will be. Memory modules usually come in sizes such as 32 MB, 64 MB, 256 MB and 512 MB, and most computers have space for either 2 or 4 memory modules. For audio applications, you should have at least 96 MB (that's one 32 MB and one 64 MB combined). However, RAM memory has never been cheaper than it is now, and this is not a place to skimp.

Prices change so quickly on computers that it is nearly impossible to quantify them in this book. If I planned to buy a new PC today with the intent of using it for audio recording, I would probably build it myself using these types of components: xp Athlon 1900 (or better) processor, 1 GB DDR RAM, 100 GB 7200 RPM Hard Drive, 24x10x40 CD-RW drive, ATI 64 MB Radeon Video Board (or better). If you build such a system yourself, expect to pay around $1800. If you don't know what you are doing with computers, save yourself the hassle and buy an off the shelf model, or pay extra and have a computer house build a computer to your specifications. Remember, you will want to have as much fast RAM memory as you can afford (or as much as your motherboard can hold) and as large a fast hard drive as you can afford.

For Mac computers, the situation is a little different. Apple is the only one who makes Mac computers, and they don't let you build them yourself. Also, you will pay more money for the privilege of owning a Mac that has roughly the same performance as a PC computer. However, all of the things I said above regarding RAM memory and disk drive speed still apply on Mac computers. If I was going to buy a Mac today for my studio, I would probably get at least a 933 MHz machine with a G4 processor, a SuperDrive (DVD-R & CD-RW drive), 1 GB SDRAM, and 100 GB drive or better.

Mac versus PC:

Well, this is a hotly debated topic, isn't it? Everyone has an opinion, and I am no exception. Having used both types of machines extensively, I definitely prefer the look and feel of the Mac Operating System (OS). I have a Mac and a PC at home, and the Mac is dedicated to my studio, but this book was written on the PC. I think the Mac is more elegantly designed, and on an equal processor speed basis, the available processors for the Mac blow away the processors for the PCs. There are also some great applications for Macs, but let's face it, about 90% of the world is on PCs. More importantly, you can get the same level of performance in a PC that would cost you twice as much in a Mac.

One factor that might help you decide which computer to buy is the software applications you intend to run on your machine. If you already have a bunch of applications you know and love that operate on one type of computer platform, then buy that type of computer. If you are going to be sharing sequencer and audio files with friends around town or even over the net, then it might help to use the same applications (and therefore computers) as they use; however, there are file standards to help promote compatibility of cross-platform file exchanges.

Audio Cards and Computer Interfaces:

If you are using a computer for audio recording, then you will need to have a way to get the analog audio into and out of the computer. The computer only works with digital bits of information (which exist in only one of two states: either a discrete logic 'one' or logic 'zero'), while analog audio exists as an infinite continuum of voltages from its negative peak value up to its positive peak value. An interface is required to digitize this analog audio and convert it into a format that the computer hardware and its software applications understand.

Enter the audio card. You can get some "el cheapo" sound cards these days, but their usefulness in a serious recording rig is questionable. If you want to go the DAW route, then my recommendation is to save enough money to buy a computer audio interface that is specifically designed with multi-track recording in mind. These units generally consist of a card that sits on the PCI bus (an internal high speed bus used for adding additional hardware interfaces to the computer) in your Mac or PC computer and have some sort of separate breakout box for all the I/O cables. I like the ones with the separate breakout box, since you don't have to climb around behind your computer to mess with cables. New PCI-based units under $200 (street price) that are worth a look are the Terratec EWS88D (~$200), M Audio Audiophile 2496 (~$160), and the Echo Mia 24/96 (~$200). More capable and more expensive PCI-based units worth a look are the Aardvark Direct Pro Q10 (~$750), ST Audio C-Port DSP2000 (~$450), Terratec EWS88MT (~$400), M Audio Omni Studio (~$400), M Audio Delta 1010 (~$600), Echo Gina (~$400), Echo Layla (~$800), and the Digidesign DIGI 001 (~$800 including Pro Tools LE software!). An upgraded Digidesign Digi-001 Factory (~$1200) system is available that has some very nice plug-in software packages included with the Pro Tools LE recording and sequencing package. If you can afford it, the Digidesign DIGI 001 Factory looks like the best bet to me.

If you are leery of opening up your computer and fiddling around with the PCI bus, you can now buy audio interfaces that simply connect to your computer's USB bus. The USB (Universal Serial Bus) is a relatively high-speed interface bus present on newer computers. Some of the USB audio interfaces available are the M Audio Audiosport Quattro (~$230), Aardvark Direct Mix USB3 (~$230), Emagic EMI 2/6 (~$350), Event Ezbus (~$700), and the Tascam US-428 (~$500). Of these USB units, the Tascam US-428 looks best to me, plus it includes Cubase's VST Audio/MIDI software for Windows. Another fast non-PCI bus option is to use the IEEE-1394 bus if your computer has one (also known as the FireWire bus). This bus is even faster than the USB bus. Mark of the Unicorn makes the MOTU 828 FireWire Audio Interface, which costs about $730 on the street new.

If you really don't want to get involved in the integration and troubleshooting of computer hardware and software, a company by the name of Carillon Audio Systems will be happy to sell you completely integrated systems ranging from bare bones platforms all the way up to cutting-edge computer systems hosting the latest software applications such as Cubase VST or Pro Tools. Putting such a system together from scratch is definitely not something for the novice computer user to try to tackle. It can be a real bear to get everything working as designed, especially on an open platform such as the PC. These systems from Carillon come standard with a whole host of extras such as custom keyboard caps for your keyboard shortcuts, over 30 different software plug-ins, Emagic's Zap audio file compression utility, and Cakewalk Pyro to burn CDs or send MP3 files over the Internet. This is certainly an excellent option to examine if you want a new DAW in your studio. Contact Carillon Audio Systems by telephone at 1-866-4carillon or via the web at www.carillonusa.com.

Multi-track Recorders:

It is going to be very difficult for me to recommend a recorder for you to buy until you have decided what format you want to go with for your home or project studio. Therefore, I will detail some good ones from each of the formats, and you can make your own decision from there. I described these various formats earlier in the book.

Reel/Reel Multi-tracks:

You won't find many new multi-track recorders on the market these days, as they have been supplanted by cassette and digital multi-tracks. Luckily, many of the older reel/reel recorders are well built, and you can still find many of them on the used market. The Teac 2340, 3340 and 3440 are good low cost 4-track reel/reel decks. You can find them for as low as $300 or more, depending on the condition. Another good 4-track reel/reel is the Ampex AG440B-4 (uses ½" tape) for about $800. The Fostex 8-track reel/reel decks (Model 80, A8, R8) are about the lowest cost 8-tracks you can buy. I've seen used Model 80s for $200. I still have a Fostex A8 that has worked flawlessly for 17 years, so I can't argue much with a "track" record like that. A step up from the Fostex machines is the Tascam 38 (or the 80-8), which may cost around $600 or so for a used machine. If you want even higher quality (and consequently much more expensive) 8-track reel/reel decks, check out the Ampex 440B-8, Otari MX80-8, Otari MX5050MKIII, Otari MX70, and the Studer A80 machines. Fostex used to make a 16-track reel/reel machine called the B16, which was probably the lowest cost of all the 16-track recorders. You can get a used one now for about $900, depending on condition. If you want to buy a used 24-track reel/reel, the two lowest cost machines are most likely the Tascam MSR24 and the Fostex G24S. Expect to pay anywhere from $3500 to $5000 depending on the condition (especially head life) and accessories. Other higher quality 16- and 24-track reel/reels can fetch $5000 to $20,000.

Cassette Multi-tracks:
The cassette multi-track deck has been around for quite awhile, probably close to 20 years. They are generally made fairly inexpensively to address the low end of the home recording market. This brings up two issues. First, they are an inexpensive means to get into home recording, even if only to get your musical ideas down onto tape. Second, since they are made so inexpensively, they don't stand the test of time very well. Therefore, buying a used cassette multi-tracker is ill advised, especially since you can get a new one for such a low price now. In this book, I am not going to detail the many extinct models from Fostex, Sony and Tascam.

The low end of the new cassette multi-tracker market is populated by the Fostex X-12 4-track and the Tascam PortaMF-P01 4-track. Both of these units cost about $100 new. You can only record one track at a time on them. You build up the 4 tracks and then mix them down in stereo to a separate mixdown (mastering) recorder with individual volume and pan controls for each track. Both units have headphone jacks built in.

The next level up in cassette multi-trackers is the Tascam Porta 02MKII ($150). It allows 2-track simultaneous record capability with 2 mic/line input channels. Tascam also has the Portastudio 414MKII ($300) and the

Portastudio 424MKII ($400). The 414MKII features 2 XLR inputs, 4 line inputs and 1 high impedance guitar input. It allows full 4 input recording to 4 tracks, and has high and low EQ for each channel, along with 2 effects send per channel. It also has a discrete sync output, so you can use it for synchronizing other devices to the audio (e.g., slide projectors). The 424MKII is similar, but it has 6 channels in the mixer section with 8 inputs. It has a more sophisticated EQ section on two of the channels (hi/lo/sweepable mids), Auto Punch In, dbx Type II noise reduction, and a logic-controlled transport.

MiniDisc Multi-tracks:

MiniDisc Multi-tracks are a relatively new fixture on the multi-track landscape. They are based on the MiniDisc (MD) technology originally developed by Sony. The distinct advantage they have over cassette multi-tracks is the much better signal-to-noise ratio (usually 95 db or better compared to around 43 db or so for cassettes without noise reduction and 85 dB for cassettes with dbx noise reduction), much better frequency response (usually 20 Hz to 20 kHz compared to 40 Hz to 16 kHz for the better cassette multi-tracks), and digital editing. These advantages translate directly into better-sounding master recordings. However, I don't think these MD multi-tracks have been widely accepted by the public.

I am not seeing the MD multi-tracks heavily advertised now in early 2002 as they were in the past. Yamaha has two MD multi-track models available. The Yamaha MD8 (about $1100 new or $700 for B stock) features up to 8 tracks of simultaneous recording and playback, the capability to bounce all 8 tracks down to 1 or more tracks (a nice feature), 8-channel mixer, 2 balanced XLR inputs, 2 balanced/6 unbalanced line inputs, MIDI capability, 3-band EQ with mid sweep, and basic digital editing capabilities. The Yamaha MD4 (about $600 new or $470 for B stock) is a 4-track version of the MD8 with similar features. Perhaps you can now pick up some of the other MD multi-tracks (Sony MDM-X4MKII 4-Track, Tascam 564 Digital 4-Track Portastudio and the Tascam 788 8-Track

Digital Portastudio) on the used market for attractive prices.

Modular Digital Multi-tracks:
In case you are confused by the naming conventions of the Modular Multi-tracks, one type uses a tape (these are known as Modular Digital Multi-tracks or MDMs), and the other type uses a computer-type hard disk drive (the Modular Hard Disk Multi-tracks or MHDMs). Tascam and Alesis fairly own the MDM market. Alesis developed their very popular series of ADAT recorders in 1991. The newest versions of these recorders use S-VHS tape as the media to carry 20-bit (24-bit for the M20) digital 8-track recordings. The three current models offered (LX-20 at $900, XT20 at $1000, and M20 at $4000) all have the ADAT Optical Digital Interface that carries up to 8 tracks at once, completely in the digital domain. Since these newer ADAT machines have been released, many of the earlier 16-bit ADAT machines are now available on the used market for reasonable prices.

Tascam has developed a competing line of MDMs that uses the Hi-8 videotape format. All of the Tascam MDMs are helical scan digital 8-track audio recorders. The DA-88 is a 16-bit recorder that can record for 108 minutes on a standard 120 tape. The DA-38 is basically a DA-88 (they share the same transport mechanics) without the capability to add the SY-88 synchronizer board. It also has enhanced track-bouncing capabilities. The DA-98 is basically a DA-88 (they also share the same transport) with synchronization built-in, a confidence monitoring function (read-after-write), internal patch bay, and an LCD display that makes operation much easier. Tascam has also developed 24-bit high resolution MDMs (DA-78HR and DA-98HR). Ballpark prices for some of these units are: DA-38 ($1900), DA-78 ($2200), and DA-78HR ($2700).

With any type of MDM or PCM (Pulse Code Modulation- a method of encoding analog information into a digital form) recorder using rotary head technology on tape, keeping the tape path clean is the only way to get error-free, dropout-free recordings. You should clean the tape path on these units when there is an indication of data loss (audio dropouts or when the error light is illuminated).

Modular Hard Disk Multi-tracks:

The MHDMs are the modular digital multi-track recorders that use internal hard disk drives instead of tape. These seem to be the most popular at the moment because they avoid some of the negative aspects associated with tape-based recording (dirty tape heads, dropouts, accidental magnetic erasures, tape stretching or breaking, etc.) and allow easy non-linear editing. Some of them come with integral mixers, microphone preamps, effects processors and even drum machines, while others are strictly just recording/playback decks. The MHDM is a good place to start if you want to get into digital audio recording in your studio because most everything you need is in just one box. Of course, all of these recorders have the capability to turn out clean, clear CD-quality digital recordings. Picking one of them really depends on what kind of budget you have.

At the very low end of the MHDM spectrum, we have the Korg Pandora PXR4 4-track ($400) and the Boss BR-532 4-track ($400). Both of these 4-track recorders have an onboard mixer, effects processor, and mic/line input capability. Both units are pseudo-MHDMs because they record to a 32 MB SmartMedia card (solid state memory that is expandable to 128 MB) instead of to a hard disk drive.

The Boss BR-8 8-track recorder ($650) has become very popular with musicians, since it is fairly straightforward to operate and gives good, clean recordings. It can record 2 tracks at once, play back 8 tracks at once, and has an onboard mixer and effects processor including an algorithmic guitar amp model. The unit uses 100 MB Zip disks for recording, plus it has a digital output for connection to CD, DAT or even MiniDisc mastering decks.

Boss also just came out with the BR-1180 and BR-1180CD digital recording studios. They give up to 80 virtual tracks and 8 playback tracks. They both come with a 20 GB hard drive, XLR mic inputs with phantom power, 2 loop processors, 1 insert processor and mastering effects.

The $1000 BR-1180CD has a built-in CD-RW drive, while the $750 BR-1180 comes without.

Fostex has several 8-track MHDMs. The Fostex VF80 ($600) is an integrated digital recorder/mixer similar to the Boss BR-8. It can record 8 hours of uncompressed digital 8-track audio on the internal 20 GB drive. It has built-in standard effects, microphone/guitar amp modelers, mastering effects, and a digital mixer. It also has inputs for 2 guitars and 2 XLR-type microphones (phantom power is included). An optional CD-R/RW drive can be added to the VF-80, making it a complete music production station. The Fostex D-108 ($650) combines digital audio recording, mixing and editing with MIDI Time Code (MTC) synchronization capabilities. It can record 1 hour of uncompressed audio on an internal 2.55 GB drive. Up to 3 D-108s can be combined to form a 24-track recorder. The Fostex D824 is a standalone recorder (no mixer) that allows 24-bit/96 kHz digital audio recording of 8 tracks onto its internal 10 GB hard drive. It has extensive synchronization capabilities.

The Roland VSR880 ($500) is a rack mount digital 8-track recorder based on the design of Roland's VS880 and VS1680 recorders. It has 8-track simultaneous record and playback capabilities, 8 analog inputs with 2 mic/line inputs, 8-channel digital input and output, optical or coaxial digital output, and MIDI In/Out/Thru. With the huge number of virtual tracks available on the VSR880 (128 virtual tracks), the flexibility and track bouncing capability is awesome. Later on, when you get more money, you can add the optional VS8F2 24-bit Effect Expansion Board into the VSR880 rack mount chassis. Note that this is a standalone recorder with no integral mixer built-in.

Tascam has the Portastudio 788 8-track digital recorder ($900) that can record 24-bit audio. The unit has an integral digital mixer and effects processor. Multiple 788s can be synchronized together with MTC. An optional SCSI CD-R drive can be purchased for about $400 to allow direct-to-digital CD-R masters.

Zoom recently introduced the MRS-1044 Digital

Multi-track workstation ($700). This unit can record to 10 separate audio tracks, has a programmable stereo drum track (think sequencer), and also has a programmable bass track yielding a total of 13 tracks upon mixdown. It can store uncompressed audio on the internal 15 GB drive. It has a built-in mixer and effects processor. For a musician who wants all of the elements of a digital home recording studio in one compact package, this might be the answer.

Korg has the D12 12-track recorder ($900) that can record up to 4 tracks simultaneously and play back up to 12 tracks simultaneously with 16-bit resolution, or 6 tracks simultaneously with 24-bit resolution. An integral 16-channel, 4-bus digital mixer is included. As with the Tascam 788, an optional CD-RW drive can be purchased with the D12 for about $450 to allow direct-to-digital CD-R masters.

Fostex offers the VF-16 16-track digital recorder for only $800. This is an excellent fully integrated unit for home or project studios. The digital mixer portion features 32-bit processing and mixing, 16 input channels (each with 3-band EQ and a parametric middle frequency), a compressor, effects send and 2 aux sends. The VF-16 records uncompressed 16-bit digital audio sampled at 44.1 kHz onto the internal 5.1 GB hard drive (which is upgradeable). The Fostex VF160 ($1150) is similar to the VF-16, except with a built-in CD-R/RW drive.

Other 16-track MHDMs available on the market now are the Akai DPS-16 ($1400), Fostex D1624 ($1200), Fostex D160 ($900), Korg D1600 ($1600), Yamaha AW1816 ($2000), and the Yamaha AW-4416CD ($2500). The 16-track MHDM certainly looks like the sweet spot of the home studio digital recording market right now, doesn't it?

Roland has an 18-track MHDM called the VS-1880HD ($1500). This all-in-one unit has 24-bit converters and comes with a copy of Emagic's Logic VS audio production and publishing software.

We are now starting to see some truly affordable 24-track digital recorders on the market. Both Alesis and Mackie have really cracked the low price barrier with the

Alesis HD24 ($2000) and the Mackie SDR24/96 (also $2000). The Alesis HD24 has the proper interfaces to fit in with any ADAT equipment in your studio. It is a 24-bit, 24-track digital recorder that can record at several different sample rates. It also has 24 analog inputs/outputs and 24 channels of ADAT Optical I/O. The equally impressive Mackie SDR24/96 is able to handle 24 channels of analog I/O and record 24 tracks of 48 kHz digital audio for 90 minutes to the internal drive (upgradeable). The SDR24/96 performs nonlinear/nondestructive editing, has 8 virtual takes per track, and can sync via SMPTE or MIDI interfaces. You will need an external mixer of some sort and external effects processors with either of these 24-track recorders.

Mackie also has the MDR24/96 Digital Multitrack Recorder. It is very similar to the SDR24/96, but with additional features including 999 levels of undo, sync via video interface, and floppy disk drive. The MDR24/96 costs about $2700.

Another impressive 24-track is the Roland VS-2480 ($3600). This is an all-in-one recording workstation that includes a 24-track/24-bit digital recorder, 64-channel digital mixer, and an internal effects processor. Additional slick features are motorized faders, mouse and ASCII keyboard inputs, and a VGA monitor output, so that you can use a computer CRT to monitor recording and mixdown operations. This is a tough package to beat at this price level.

Rounding out the 24-track recorders are the Tascam MX2424 ($3600) and the Mackie HDR24/96 ($4000). Both of these units can record at either 48 kHz or 96 kHz (with a lesser number of tracks on the MX2424 and a required software upgrade on the HDR24/96) with full 24-bit resolution. With both of these units, external mixing and effects processing is required.

So, we are seeing new and more powerful multitrack recording units come onto the market constantly. Trying to keep up with what is the latest and greatest is like having bees live in your head. They don't call it "The Bleeding Edge of Technology" for nothing! Perhaps a good strategy to use if you are going to buy an expensive multi-track deck is to buy one that has already been on the market for a fair amount of time. Find one that has been readily accepted by the masses, has a large installed base, and has all of the early software and hardware bugs upgraded out of it. This might save you quite a bit of anguish and down time in the studio.

Mastering Recorders (2-Tracks):

Mastering recorders are the units that record the final 2-channel mixdown from a multi-track recorder. There are many options here, and again they are largely governed by budget. If you are making a serious demo tape to send to a record producer, then I recommend that you spring for a CD-R/RW mastering recorder (either standalone or as part of your PC workstation). I am not going to detail every 2-channel recorder available on the market, but I will discuss some of the options you have here.

If you are financially embarrassed, you can use the cassette recorder from your entertainment system in the living room to record your 2-track master. This has some fairly serious limitations (tape hiss, lack of frequency response and distortion being the major ones). Here is a much better solution, in my opinion. Buy a VHS stereo Hi-fi VCR (or use the one you already may have in your living room) and use it as your mastering deck. You will achieve much better frequency response, less distortion, and much less tape hiss than most cassette decks. In fact, with the rotary head technology in VCRs, the performance is more like a reel/reel deck with an effective tape speed of over 200 inches per second! For example, you can buy the Toshiba W512 Stereo Hi-fi VHS VCR on the Internet for somewhere between $57 and $75, depending on the vendor. I doubt rather seriously that you will find any new 2-channel audio recorder on the market that can outperform it at that price point (but I am prepared to be pleasantly surprised). As an added bonus, you can record from 2 to 8 hours of music on just one VHS tape. Try that on a cassette! Note that the tape speed difference between the SP and SLP video recording modes doesn't really affect the audio quality much at all, but there is a higher chance that the recording will be negatively impacted by tape drop-outs at the slower SLP speed. With VHS tapes costing less that $2 each, record at the SP speed.

Of course, you can buy any one of the thousands of used reel/reel recorders on the market and use it as your mastering deck. You can get good results in frequency response and lack of distortion, but tape hiss will generally be a big negative impact with this format. You can mitigate that somewhat if you use an external Dolby or dbx noise reduction system. Even a single pass noise reduction system (a device usually designed with a smart sliding filter that tries to remove the hiss in the higher frequencies when the music is at too low of a level to mask the hiss) can remove some of the tape hiss upon playback, with the unfortunate side effect of taking some of the high frequency audio content with it. The hiss problem becomes less objectionable with the more expensive 30 inches-per-second tape machines.

Another option for a mastering deck is a MiniDisc (MD) recorder. They usually sound very good (especially the newer generation machines), and the media format is a dream (small, compact, relatively cheap). One drawback here is that the MD format uses a lossy compression algorithm that removes some of the audio information in an effort to save digital memory space when it converts it from the analog domain to the digital domain. This occurs even if you perform a digital transfer (via optical digital or coax digital connection) from a CD or hard disk player to the MD recorder. Once this audio information has been discarded by the audio compression scheme, it is gone forever and can't be magically reconstructed somehow. That is why it is called lossy compression (as opposed to lossless compression which does not throw any important data away). The mitigating factor is that these lossy audio compression algorithms are very good now, and it is difficult to tell the difference between the original recording and a 1st generation MD recording. Another drawback is that nasty SCMS signal that only allows one copy off of the master.

I think the best option for the mastering deck is the CD recorder. You can get them as standalone decks, or they can be configured as part of your computer system. The best approach is to perform a digital-to-digital transfer from the multi-track to the mastering deck, if at all possible. This avoids adding extra distortion and noise in the additional audio conversion processes required because the data always stays in the digital domain. Be aware that consumer CD recorders have a nasty little feature called SCMS (Serial Copy Management System) that prevents making additional digital copies of your digital masters. Pro and Semi-Pro CD recorders avoid this delightful inconvenience (but they cost more, of course).

Mixers:

Mixers come in all sorts of different configurations and complexities. You can get mixers that are designed to only mix microphones (called mic mixers) and mixers that are designed to only mix line level equipment (surprisingly called line mixers). You can get portable battery-operated mixers. You can even get passive mixers that mix together signals using just a network of resistors and no active electronic circuits. In this section, we are going to concern ourselves mainly with mixers that cost under $1000 and have both line- and microphone-level input sections, at least 8 mixer channels, and at least two internal buses. You can certainly spend more (lots more!) for a mixer (sometimes called a console when they get larger and more expensive) with very little effort. I am going to assume that if you are reading this book, you don't have $20,000 to spend on your mixer.

You have probably seen pictures of mixers that are 10 feet long and have what looks like 10,000 knobs and buttons on them. These are intimidating at first glance, but basically they have the same functions replicated over and over for each channel. So, once you understand the signal flow through one channel, then you will have a good grasp on the signal flow through all the other channels. The same logic applies to the mixer you buy for your home or project studio. Most all of these mixers will have some combination of microphone preamplifier and/or initial gain stage, equalization, internal bus assigning, panning and volume control for each channel (sometimes called the channel strip).

The microphone preamplifier and initial gain stage are used to boost microphone signals and weak line level signals to useable levels. This amplification is also used to boost the signal level so that some of the signal can be sent to headphone amplifiers, effects devices and other destinations without loading down the original signal. Setting this initial amplification level and the subsequent levels of amplification is called gain staging. Proper gain staging (also called gain structuring) is critically important in that it will allow you to have control over how much headroom you have (i.e., the amount of additional signal level you can have before clipping of the signal occurs) and how much noise floor you have (i.e., the amount of noise that is audible even when no audio signal is present).

Any audio signal point in your studio (not just on the mixer) where there is a preamplifier or volume control that can change the signal level of your audio can be considered a gain stage. The owner's manual for your mixer should have a discussion on how to set the proper gain structure for that particular piece of equipment. Later in the book, I give a basic procedure for setting the gain structure (see Setting the Gain Structure) of your mixer and connected equipment. If you want to learn more about gain staging (and you should!), or if your owner's manual is history, go to this website (http://cara.gsu.edu/courses/MI_3110/gainstaging/gain1.htm) and read through Georgia State University's School of Music online gain staging course. Other web sites that will give you a thorough understanding of gain staging can be found here:

- http://www.musicianstechcentral.com/10mixtips.html
- http://www.guitarmag.com/issues/9808/recguit.html
- http://audio1.ultrainteractive.com/guide2/sld011.htm
- http://members.aol.com/uniquenyc/key23.htm
- http://archive.bassplayer.com/z2001/0103/

anderton.shtml
*   http://www.professional-sound.com/sound/
    aug01.htm
*   http://www.soloperformer.com/Studio_Talk/
    cleaner.html
*   http://www.tape.com/techinfo/badsound.html
*   http://www.sweetwater.com/insync/
    techtip.tpl?find=04/03/2001
*   http://www.365proaudio.com/prod_tools/ten.shtml

A mixer might have one or more types of equalization available as part of its channel strip. The equalization (EQ) is generally provided to compensate for certain
spectral deficiencies in the audio signal. EQ can also be
used to produce special effects or remove noise from the
signal. The typical types of EQ you might encounter in a
mixer are shelving EQ (where a large portion of the high or
low frequency spectrum is boosted or cut all at once), multiband EQ (where slider or rotary pots boost or cut at specific frequencies), and parametric EQ (where the center
frequency, the number of adjacent frequencies, and the
amount of boost or cut are all continuously variable).

In my opinion, EQ is great when you really need it,
but too many people use it when they don't need it, and
they end up ruining the sound because of it. All EQ causes
a phase shift at certain frequencies when it is used. If I
find that I need to EQ a signal on the mixer, I will first see
if the source sound can be adjusted somehow without
reaching for the EQ knob on the mixer. For example,
maybe the microphone can be adjusted differently to pick
up more highs or lows, or maybe the synthesizer patch
can be adjusted to provide a different spectral sound. If I
really must use EQ on the mixer, I will try to do so by
cutting the other sounds around the frequency of interest
rather than boosting the frequency of interest. For example, if a sound doesn't seem to have enough high frequencies in relation to the low frequencies, I might cut the
low frequencies and then boost the overall volume of the
signal; this will essentially have the same effect as boosting the high frequencies. Just remember that there are

options other than immediately twiddling EQ knobs to alter a sound's character.

Inserts are the points in the mixer channel strip flow where the signal chain can be broken to insert signal processors. Using an insert, for example, a signal can be taken from the mixer board at the insert jack, run through an external equalizer or compressor device, and then brought back into the mixing board to continue its flow through the mixer channel strip.

Most mixers have other internal buses to complement the master (main) output buses and facilities for routing signals to those internal buses. There may be one or more of these buses for mixing a separate headphone mix (also called the cue bus), listening to certain channels in isolation (also called the solo bus), sending signals to outboard effects processors (also called the send bus), and receiving signals from outboard effects processors (also called the return bus). Some of these buses are also called aux (short for auxilliary) buses. There can also be other output buses for sending signals off the board to other recorders or mixers (sometimes called submaster outputs or just subs).

Panoramic Potentiometers (panpots for short) are used to steer a signal among one or more output channels on a mixer. The channel fader or volume potentiometer controls the amount of audio signal from that channel that makes it onto the output buses which are selected to receive that signal.

With all these signals running around, it is easy to see why large studio mixers can be intimidating. The key to understanding the mixing on your (or any) mixer is the mixer block diagram and the mixer channel flow diagram. The mixer block diagram will show a graphic representation of all the inputs and outputs that are available on the mixer for signal routing. The mixer channel flow diagram will show what the circuits are in a typical channel strip for that mixer, and it will show the signal flow order in which they appear on the strip (usually from top of the strip to the bottom). I recommend that you make copies of these diagrams and post them near your mixer, especially if other people are going to be using your equipment in a project studio.

Let's take a look at what kind of mixers are available today for home and project studio. One of the lowest cost 8-channel mixers with two aux buses is the Behringer MX802A. The unit has 4 mono inputs and 2 stereo inputs giving a total of 8 inputs. Four of the inputs have microphone preamps integrated into them, and each of the channel strips have a 3-band EQ integrated into them. The MX802A has 2 mono aux sends and 2 mono aux returns. Physically, the unit has a steel case instead of the plastic case you might expect at the price point of $100. If you need a slightly larger low-cost mixer, Behringer also makes the MX1604A mixer, which is very similar to and larger than the MX802A. The MX1604A has 4 mono and 4 stereo inputs (12 inputs total), 4 microphone inputs with +48V phantom power, 2 mono aux sends and 2 stereo aux returns. The MX1604A costs about $170. And if you need a still larger and more sophisticated low-cost mixer, then you can buy the Behringer MX2642A for about $400. It has 8 mono mic/line inputs and 4 stereo inputs, 6 aux sends and returns, and an additional 4 stereo line inputs (26 inputs total). Plus, this unit has inserts and direct outs. Inserts are jacks in the signal chain that allow the signal chain to be broken and another piece of external equipment patched in at that point. Direct outs are jacks that allow the signal from each individual channel strip to be accessed separately on its own dedicated jack. These features are handy when bouncing tracks and during mixdown. The MX2642A also has much better EQ circuitry with high/low shelving, semi-parametric and 4-band EQ on various channels.

Probably the most popular low-cost mixers these days are the Mackie mixers (www.mackie.com). The reasons for this popularity are their well-designed microphone preamps and generally low-noise electronic signal paths. The microphone preamps rival many standalone microphone preamplifiers, which is usually not the case in multifunction mixers in this class and price range. The 1402VLZPRO is a 14-channel mixer (6 mic/line mono inputs and 4 stereo inputs). The 6 microphone preamps have excellent specs such as distortion under 0.0007% (over the full 20 Hz-20 kHz range), a 130 dB dynamic range, and a wide 0-60 dB gain range. With this mixer, you won't need a separate standalone microphone preamplifier to get the best out of your microphones. The channel strips have a 3-band EQ and 60mm faders (volume potentiometers). The longer the faders, the easier it is to move them for a slow fade out. This mixer has 2 aux sends and 2 stereo aux returns. It costs about $530.

If you don't want to spend quite that much for a Mackie mixer, you can buy the 1202VLZPRO for about $380. It has the same type of excellent specs as the 1402VLZPRO, but with only 4 mic/line inputs and 4 stereo pair line inputs (12 inputs total). And if you can afford it, Mackie also sells the 1604VLZPRO mixer, which has 16 mic/line inputs, 6 aux sends with 4 stereo aux returns, and a true 4-bus internal design with subgroup and stereo bus assign. This may be the best analog mixer you can buy for under $1000 (and $1000 is about what you will pay for a new one on the street).

Not to be overlooked in the bang-for-the buck mixers are the Carvin mixers. Carvin is a company in Southern California that sells its equipment directly to you without the middle man distributor's cut. They have a reputation for low-cost, solid and high quality gear. Check them out at www.carvin.com, or call and order a catalog at 800-854-2235.

If you want to stay within the digital domain when you do your mixing, you can buy a digital mixer to go along with your digital recorder. Several companies make them now, including Fostex, Roland, Tascam and Yamaha. The advantage of using digital mixers with digital recorders is that every time you transition between the analog domain and the digital domain, circuits called analog-to-digital (A/D) and digital-to-analog (D/A) converters are used. These types of circuits can add non-linearities, distortion and noise to the signal, and the more times you make the transition between analog/digital/analog, the more the signal will degrade. The reasoning is that if you can make just one transition from analog to digital in the beginning (e.g., when recording from a mic), do all the recording, mixing, processing, and mastering in the digital domain, and then make just one more transition from the digital domain to the analog domain at the very end of the process (e.g., when you play your CD on your stereo), then you will be much better off. This may well be true; however, this approach can be more expensive than analog recording, especially if a large number of tracks and mixer channels are involved.

If you want to go the digital route, make sure that input and output buses on your mixer match the format and signal type on your digital recorders and your digital signal processors. Be aware that the newer digital recording standard (24-bit, 96 kHz sampling) will give a better and more accurate digital representation of an analog signal than the older digital recording standard (16-bit, 44.1 kHz). Also be aware that in the end, however, the consumer is most likely going to listen to your material on a 16-bit, 44.1 kHz CD player (or worse, on an MP3 player). A good example of a digital mixer is the 32-channel Behringer DDX3216 with a list price of about $2000. Another example is the Tascam DM-24, a 24-track, 24-bit, 96 kHz mixer that lists for $3000.

If you are looking for a larger, more expensive, new analog mixer, a good one is the Soundcraft Ghost LE. It has 24 or 32 input channels that can double at mixdown to provide 48 or 64 line inputs, along with 4 bands of equalization on each channel, 2 bands of which are fully parametric. This unit costs about $4000. If you are looking for a larger used console, the Trident 65 Series is good. It has 20 inputs and 8 outputs (expandable to 24 in, 16 out), 4 bands of semi-parametric EQ, low end roll off, 8 aux sends & returns, meter bridge, and a monitor section. You will pay about $5500 or $6000 for one of these. If you buy a used mixer, however, you may be buying someone else's headache. Chances are that the switches and pots will need to be at least cleaned and possibly even replaced, which could be a big cost. Mixers over about 10 years old start to have these problems.

Microphone Preamplifiers:

If you are going to be recording from a microphone, then there are three very important items that critically affect the sound you are going to record (the performance of the musician or artist notwithstanding): the microphone preamp, the microphone itself and the room acoustics where the recording is being done. You may not need a standalone microphone preamp in your recording system because some of the computer interfaces described above, certain standalone recorders, and most mixers (except line mixers) contain their own microphone preamplifiers in them.

Previously, I discussed my selection for a low-cost used microphone preamp, which is the Symetrix SX202. This dual microphone preamp has high-end performance at a low-end price. The list price for a new unit was $319 when it was being manufactured, but you can find them as low as $100 on the used market. Even if the tape recorder you are using has microphone inputs, chances are very slim that the microphone preamps in your recorder will have anywhere near the performance of the SX202. This is because the manufacturers of the recorders (cassette multi-tracks, digital multi-tracks, and even reel-to-reels) cannot afford to put high-end microphone preamps in their machines and expect to remain competitive on price. Even most of the low-to-mid priced mixer manufacturers don't have microphone preamps that outperform the SX202 (some of the Mackie mixers notwithstanding). So, for recording the key performances (such as vocals and lead instruments), having at least one SX202 on hand makes some sense. At about $120-$150 each for a used unit, it is not a budget killer. If you want to buy the newer version of this awesome microphone preamp, you can buy the Symetrix 302 for about $240. It has essentially the same features and specs as the SX202 (and the EIN is even better at −128 db!).

There are other low-cost standalone microphone preamps out there now. Standalone microphone preamps with tubes in them are now becoming very popular. For instance, dbx now sells a Mini-Pre Tube Microphone

Preamp for around $100. This single-channel preamp uses a 12AX7 vacuum tube as the main circuit component. ART offers a 12AX7 microphone preamp called the Tube MP Studio for about $110. Presonus makes the Bluetube two-channel microphone preamp with dual Sovtek 12AX7 tubes for about $160. Bellari has the single-channel MP105 Round Sound Tube Mic Preamp for about $100. Behringer sells the two-channel MIC2200 Ultragain Pro Tube Mic Preamp for about $170. Take a look at the spec sheet and see how these newer units measure up to the SX202. If the specs look good on paper, go to your local Pro Audio vendor and try the microphone preamp with your favorite microphone as the final verification before you buy it.

There are plenty of high-cost standalone microphone preamps out there, too. You can easily pay up to several thousand dollars for just one or two channels of microphone preamplification (Focusrite, Avalon, Millennia Media, etc.) if you have a thick wallet! One of the latest trends is to combine a high quality microphone preamp with other processing elements in one box. The ART 259 Tube Channel provides a single channel tube preamp, optical compressor and tube parametric EQ for about $400. The dbx 376 Tube Channel Processor combines a tube preamp, a 3-band parametric EQ, a compressor and a de-esser for about $500. (Note: a de-esser is an equalizer function combined with a dynamics processing function to remove sibilance— that annoying sssssss sound— from miked vocals.) Behringer has cracked the low-cost tube channel barrier with the VX2000 Ultra-Voice Pro for about $130. It has a microphone preamp, EQ, compressor, expander, de-esser and a "tube emulation" to add warmth to your sounds. As you can see, there are plenty of microphone preamp offerings in many styles and price ranges, and I only mentioned a few of them. I recommend that you use the Symetrix SX202 as the baseline to compare price and performance, and see how the microphone preamp you are evaluating compares to it.

Microphones:

Microphone prices can go from dirt cheap to astronomically high, and to a large extent, you will get what you pay for them. Here is a quick primer on microphones.

There are basically two types of microphones available to the home studio: dynamic and condenser. The dynamic microphone is a magnetic device that uses a very thin diaphragm attached to a moving coil. The coil is placed into a narrow magnetic gap, and when sound pressure causes the microphone diaphragm to move back and forth, the motion of the coil within the magnetic field of the gap induces a voltage that is proportional to the velocity of the diaphragm. In this way, the microphone turns sound waves into electrical signals. The efficiency of the permanent magnets, the sensitivity of the diaphragm, and other factors all conspire to affect the microphone's response and audible performance. The condenser microphone (also known as a capacitor microphone or electret condenser microphone) also has a diaphragm, but instead of being attached to a coil, the diaphragm is actually one plate (electrode) of a capacitor. As the incoming sound wave moves the diaphragm, the capacitance of, and hence the voltage stored in, the capacitor changes. As a very general rule of thumb, the condenser microphones are more sensitive than their dynamic counterparts, but the dynamic types are usually more able to withstand high sound pressure levels without distortion or breakup.

Each microphone can be capable of one or sometimes several different polar response patterns. The polar response pattern shows the ability of the microphone to pick up sounds waves emanating from sources in front of, behind or even to the side of the microphone (with respect to the microphone's on-axis sensitivity). The omnidirectional microphone is equally sensitive in all directions. The cardioid microphone (also known as unidirectional) is mainly sensitive to signals in front of it, and rejects sounds emanating from behind it. The hypercardioid picks up a minimum amount of sound from the sides, and mainly picks up sounds from the front, and to a lesser extent, the rear (180 degrees off axis). The supercardioid microphone has the highest ratio of front sensitivity to off-axis (reverberant) sensitivity. The bi-directional (also called the Figure 8 microphone) microphone is equally sensitive at 0 degrees on-axis and 180 degrees off axis. Parabolic and shotgun microphones are special cases that we won't cover here, since they are rarely used in the home studio.

Recommending a microphone is like telling someone they should buy a Ford vehicle versus a Chevy versus a Japanese import. My personal opinion is that you should have at least one reasonably good condenser microphone and one good dynamic microphone (buy the condenser first). If you can afford more microphones than those, then great. If you are going to be multi-tracking instruments one at a time, you can get away with just having a couple of good microphones. If you are going to be miking a whole drum set and several guitar amps for a real-time, live recording, then two microphones is probably not going to get the results you want (especially if control over each instrument's sound is what you desire). Since I am writing this to be useful for the absolute beginner also, I will recommend one of each type of microphone. If at all possible, you should go and audition several microphones, but if you can't or you are ordering used equipment by mail, you can go with these recommendations. If you really can only afford to buy just one microphone, then buy the condenser microphone.

The AKG C1000S is a good low-end condenser microphone. It is known as a small-diaphragm condenser microphone. The list price for this microphone was $429 up until recently, but with the glut of new low-cost microphones, you can find a used C1000S in the $150 neighborhood, or maybe even less. I personally don't think you can pay $150 and get a better microphone for recording vocals, acoustic guitar and other acoustic instruments. It is very sensitive and has a good frequency response (50 Hz to 20 kHz). It has an insert that you can put inside of the microphone to change it from a cardioid response pattern to a hypercardioid pattern. It can be powered from an internal 9V battery, or it can be phantom-powered with +48V from your mixing console. (Some mixers provide phantom power to energize condenser-type microphones, so that batteries aren't required inside of the microphones. The SX202 and many other microphone preamps provide their own phantom power to the microphone.) This microphone can handle a maximum SPL (Sound Pressure Level) of 137 dB, which is fairly good for a condenser microphone, but you probably won't want to use it to microphone your favorite drum set (unless it is from a distance overhead), especially the kick drum. If you can afford to pay a little more for your first microphone, then buy one of these new microphones: AKG C2000B (~$200) (or the Rode NT1 at $200), AKG C3000B (~$300), Rode NTK Tube ($500), or the AKG C4000B (~$600). Buy the best microphone you can afford, as it *will* make a difference in the quality of your recordings. One of the finest vocal microphones under $1000 is the AKG C414B (~$800). It's a real gem, if you can afford it. Even better is the Neumann U87 large dual-diaphragm condenser microphone (~$2000).

On the dynamic microphone side, I am recommending the Electro-Voice N/D 767A. This is a supercardioid microphone, which uses a neodymium alloy to form the magnetic material inside the microphone. This neodymium material gives the microphone very good sensitivity for a dynamic-style microphone. It also has a built-in pop filter to reduce wind noise and vocal pops. This is a good vocal microphone that can also be used for miking amplified instruments such as guitars and basses. The close field response goes down to 35Hz, and the high end tops out at 22kHz. It can handle SPLs up to 156dB. Dynamic microphones have a phenomenon known as the proximity effect, which boosts the bass response of the microphone when it is within 12" or so of the sound source. The 767A has a switch to roll off this increased bass response during close-proximity applications (which is generally a good idea to use unless you are collecting low-frequency sound samples). This is also a good microphone to use for live vocal performances; the microphone has special materials to reduce the conduction of handling noise into the diaphragm. This microphone has a street price of ~$140.

Another good (but lower-cost) microphone that you can buy new or on the used market is the Shure SM-57. This microphone has been the industry standard for miking instruments for many years. It is recommended for miking electric guitar amplifiers. You can find one of these new for ~$80 and used for even less than that.

Now that you know more about microphones, let me tell you that no one microphone is going to be the answer in all microphone situations. Probably the best strategy is to amass a balanced collection of condenser, dynamic and ribbon (another name for Figure 8) microphones as time progresses and your pocketbook recovers from the last purchase. Try to buy microphones that can handle both of the main polar pick-up patterns (cardioid and omnidirectional). Also, buying new microphones might be a better strategy than buying used microphones. It is hard to know which used microphones have been banged around out on the road or misused in studios. Have you ever seen The Who in concert?

Effects Processors:

Effects processors have become something akin to the Swiss Army Knife— they do just about everything now. You can get processors that manipulate the audio to provide effects such as reverb, echo, pitch shift, chorusing, flanging, phasing, delay, equalization, tremolo, panning, vocoding, detuning, and a ton of other stuff. (I explained these kinds of effects earlier in the book.)

If I had to buy just one signal processing device, and I had a *very* limited budget, then I would buy the Alesis Nano Verb. The list price is $135, but you can get one new for about $100 or so, and a used one for even less (~$50). Don't be fooled by the low price and the diminutive packaging; this unit has impressive specs. It has several hall, room and plate reverbs, and they sound reasonably good. (One way to judge the quality of a reverb is to listen to the "tail" of it. Does it get grainy and choppy towards the end, or does it smoothly fade out to silence? This is an indication of how good the algorithm is that generates the reverb.) The Nano Verb also has gated reverb, chorus, flange, delay and rotary speaker effects. The unit is very clean with a total harmonic distortion spec of 0.02% and a dynamic range of over 90dB. It covers the full frequency bandwidth of 20Hz to 20kHz. There are many effects devices on the market, but this one surely stands out in the bang-per-buck category. Another good low-end effects processor is the Zoom RFX-300 ($100 new). I like the fact that it has a microphone simulator that will allow one microphone to sound like several different ones. It also has a compressor/limiter function, which is a necessity to get a consistent amplitude when recording with a microphone. If you have a little more money to spend, then a good choice might be the Alesis Wedge, but you can only find these on the used market now. And if you have even more money to spend, I would spend it on one of the Lexicon effects processors. Lexicon is a very respected name in signal processing, and they have recently been introducing lower-cost equipment into the market. Depending on what your budget permits, you can expect to pay these street prices for new Lexicon gear: MPX 100 (~$200), MPX 110 (~$250), MPX 200 (~$300), MPX 500 (~$400) and the MPX 1 (~$700). Buy the best one you can reasonably afford.

If you want one of the best reverbs on the market, it surely must be the Sony S777 Digital Sampling Reverb. This awesome device allows you to sample the reverb attributes (early reflections, delays, timings, amplitudes and frequency response) of your favorite acoustic space and then use that reverb algorithm to mix your audio! For example, you could sample the acoustic space of a church or concert hall, and then use those characteristics for the reverb on your vocal tracks in your studio. The unit can also be configured with other sampled acoustic spaces available on CDROMs. As you might guess, it is not cheap.

There are many effects processors on the market now, not only new ones coming out each week, but tons of older used ones. For example, two used units that are very good are the Lexicon PCM60 reverb (~$550 used) and the Yamaha REV7 reverb (~$500 used). You will eventually end up with several effects processors in your studio, mainly because of the low cost of digital processing now. So, my advice is to get a reasonable Swiss Army Knife-type first (if you can find and afford a used Alesis Wedge, buy it first). Next, add on processors that you will use for specialty processing or possibly a dedicated unit that has exceptionally good reverbs (such as the used Yamaha REV7 or even the new Sony S777), and make that your dedicated reverb box. Gear lust will overcome you, and you will eventually be buying other effects processors as time progresses. Gear lust gets us all eventually.

Dynamics Processors:
It is possible to make reasonable recordings without a compressor, but most of today's music uses a compressor somewhere in the chain. Compressors are used to even out the dynamics in a recording. As a minimum, they are generally used on the lead vocal of the song. Other areas usually requiring compression are drums, certain percussion and the bass. Probably the best, low-cost 2-channel compressor in the world is the RNC1773 from FMR Audio. This unit has a 100kHz bandwidth and can provide stereo dynamics processing with control over ratio, attack, release, and threshold. It also has a unique proprietary mode that layers 3 separate compressors together to minimize compression artifacts like pumping and breathing. This mode sounds super smooth, and is appropriately called Super-Nice Mode. The list price is $199, but you can buy a new RNC1773 for only $180 directly from FMR. I don't recall ever seeing a used one for sale (what does that tell you?). OK, so my memory is bad, but this compressor is a good deal, folks. I have one in my rack and I use it on nearly every recording with excellent results. You can easily pay much more money, but not get better quality in a compressor. You can check out the RNC1773 at FMR's web site: www.fmraudio.com. You can call them at (800) 343-9976 in Austin, TX. By the way, RNC stands for Really Nice Compressor.
Another good low-cost compressor is the Alesis 3630. This unit can provide stereo or dual mono dynamics processing and can provide RMS and peak compres-

sion, limiting, noise gating, and ducking functions. You can find them used for under $100, and this is a good deal. (In my opinion, the Alesis 3630 is not sonically as good as the RNC1773, but it is more of a Swiss Army Knife compressor.) You can check out the 3630 and other Alesis products at the company's website: alecorp@alesis1.usa.com.

Enhancers and Exciters:
    A couple of different manufacturers make psycho-acoustic enhancers. Basically, these are signal proces-sors that make your mixes (or individual instruments) sound better (clearer, more definition, etc.). The two main ones are the BBE Sonic Maximizer and the Aphex Aural Exciter. I have versions of both of these units. If you are going to buy just one, then make it the BBE Sonic Maxi-mizer. You can run your final mix through it to make the mix sound even better. It is very simple to operate, and the lowest cost one (Model 264) is about $40 new. It really does make a positive difference in the sound (if you don't overdo it!).

Reference Monitors (Speakers):
    As I mentioned earlier, I highly recommend that you get a set of reference monitors with which you are already familiar, or buy a set of monitors and then become very familiar with them through listening to your favorite com-mercial recordings on them. Eventually, you will come to understand their shortcomings and how they color the sound in your particular room or studio. This is a very critical point, because when you know what things are supposed to sound like through those monitors, then you can strive to make your own mixes emulate those sounds. For a long time, I used a set of Yamaha NS-044 speakers (forerunners of the ubiquitous NS-10s that you see on ev-ery professional mixing console in the country). The NS-044s most definitely color the sound, no question about it. At the time I purchased them (close to 20 years ago), it was all I could afford. Right now, I am using a pair of NHT SuperZero speakers (NHT recently replaced these with their

SuperAudio line of speaker systems— see http://www.nhthifi.com/products home.asp). These speakers are made for the consumer home stereo market; however, they are ruler flat from 100 Hz on up to 20 kHz, and they have a "transparent" sound quality. Plus, the price was right (about $120 each on the street). They sound great with an added subwoofer to fill out the bottom octave. Also, I have another pair with a subwoofer in my living room, so I am intimately familiar with how they sound.

There are other ways to go, of course. The market is rich with studio monitor offerings from Roland, Event, Tannoy, JBL, Yamaha, Mackie, Krok, Paradigm, NHT, Samson, and others. The reason for all these products is the big surge in home and project studios. These manufacturers recognize that if someone has converted a bedroom into a studio, they probably aren't going to have room for a huge set of monitors (nor will the room dimensions be able to support such an approach acoustically). Hence, the close field concept has become the standard in these situations.

Most all of the monitors in this genre have either a 6.5" woofer or 8" woofer, plus a small tweeter. Pricing on the street is from $200 per pair at the low end (for non-powered monitors) on up. For example, you can get the Hafler M5 monitor speaker for about $100 each. You can also get self-powered monitors (i.e., the audio power amplifier is contained within one or both speakers cabinets), which will free you from having to buy, mount and hook up a separate power amp. If you are going to have your monitors mounted on a desk near a computer CRT monitor or television, then I highly recommend that you buy magnetically shielded monitors. Otherwise, the magnetic field from the speakers will distort (potentially permanently) the display orientation and colors on the CRT. Also, the CRT might induce hum or noise into your monitors. (See the tip near the end of the book on shielding non-shielded monitor speakers.)

NHT (an acronym for Now Hear This) has developed the NHTPro A-10 and A-20 series of powered studio monitors. The A-10 system (~$500) includes a pair of 2-

way, acoustic suspension monitors (6.5" paper-cone woofer and a 1" soft-dome, liquid-cooled tweeter) with a rack mount dual-mono 150W RMS/300W peak power amplifier. These monitors will get down to 57 Hz and up to 20 kHz (+/-2 dB) from one meter away on axis. The A-20 (~$1000) series is similar, but with a more powerful amplifier (250W RMS/400W peak) and a response down to 45 Hz. I have not listened to the NHTPro series of monitors and subwoofers, but if they are anything like NHT's SuperZero speakers (ruler flat, low distortion and transparent sound quality), then you should consider them for use in your studio. Check out the entire NHTPro line of speaker systems at http://www.nhthifi.com/products_pro.asp.

If you want a fine, no-nonsense pair of studio monitors, then consider the Mackie HR824 Active Biamped Studio Monitors (~$1400 new). These monitors have power amplifiers and crossovers built right into the speakers. They are bi-amplified, meaning the low frequency woofers are driven from a separate amplifier than the high frequency tweeter. This helps the clarity of the sound because big transients (i.e., heavy current draws on the amplifier) in the bass frequencies don't affect the high frequencies. The overall effect of biamplification is better transient response and lower distortion. The Mackie HR824s have a flat frequency from 42 Hz up to 20 kHz.

Power Amplifiers:

As I have mentioned previously in this text, if you already have an old power amp, integrated amp or stereo receiver laying around, there is no reason that you can't put this to good use in your home studio. Maybe the worst thing is that you have to buy some contact cleaner to clean up that scratchy volume control. You can find plenty of these older power amps at the swap meet, flea market, or each week in the classified ads of your newspapers.

Now, here are a few technical aspects to understand about monitor speaker and power amplifier specifications. The impedance of a speaker is the measurement of how that speaker impedes the flow of current over frequency. The impedance value is generally a nominal number only, and the actual impedance of the speaker can vary from down to 2Ω up to over 50Ω, depending on the frequency of interest. Most of the speakers you will be evaluating are 4Ω, 8Ω or 16Ω. The speaker also usually is given a maximum power rating, and this is the value at which the speaker can safely be operated without damage. (Note that this maximum power value is usually determined by using a nice clean sine wave as the input waveform, and not a clipped or distorted audio signal. We'll come back to this.) Power amplifiers usually have a specification of so many watts driven into some load, with both channels driven over the full frequency spectrum with no more than a certain amount of distortion.

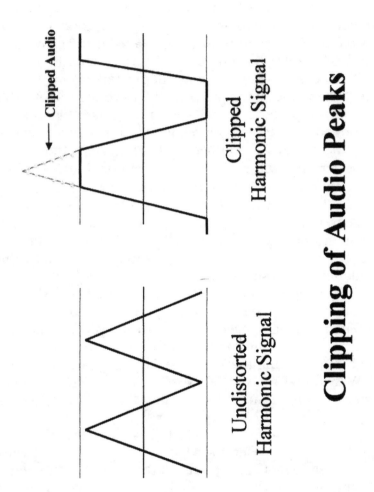

Figure 6: Clipped & Unclipped Waveforms

The reason that so many stipulations are put onto the power amp spec is that there has been extreme "salesmanship" involved in amp specifications over the years, and the industry has tried to nail down what the output power of a certain product really is. So, you may see an amp specification read as "50 Watts per channel into 8Ω, both channels driven, from 20 Hz to 20 kHz at no more than 0.05% total harmonic distortion." This is a good spec that tells you how the amplifier is really going to perform. The same power amp might have a spec of "250 Watts music power." If you see a rating like this (thankfully not so common anymore), ignore it, because it is basically meaningless. Another interesting fact is that a certain power amp will put out 200 W/channel into 4Ω, but it will only put out about 100 W/channel into 8Ω. This is because the power amp is putting out basically the same voltage in both cases, but the load impedance determines the amount of power dissipated in the load (using the formula: the power equals the voltage squared divided by the impedance of the speaker.)

So how do you match up a power amplifier's output rating with a speaker's rating? I have read in many different magazines over the years that you should not connect a power amp to speakers if the power amp has a higher power rating than the speakers (e.g., connecting a 100 W/channel amp to 50 Watt max speakers). I don't agree with this. I am of the opinion that you can just as easily damage a 50 Watt speaker with a 25 W/channel power amp if you run a distorted signal through it for extended periods. Here is why: a distorted signal with excessive clipping (i.e., clipping off the tops of each electrical signal peak so that the signal ends up pegged to either the most positive value or most negative value) is going to heat up the voice coils in the speakers. See Figure 6. The voice coil is a small winding of thin wire that becomes an electromagnet when the audio signal is passed through it. When the audio signal is a highly distorted and clipped signal, the speaker cone starts to be fully extended in one direction or the other *all* the time. Over a period of time (sometimes a very short period of time!), the voice coil wire will start to melt, short out, and you then have a burnt out speaker that needs to be replaced. This can happen with a power amp and speaker combination even though the power amp's output is rated less than the speaker's maximum input power.

Of course, you can also easily burn out your speakers with too much power (e.g., connecting a 200 W/channel amp to 50 Watt max speakers) if you turn up the volume control too much. I operated my 40W maximum Yamaha speakers for over 10 years with an 80W/channel Kyocera power amplifier with absolutely no problems. I was very careful not to run highly distorted audio through the speakers at high levels for extended periods, and I never changed signal cables to the power amp with the volume up on the speakers. So, the moral of the story is that you can use a power amp with a higher power rating to drive the monitor speakers in your studio— if you are careful not to overdrive the speakers with too much wattage. And, you can use a lower powered amp to drive the speakers, but you still have to be careful not to drive clipped audio through them for extended periods!

If you want to buy a used amp made specifically for recording studios, then the Alesis RA-100 is a good choice. It puts out 100W per channel into a 4Ω load. You can find these for about $150 now at many of the used equipment web sites I list in this book.

If you want to buy a new power amp, there are also some good studio amps out on the market now for reasonable prices. Alesis now has the RA150 (45 W/ch) for about $200, the RA300 (90 W/ch) for about $280, and the RA500 (150 W/ch) for about $380. Symetrix has the 420 for about $350, which puts out 20 W/ch into 8Ω and comes with a front panel headphone jack. Hafler has the TA1100 (40 W/ch) for about $200 and the TA1600 (60 W/ch) for about $250. The Hafler amps are convection cooled (no fans = quiet!), and have a soft-start circuit that protects speakers from that damaging initial turn-on thump.

Headphones:

Here is a fact of life: it is tough to pay under $40 and get a set of headphones that doesn't drastically color the sound somehow. If all you have is about $40 to spend, then buy the AKG K66 Semi-Open Dynamic Headphones, or the AKG K100 headphones for $50. If you have ~$100, then get the industry standard AKG K240M or Sony MDR-7506 headphones. If you have $200 to $240, listen to both the Sony MDR7509 (~$200) and the AKG K270S (~$240) and see which one sounds best to you and is most comfortable to wear for extended periods.

If you are a one-man band, and you multi-track yourself while listening to previously-recorded tracks on headphones, be aware that "open-air" types of headphones can bleed into the microphone much more readily than "closed" types of headphones. The AKG K270S and the Sony MDR7509/MDR7506 are closed types, while the AKG K240M and the AKG K66 are open types. If you are buying a second set of headphones for other musicians to use in your studio while you record them, make sure you buy the closed type of headphones to prevent bleed into the microphones.

Headphone Amplifiers:

Headphone amplifiers are little standalone boxes that have one or more headphone jacks in them for the purpose of allowing the recording engineer and/or the musicians to monitor the audio. Generally, they have one or more line level input jacks on the back for connecting the output of the mixer or other audio device that you want to monitor. On the front, they have at least one volume control to control the level of the audio in the headphones. Some headphone amplifiers have all sorts of other features, allowing each individual listener to set up a personal mix in the headphones to his or her liking. (And, you know how those musicians can be.)

If you want to buy a used headphone amplifier, the Alesis Micro Cue Amp is a simple and solid performer. It has two headphone jacks, and each listener can modify the relative volume mix between two stereo sources. There is also a connection to allow other Micro Cue Amps to be connected in series. You can find these for as little as $30 on the used market. How can you go wrong? Another good used headphone amp is the Symetrix SX204, which you can find on the used market for around $150. This is a one input-four output unit, allowing you to set different volume levels for each headphone. Symetrix has improved on this design with their new Model 304 Headphone Amp. You can get these new for about $235.

Rolls Corporation has a low-end headphone amp called the HA43 for about $72. This is another one input, four output headphone amp with individual volume controls. Probably the best low-end deal on a new unit is the Behringer HA4400 headphone amp. It can drive up to 12 sets of headphones with 4 different mixes (3 headphones each). It has buttons for Mono/Left Mute/Right Mute selection, LED power meters for each section, a separate stereo AUX IN jack, plus balanced and unbalanced output jacks. All this for about $80!

If you need a headphone distribution system, you can get the Furman HDS6. This system allows you to have a rack mount audio distribution box and up to 8 remote mixers, one for each musician. The remote mixers are connected to the main box by 25' cables. The remote mixers have 4 monophonic volume controls that allow each user to create their own custom mix of up to 4 channels from the console or mixer bus, and each remote mixer can drive two sets of headphones. The main box goes for around $260, while each remote mixer box costs about $100.

Headphone Amp Kits:

If you don't want to buy a commercially available headphone amplifier, you do have the option of buying a headphone amplifier kit and assembling it yourself for a reasonably low price.

PAiA has a headphone distribution amp kit that will allow you to drive up to 6 sets of stereo headphones at once. Headphone impedance can be 8 to 600Ω and each headphone has its own volume control. The 9206/k HDA kit costs about $80 unassembled.

Another company that has a stereo headphone amplifier kit is Ramsey Electronics. You can check them out at www.ramseykits.com. They sell the SHA1 kit for $20. This kit takes stereo RCA line level inputs and drives one stereo headphone with a pair of 250mW audio amps. You can get a matching case and knob set (CSHA) for $15, or you can buy the whole kit assembled and tested with case and knobs for $50. The unit runs on 9VDC to 15VDC wall wart (not supplied with kit).

If you want to add a small headphone buffer amp right inside one of your pieces of studio equipment, you can do so with the PAiA Headphone Buffer Amp kit. This is a slick little PCA (Printed Circuit Assembly) that you can build and mount right inside a cassette deck, reel/reel, synthesizer, effects box or any other device that uses a line level (preamp level) signal. The 9605/k Headphone Buffer Amp kit costs about $25. You can see the schematic and description for it at http://www.paia.com/headbuff.htm.

The Bottom Line:

All in all, you will need to have good recording techniques and good equipment to achieve a reasonable recorded sound (not to mention actual musicianship). One thing that I recommend you do is to continually trade up in equipment quality and performance as your budget allows. You may have to start out with low-end, used equipment (everyone has to start somewhere), but as technology progresses, today's hot new item is tomorrow's low-cost deal.

RECOMMENDED BASIC SYSTEMS

In this section, I will make some recommendations on what equipment to buy for various studio budget levels. If a friend of mine came to me and told me he had a certain budget to spend on new studio equipment, these are the items I would tell him to buy. If you really don't know where to start, and you would like a recommendation from someone who is not a salesman for some store, then these recommendations might be a good place for you to start. For these systems, I am going to make the following assumptions and stipulations:

- You are going to be recording just one person at a time (probably yourself), therefore just one microphone is required.
- You don't have any other studio equipment, but you do have a reasonably equipped entertainment system that can play/record cassette tapes and play CDs. Most people have at least that capability these days.
- All the equipment is going to be purchased new.
- Studio infrastructure and accessories (i.e., acoustic treatments, power distribution, studio furniture, cables, tapes, etc.) will be largely ignored.

These recommendations are based on what you might expect to pay for the equipment on the street, not the list prices. (Big Hint: you should never be paying list price for your studio equipment!)

If I don't draw the line somewhere, the number of permutations will quickly get out of control here. Each system will have a multi-track recording capability, a microphone, a mixer, a way to impart effects onto the signal, a recorder to mix down to a stereo master, and a way to monitor the audio.

Recommended System under $500:
- Microphone: Shure SM-57 Dynamic Microphone, $80.
- Mixer: (Built into the multi-track recorder, $0.)
- Multi-track Recorder: Tascam Porta 02MKII Cas-

sette Multi-track Recorder, $150.
- Audio Processors: BBE 264 Sonic Maximizer, $40; Zoom RFX-300 Multi Effects Processor, $100.
- Stereo Master Recorder: Toshiba W512 Stereo Hi-Fi VHS VCR, $57.
- Monitors: AKG K66 Headphones, $40.

At this price level, it is tough to get anything better than a cassette multi-tracker (unless of course you go with used equipment). The cassette multi-tracker is definitely going to be the weakest link in this signal quality chain. The Shure SM-57 is an excellent, low-cost workhorse of the recording industry. You won't go too terribly wrong with this microphone. Even high-end studios use it. The Tascam allows microphone or line inputs, so an external microphone preamp is not required (but a low-to-high impedance converter is required). I chose the Zoom RFX-300 effects processor because it not only has some good effects in it, it has a microphone simulator that will allow one microphone to sound like several different ones, which is an added bonus. It also has a compressor/limiter function, which is a necessity when recording with a microphone. The AKG K66 headphones will allow you to monitor what is being recorded and mixed down on the Tascam. At this price range, we can't really afford a separate set of studio speakers and an amplifier (or a set of powered speakers). I think it is more important to have the headphones, and then listen to the mixes on your living room stereo. The BBE 264 Sonic Maximizer only costs $40, but it will make a huge difference in the final sound quality of your mix. I would use it at the output of the Tascam when you go to mix down to the final master recording. And why did I choose a VCR for the master deck? You will never be able to find any new audio recorder for $57 that will sound better than a VHS Hi-Fi VCR. (When I wrote this text, J&R Music World was selling this VCR for $57.) The good thing about this choice is that you get full bandwidth frequency response and extremely low noise (both far in excess of the capabilities of any cassette multi-tracker) at a rock bottom price. You can store hours of masters on one inexpensive tape. Plus, you can watch your favorite movies on it when the recording session is over!

Since you have a cassette recorder/player on your living room stereo, you have even more options available to you. After you have mixed down and recorded the master to your VHS Hi-Fi tape, you can dupe a copy onto your cassette deck for playing in the living room, in the car, or to give to your friends (or as a demo tape). You can also mix down 4 tracks on the Tascam to your stereo cassette recorder, and since the Tascam runs at the normal cassette speed, you can take the mixed-down 2-channel tape out of your cassette player, put it into the Tascam, and then record two more tracks to it before mixing down to the final master recording. This gives you the capability of getting 6 tracks of recording from this system. If you bounce tracks around on the Tascam, you can get even more tracks than that (but audio quality and noise level will suffer). By bouncing tracks, I mean taking what you recorded on say tracks 1, 2, and 3, then combining those and recording them onto track 4. Now you can erase tracks 1, 2, and 3, because all of that audio is now on track 4. This frees up the first 3 tracks for more audio.

Note that the frequency response of this multitracker is only 12.5 kHz at the high end, and it has a signal-to-noise ratio (the ratio of the loudest signal in the recorder to the noise floor) of only 43 dB. This is in comparison to today's digital recorders that generally have a high-end frequency response of 20 kHz and a 96 db signal-to-noise ratio. One way to combat this problem is to pre-emphasize the high frequencies when you record them to a cassette multitracker (or to an older reel-to-reel recorder). This technique was originally discovered a long time ago when the Bell Lab engineers were looking for a way to push voice signals farther distances along copper wire. Since copper wire has inherent losses associated with it, the Bell engineers pre-emphasized the frequencies that would be lost in transit, therby allowing a coherent audio signal to travel further down the cable. Similarly, if you premphasize the high frequencies above 10 kHz as you record them to the cassette tracks, you may be able to get just a little more brightness and clarity out of the top end of your cassette multitrack recordings. You can always reduce the high end upon playback and mixdown if the high frequencies become too strident. This reduction of highs during playback will also have the effect of reducing tape hiss, which is always a good thing.

Recommended System under $1000:
- Microphone: Rode NT3, $150.
- Mixer: Behringer Eurorack MX802A Mixer, $100.
- Multi-track Recorder: Roland VSR880 8-track Digital Recorder, $500.
- Audio Processors: BBE 264 Sonic Maximizer, $40; Zoom RFX-300 Multi Effects Processor, $100.
- Stereo Master Recorder: Toshiba W512 Stereo Hi-Fi VHS VCR, $57.
- Monitors: AKG K100 Headphones, $50.

Being able to squeeze the Roland VSR880 8-track hard disk recorder with 24-bit sound quality and powerful digital editing into the $1000 system will result in a quantum leap in sound quality over the $500 system. The price of the VSR880 has recently been reduced to the $500 level (presumably because of the large number of competing digital recorders). Also, with the huge number of virtual tracks available on the VSR880 (128 virtual tracks), the flexibility and track bouncing capability is vastly better than any cassette multi-tracker. Later on, when you get more money, you can add the optional VS8F2 24-bit Effect Expansion Board into the VSR880 rack mount chassis.

The Behringer Eurorack MX802A is a nice little mixer for only $100. It has 4 mono mic/line inputs and 4 stereo line inputs. It also has two send buses with two stereo return buses, and additional 2-channel deck input and output, separate main and monitor outputs, and a headphone amplifier onboard. It is definitely tough to beat at the $100 level. (I considered including how to build a small, cheap mixer for the DIY (Do It Yourself) folks, but there is no way to beat the Behringer Eurorack MX802A mixer at that price point.) The Rode NT3 condenser microphone gives full 20 Hz-20 kHz bandwidth sound and low self-noise (additional noise generated by the mic itself). It is a good responsive microphone for the $150 level. I kept the Zoom RFX-300 because of the microphone simulator and compressor/limiter functions. The BBE 264 Sonic Maximizer and the Toshiba W512 Stereo Hi-Fi VHS VCR are the same as described in the $500 system above. The headphones have been upgraded to the AKG K100 Headphones, which are able to reproduce the full 20 Hz to 20 kHz audio spectrum.

Even though the Roland VSR880 can only play back 8 tracks at a time, the fact that it has 128 virtual tracks really opens up the possibilities in this system. You could conceivably record 7 tracks of audio on the first 7 real tracks and then mix those down to real track 8. When that is done, you exchange all 8 real tracks for a set of 8 virtual tracks. Then, you could record another set of 7 tracks of audio on real tracks 1-6 and 8, and subsequently mix those to real track 7, and so on. In this manner, you could build up 7 tracks of audio on each of the 8 real tracks on the VSR880. This would give you up to 56 high quality tracks at mixdown time, since the audio tracks on this digital recorder would suffer only the slightest degradation as you bounce them to other tracks.

I still maintain that you will get the best mastering results with the Toshiba W512 Stereo Hi-Fi VHS VCR as your stereo master deck as compared to a cassette deck. Maybe once you get up into the 3-head cassette decks priced over $300, you will start to see comparable audio recording quality. Again, after you have mixed down and recorded the master to your VHS Hi-Fi tape, you can dupe a copy onto your living room cassette deck.

As an alternate $1000 system, you could replace the Roland VSR880 and Behringer Eurorack MX802A with the new Fostex VF80 8-track Digital Recorder (for about the same $600). You may get better sonic results with the Fostex VF80, as the signal is kept in the digital domain between the recorder and the mixer. Plus, you can add the optional CD-R/RW burner to the VF80 later on when you get the money.

Recommended System under $1500:
- Microphone: AKG C3000B Condenser Mic, $300.
- Mixer: (Built into the Fostex VF-160 multi-track recorder, $0.)
- Multi-track Recorder: Fostex VF-160 16-track Digital Recorder with CD Burner, $1149.
- Audio Processors: BBE 264 Sonic Maximizer, $40. (The Fostex VF-160 has its own internal effects processor.)
- Stereo Master Recorder: (Built into the Fostex VF-160, $0.)
- Monitors: AKG K100 Headphones, $50.

Adding another $500 to the budget allows us to add quite a few more capabilities. For starters, we now have a 16-track digital recorder with its own integrated digital mixer and internal effects processor (including a compressor). The VF-160 also has phantom power for condenser microphones. To keep the complete audio path pristine, we are now using the VF-160's built-in CD-R/CD-RW digital recorder for the stereo mastering deck. And we have added the highly acclaimed AKG 3000B condenser microphone. These are very nice microphones for the money— nice enough to cause me to buy two of them for my own studio. And OK, I went over the $1500 limit by $39. If you are looking for a source for the VF-160, try JD Sound at www.jdsound.com or 877-JDSOUND.

Recommended System for about $2000:
- Microphone: AKG C3000B Condenser Mic, $300.
- Mixer: (Built into the Fostex VF-160 multi-track recorder, $0.)
- Multi-track Recorder: Fostex VF-160 16-track Digital Recorder, $1149.
- Audio Processors: FMR Audio RNC1773 Compressor, $180. (The Fostex VF-160 has its own internal effects processor.)
- Stereo Master Recorder: (Built into the Fostex VF-

160, $0.)
- Monitors: Combination of Hafler TA1100 power amplifier with two Hafler M5 Monitors, $380, AKG K100 Headphones, $50.

At the $2000 level, we can add the FMR Audio RNC1773 Compressor.   This will help immensely in leveling out the dynamics in your recorded material, especially vocals and bass lines.   Also added is the combination of the Hafler TA1100 power amplifier with two Hafler M5 Monitors.   This will allow audio playback through speakers in the studio instead of using speakers in the living room or elsewhere to monitor the mixes.

Recommended Standalone Studio System for $5000:
- Microphone: Rode NTK Tube Mic, $500.
- Mixer: (A digital mixer is built into the Roland VS2480HD Digital Workstation, $0.)
- Multi-track Recorder: Roland VS2480HD 24-Track Digital Workstation, $3600.
- Audio Processors: FMR Audio RNC1773 Compressor, $180. (The Roland VS2480HD has its own internal effects processors.)
- Stereo Master Recorder: TDK DA-3826 Dual-Well CD-R Recorder, $300.
- Monitors: Combination of Hafler TA1100 power amplifier with two Hafler M5 Monitors, $380, Sony MDR7506 Headphones, $100.

This system is built around the Roland VS2480HD 24-Track Digital Workstation, which is a fairly sophisticated piece of equipment (24-track/24-bit digital recording with 64-channel digital mixing). An optional CD burner can be purchased for the unit, which I would recommend over the outboard consumer CD-R recorder mentioned above (I believe the cost is around $500 for this option). The Rode NTK Tube Mic is a highly regarded Class A twin-triode (i.e., tube-based) microphone with a 1" gold-plated membrane that gives exceptional quality and warmth at this price range. This $5000 standalone system has the capacity to turn out high quality digital recordings.

Recommended Computer Studio System for $5000:

- Microphone: Rode NTK Tube Mic, $500.
- Multi-track Recorder and Mixer: Digidesign Digi-001 Factory 24-bit Audio Interface and Software Package ($1200).
- Effects Processor: (included as part of the Digi-001 Factory package)
- Stereo Master Recorder: (included as part of the computer).
- Monitors: Mackie HR824 Active Biamped Studio Monitors, approx $1400, Sony MDR7506 Headphones, $100.
- Computer: xp Athlon 1900-based PC Computer with the following equipment: 1GB DDR RAM, 100GB 7200RPM Hard Drive, 24x10x40 CD-RW drive, ATI 64MB Radeon Video Board (approx $1800 total).

This is a computer-based system that uses a PCI card for the interface to the computer. These components mentioned in the computer are merely suggestions as a starting point, but you will definitely want some high performance electronics in there similar to what I have listed. The CD-RW drive will allow you to make CD-R or CD-RW master disks of your recordings. The large and fast hard drive and RAM memory are highly recommended for any serious audio recording. The Digidesign Digi-001 Factory 24-bit Audio Interface and Software Package is one of the best recording systems for about a kilobuck. The hardware portion includes the PCI card and an I/O breakout that includes 8 channels of analog I/O, 8 channels of ADAT optical I/O, 2 S/PDIF I/O channels, MIDI In, MIDI Out, a pair of analog monitor outputs, and a headphone output with separate volume control. The software portion includes recording, mixing, editing and effects software such as Pro Tools LE software, Bomb Factory's 1176 and LA-2A Classic Compressors, the Moogerfooger low-pass filter, Waves' Supertap delay, Q10 EQ, and Metaflanger

flanger effect, Native Instruments' Dynamo software synthesizer/sampler, Digidesign D-Fi sound design tools, D-Verb reverbs, Maxim peak limiting and maximizing tool, and Digidesign RTAS and AudioSuite plug-ins. That is a tough package to beat! (There is an alternate (and excellent) system you can buy for your computer at a lower price: the Mark of the Unicorn 828. It requires an IEEE-1394 FireWire interface on your computer. The Mark of the Unicorn 828 cost is about $730.) The other big upgrade here is the Mackie HR824 Active Biamped Studio Monitors. This $5000 computer-based system is highly flexible with all the software plug-ins that come with the Digidesign package. Also, there is an upgrade path to the full-up Pro Tools software package from this system. Pro Tools is one of the best recording/sequencer software packages available on the market at any price. In fact, Digidesign has just updated their Pro Tools package to 96/192 kHz performance with the Pro Tools HD.

Now that I have gone out on the flame-war limb and recommended some new studio systems for various budget levels, let me remind you that you can often get much better performance and functionality on the used equipment market. For example, you simply will not realize as high a quality recording on a new cassette multitracker as you will on a reasonably well maintained used reel/reel multi-track recorder, in my opinion. I've seen used 8-track reel/reel recorders for around $250 on the used market.

Recommended Systems Over $5000:
In this book, I am focusing on low-cost solutions for home studios. Therefore, I just detailed some recommended systems for $5k or less. If you want some recommended systems for $10k, $25k or even $50k, then check out the March 2002 issue of *Mix* magazine. Go to www.mixonline.com, click on the March 2002 issue, and then scroll down to the article entitled "Building Your System" under "The Project Studio" section. Or you can just direct your browser to http://industryclick.com/magazinearticle.asp?magazineid=141&releaseid

=9915&magazinearticleid=142014&siteid=15. If you can find a copy of the July 2002 issue of *Electronic Musician*, it details 8 recommended systems from $2.5k to $30k; you can also order it as a back issue from *Electronic Musician*.

BUYING NEW & USED EQUIPMENT

Let's start with used equipment first. There are many, many sources for used equipment. Your local newspaper is one place to start looking for good deals on used equipment. In my city, there is a free weekly publication that comes out that has a special section for "Music." In it are tons of entries for people either wanting to sell their studio or stereo equipment, or wanting to buy yours. If you have any music stores in your city (e.g., Guitar Center, etc.), they may be willing to sell at a reduced price any demo models they have, any dented & scratched equipment, or any equipment with open boxes (sometimes they refer to these items as "B" stock). You can usually get the full warranty on this equipment, which is always helpful. The good thing about local transactions for used equipment is that you can view the equipment with your own eyes, and possibly even hook up the equipment and put it through its paces to make sure it operates correctly (or at least well enough for your purposes).

As for new equipment, I only buy it when it goes on sale. And I am talking a *good* sale! Usually, this is when they are closing that particular unit out to make room for the next great thing. To know when you are getting a good deal on new equipment, you need to stay abreast of what has come out recently and what the going prices are. The best way to do this is to get on several different catalog mailing lists. Go to the websites for Musician's Friend (www.musiciansfriend.com), Guitar Center (www.guitarcenter.com), Sam Ash (www.samash.com), American Musical Supply (www.americanmusical.com), and Broadcast Supply Worldwide (www.bswusa.com) and get signed up for their catalogs and flyers. If you physically go into a store and use up the time of some saleman to show you new equipment, then you should absolutely buy your equipment from that salesman.

Usenet:

If you have access to a computer (and there is no excuse not to have access— go to your local library!), then the used equipment options open to you are astronomi-cal. One thing you can do is go to the classified ads on Usenet. For studio-related equipment and musical instru-ments, go to rec.music.makers.marketplace, or do a search on Google for rec.music.makers.marketplace. (See the next section for a discussion of search engines on the Internet.) If you are new to Usenet, you can refer to a FAQ (Fre-quently Asked Questions) that explains it at http:// www.faqs.org/faqs/.

Search Engines:

You can use search engines online to help you find a specific piece of gear, if you know what you are looking for. The absolute best search page to have book-marked on your computer is the All-In-One Search Page. This fantastic search tool has just about every search engine known to man catalogued and ready for you to use. You should know that each search engine uses a special blend of search algorithms to find the information you seek, and many are optimized for different types of search tasks. The good thing about the All-In-One Search Page is that it tells you in what way each search engine is optimized. To access the All-In-One Search Page, go to http:// www.allonesearch.com/all1www.html#WWW.

A favorite specific search engine of mine is Google (www.google.com). It is usually ranked as the number one generic search engine among engineers and scientists. It has over 1.387 billion web pages indexed. (Source: Karen Auguston Field, Chief Editor, *Design News*, 10/15/2001). Of course, with such a large search engine you may end up getting all sorts of information that doesn't really re-late to your search, but usually you will find some very relevant hits, and you can follow up on those. You can also access this search engine at the All-In-One Search Page. If you use Internet Explorer as your web browser, you can have a Google toolbar installed right onto your Internet Explorer toolbar. Go to http://toolbar.google.com and follow the instructions to download the Google toolbar onto your machine. This gives instant access to the most extensive search engine available.

A secondary favorite specific search engine of mine is MonsterCrawler. You can get to it at the All-In-One Search Page, or you can go to http://www.monstercrawler.com. If you want a technical search engine that is focused specifically on relevant electrical and mechanical design topics (for you DIYers), you can try www.dnsearchengineer.com. This is a technical search engine developed by the folks at *Design News* magazine.

If you need a definition of a technical term, especially if it is related to computers, the Internet, software, networking and Telecom, then you might be able to find it at http://whatis.techtarget.com.

Judging the Condition of Used Gear:

If you are buying or selling gear online, it helps to have a common set of criteria to judge the condition of the equipment. DAC Crowell, from the Aerodyne Works Studio for Electronic Music, has written some guidelines for this purpose, and this copyrighted material is posted at Mark Pulver's website at http://www.midiwall.com/buyingsafe/judging.html. There is also some good advice there regarding CODs (Cash On Delivery) and safe transactions with unknown people.

New and Used Gear Lists:

On the Internet, there is a web site that lists the prices that people paid for new equipment. You can access it at http://www.princeton.edu/~casey/newgear.html. This is the USA New Gear Price List, and it was once maintained by Casey Palowitch. The problem with this list is that it does not seem to be actively supported any more by Mr. Palowitch, so the information is dated. Too bad, as this was a great resource to use when bargaining the price on new equipment. Similarly, you can go to http://prepal.com to access a list of the used prices paid on used musical instruments and recording gear. These guys did a great job on their web site. They list the year the equipment came out, what the original list price was then, the average price it goes for now, the trend (up or down) in which the used price is currently moving, the number of transactions tracked for the equipment, the resale popularity of the equipment, and where you might go to find that piece of equipment. They say that the info in their web site is updated daily from various sources on the Internet, so this is a great up-to-date resource for you to check out.

Another good equipment site to check out is http://musicians.about.com/cs/buyinggear. These folks have researched quite a few sources for buying new and used equipment. If you are brave and/or patient, you can check out some of the online auctions devoted to musical instruments and recording equipment (www.digibid.com and www.musichotbid.com), and the ubiquitous eBay (www.ebay.com).

If you are looking for prices on just new gear, then check out http://www.gearprice.com. The gearprice tool may be able to give you the best price on some equipment and where to find it. Another web search tool for new and used gear can be found at http://www.gearsearch.com/main.htm. And, here is a search tool (with a cool graphical user interface (GUI)) that searches 8 retailers for the best price on new recording gear: http://xmidi.com/cgi-bin/xmeta.

One thing that I have found in my searches for good deals on used equipment is that some companies and vendors don't even actively advertise that they have the used equipment for sale. You have to do some searching on your own. One good thing to do is to locate the web sites for various online gear sellers, and see if they have a link on their page that takes you to a list of the used, dented, scratched or otherwise price-reduced gear they have for sale. Many of the ones I have visited in the past are detailed in the next section below.

Used Equipment Web Sites:

As you learn how to use search engines effectively, you can zero in on the sites where used equipment is available. Usually, buying from an online equipment dealer is relatively safe (but not always!). They have a reputation to maintain, and if they screw you, the word gets out on the various audio- and studio-related lists relatively quickly, adversely affecting their sales. If you are buying from a private party/individual that you don't know, make sure you get good information on his location (not just an email address or a P.O. Box), get JPEG pictures of the equipment you are buying ahead of time along with a description of any equipment defects, and if you can, use a 3rd party escrow service. The escrow service will hold your money (for a small fee of course) while you evaluate the equipment you are going to buy. If the equipment meets with your approval, then the money is sent to the seller from the escrow service, and you retain the equipment. If not, then you get your money back (minus the escrow fee), and the seller gets his equipment back.

Here are some of the web sites to investigate for good deals on used equipment. This is by no means a complete list.

- American Music (www.americanmusic.com/usedgear.htm)
- Audio Village (http://www.audiovillage.org)
- Big City Music (www.bigcitymusic.com)- some vintage stuff here
- Caruso Music (www.carusomusic.com)
- Daddy's Junky Music Stores (www.daddys.com)
- The Electric Keyboard (www.electrickeyboard.com)- used keyboards and MIDI equipment
- ElectroGear (http://ep.com/js/csp/c0?csp=3026)
- Filament Audio (www.filamentaudio.com/used.htm)
- Grandma's Music and Sound (www.grandmas.com/used.htm)
- HTICS Pro Audio (http://www.hticsproaudio.com)
- Kraft Music (www.kraftmusic.com/catalog/usedgear)
- Lentine's Music (www.lentines.com/used.stm)

- The Music Brokers (http://216.119.87.84/}
- The Music Marketplace (www.midifarm.com/market/)
- Oak Tree Enterprises (http://www.oaktreeent.com/)
- Odyssey Pro Sound (http://www.odysseyprosound.com/used.html)
- ProMusicFind (www.promusicfind.com)- a worldwide marketplace for buying and selling equipment
- Recycler Classifieds- Music (www.recycler.com/asp/Class.asp?iC=12000)
- Rehoboth Beach Music (www.rehobothmusic.com/used/index.html)
- Rogue Music (www.roguemusic.com)
- Sonic State (http://www.sonicstate.com) This is an awesome online resource for electronic musicians and home studio owners.
- The Starving Musician (www.starvingmusician.com)
- Sweetwater Sound Trading Post (www.sweetwater.com/tradingpost/home.tpl) –buy and sell equipment with no fees here
- Synthony Music Online (www.synthony.com/used.html)
- Used Gear By Mail (www.ugbm.com)- an unbelievable amount of stuff here

PART TWO: STUDIO LAYOUT AND FURNITURE

ACOUSTICS IN YOUR STUDIO

Most people who seek to build up a home studio or project studio are relegated to a spare bedroom, the garage or an area of the basement. That's because it is a home first and a studio second (or possibly last as far as your spouse might be concerned!). If you find yourself in this situation, all you can do is make the best of it. If you have the money to build a separate structure out back to contain your studio, or you "floated" a room within a room in your house, then fantastic, but that's not what most home studios are. In this section, we will discuss some strategies for improving the acoustics within your studio space. The real objective is to achieve a neutral sound in your studio space (and this may only occur in just one "sweet spot" in the entire room!), so that the studio doesn't color the sound in any unintentional way as you record or monitor the audio. Unfortunately, this is much easier said than done!

Just like everything else concerning recording studios, with acoustics you can really jump into the deep end, or you can try to improve what you have based upon your available budget. And when I say deep end, I really mean deep end. One book I bought about 15 years ago recommended that I procure a copy of the *Compendium of Materials for Noise Control*, which is a 380-page, 8.5 x 11 inch government publication summarizing the basic acoustical data materials available from 146 different companies. Yikes! While the book does have some excellent information in it, and I suppose the Compendium is a great place to start if you are putting together a professional recording studio with a fat budget, I don't think most home studio owners are going to wade through it.

If you really want to do some reading on the subject of acoustics, then I suggest you spend some time at the Auralex web site (www.auralex.com). There, you will be able to read through an excellent piece of work written by Eric T. Smith, Founder and President of Auralex Acoustics, Inc. It is called Acoustics 101, and it goes into way more detail than I am prepared to discuss in this text. I recommend that you print it out and keep it as a reference source. Now granted, Mr. Smith does have products to sell, so he does put in some plugs for Auralex foam, but this is still an excellent source of information pertaining to room acoustics. I am going to assume that if you are prepared to do demolition, construction and reconstruction in the hopes of putting together the perfect home studio, then you are prepared to follow the advice he gives on lumber, construction materials, adhesives and caulks, sound barriers, floor decouplers, the proper way to run stringers, angled ceilings, heating and cooling systems, window treatments, doors, stairwells, garage doors, and countless other subjects. (See, there is quite a bit to the subject of studio acoustics!) Another source of good information on acoustics as they pertain to recording studios is *Recording Spaces: A Must Read for Studio Builders, Designers* (Newell, Phillip, Focal Press, 2000).

But what can you do if you are unwilling to (or don't have the money available to) rip the studio space apart and start new construction from scratch? You will need to make some compromises. Let's first start with some of the physical limitations you will encounter in a small room. With sound waves traveling at around 300 meters/second (or 1130 feet/second), you can easily see that it does not take long for the sound to reach the other wall and bounce back (and forth and back and forth) in a 10' x 10' room. This creates a couple of problems. First, the small room sounds like a "small room" because the early reflections of the sound never really get a chance to develop. Sound theory tells us that the first reflections (or early sound field) reach the listener before the remainder of reverberant sound field, and this is what gives a concert hall (or a recording room) its lively, tight, dead, mushy (insert your own descriptor here) character. In your 10' x

10' bedroom, there is going to be very little early sound field before all the bouncing around starts to muddy things.

Another serious acoustical problem is that with the sound bouncing back and forth within this 10' x 10' little box, the room sets up what are known as normal modes. These normal modes are a function of the room dimensions. You can simulate what these room modes are by taking a piece of string, tying it to a door knob on one end, and then shaking the other end back and forth at a constant rate. Eventually, you will see the string set up a standing wave at its resonant or preferred frequency (which is a function of its length). This is the same thing that happens in a room with sound waves. Every room has a set of natural resonant frequencies that tend to be accentuated and a different set of natural frequencies that tend to be suppressed. They look like peaks and valleys on a graph of amplitude versus frequency. The overall sonic effect of these peaks and valleys on the sound in the room will be more pronounced in a room that has little acoustical absorption than in one that has been properly configured with absorptive materials. In addition, most of these individual peaks and valleys occur at frequencies below 250 Hz. (This is the critical reason why most small control rooms and mix-down rooms in professional recording studios that sound "good" are the ones with adequate low-frequency absorption and adequate high-frequency absorption.) The upshot of all this: these normal modes will color the sound (accentuating some frequencies and subtracting others); a song played back in similarly-sized rooms with different dimensions will necessarily sound different in each room; different listening locations within the same room will sound different and have different sound pressure levels; and the sound pressure levels will be highest in the corners of the room and lowest in the center of the room. So, you can see that physics plays a large roll in how your small home studio is going to sound.

What can be done to mitigate the effects of physics in your studio? There are two approaches to taming this problem, and you can try both of them. One approach involves adding materials to the walls and ceiling within the studio to overcome the acoustic problems. The other approach involves filtering the audio before you send it out through the monitor speakers to overcome the acoustic problems in the studio.

The first problem solving approach is to apply acoustic foam products to try to mitigate the effects of physics. There are many suppliers of wall wedges, baffles, barriers, bass traps, diffusers, and even isolation enclosures. Some of the manufacturers of these products are Acoustical Solutions, Auralex, db Engineering, RPG Diffusor Systems, Cutting Wedge, Profoam, Sonex, Tecnifoam, and WhisperWedge. You can look at the specifications and pricing for most of these competing products at Silent Source (http://www.silentsource.com/index.html). But, that approach can be confusing.

I think the simplest approach to tame a small room for recording purposes is to buy a kit from Auralex and install it yourself. Remember that the goal here is to make your room acoustically neutral, not acoustically dead. If you go to the Auralex website (http://www.auralex.com), and then click on the Auralex.com button, you will get a list of their products. Next, click on the Roominators product category link. The Roominators are sound control kits that Auralex has assembled for variously sized rooms. The kits are Alpha-1, Project-2, Deluxe Plus and Pro Plus. Look at those links and choose the Roominator product that matches the description of your room. With the kit, you get various foam products to mitigate your room's sound problems, foam adhesive to apply the foam, and instructions on how to proceed. Expect to pay approximately $300 (for the Alpha-1) to $900 (for the Pro Plus), depending on your room requirements. Well, I didn't say it would necessarily be cheap to overcome the laws of physics.

Another free pamphlet you can get is entitled *Noise Control Solutions* from NetWell Noise Control. You can call them at 800-638-9355 and request it. The pamphlet covers noise absorbers, architectural acoustics, blankets, curtains, barriers, composites, enclosure linings, flooring, and even intake/exhaust silencers.

The second problem solving approach is to actually

filter the problematic frequencies in your home studio with an equalizer before they are amplified and driven out of the studio monitors. See the section in this book entitled Spectrum Analyzer and RTA for more on this technique.

Be aware that pasting acoustic foam products on the walls of your studio generally will not affect the leaking of sound into or out of your studio. The foam products discussed above are designed to tame problems above 200 Hz. The only thing that stops sound (especially low-frequency sound) from escaping or entering your studio is mass. By mass, I mean a second wall, heavy curtains, thick blankets, a second door, double-paned windows with a vacuum between the panes, etc. The low-frequency sound energy of the audio is converted into heat as it passes into and through these heavy mass objects, and that heat is then conducted through the mass and dissipated. That is the *only* way to overcome the physics of the situation. If you have neighbors complaining that they can hear your studio in your garage, or if noise from the local airport is leaking into your microphones, then you will need to correct the problem with a judicious application of mass.

Since we've covered removing various acoustic anomalies from your studio to achieve a neutral sound, let's now discuss the natural liveliness of an acoustic space. Sound is really just acoustic energy, and when that transmitted energy encounters some kind of barrier (wall, ceiling, floor, you), it is either reflected or absorbed, or more likely, some combination of both. Obviously, thick drapes are going to mainly absorb sound energy (at least at the mid and upper frequencies), while a tile floor is mainly going to reflect sound energy. You may have an area in your house that really lends itself to recording with a microphone because of the acoustic qualities it has. For instance, you may be able to set up a microphone at one end of your hallway and record someone playing acoustic guitar or perhaps singing a vocal line, while using the natural reverberant space of the hallway (especially if there is no carpet) to provide an openness and reverb quality without electronic reverb. Other rooms where this might work are a large bathroom or the kitchen, since these rooms have many reflective surfaces in them. It is worth experimenting to see if you can capture a performance in one of these spaces that doesn't sound suffocated, using the natural reverb of the space to enhance the sound of the musician.

You will need to experiment with microphone placement, since the sweet spot with the nice-sounding reverb may only be in one spot. The best way to do this is to walk around and use your ears to listen at various spots while your partner plays the guitar or sings. Place the microphone where you hear the most open and airy sound. If you are doing this experiment by yourself, perhaps you can record a dry rendition of your performance to tape, then place a speaker in the position in the hallway or kitchen where you will be playing the guitar or singing. While the speaker is playing back the dry performance you just recorded, walk around and see if you can find a sweet spot to locate the microphone. Experimenting in this manner costs nothing, but long microphone cables will definitely assist in the effort.

Recording in a small room in your home is going to be a compromise on a number of different levels. In this book, I have outlined several approaches to help tame the problems you will encounter (close field monitoring, removing acoustic anomalies, using acoustic anomalies to your advantage, preventing audio leakeage, controlling noise, etc.). No single approach is going to eliminate all the problems, and quite possibly all the approaches applied together may not eliminate the problems; however, they should go a long way towards helping to improve the overall sonic quality of your home studio.

References:
Eargle, John, *Sound Recording*, Van Nostrand Reinhold Company, 1976, pp.29-32.

STUDIO FURNITURE

Since I started connecting home studio equipment together in a bedroom over 25 years ago, I have really run the gamut with studio furniture. A $40 table that I purchased at a home improvement store supported my initial system. And that was the whole studio! (Hey, any port in a storm when you are young and broke.) I just stacked my reel/reel, mixer, cassette deck and a couple of effects processors on the tabletop, and it was a functional system (but hardly aesthetic). I didn't have any monitors back then, just a set of headphones, so I didn't have the problem of mounting monitor speakers.

Since my main instrument is keyboard, it didn't take too very long to displace the recording equipment off of the table after my second keyboard was purchased. I needed a way to handle the keyboards separately from the recording equipment. So, I purchased a tubular support stand (the A frame variety).

As mentioned earlier in this book, I received good mileage from the tubular support stand after I made some modifications to it. I purchased some short tubular arms for it to hold my new close field monitors at head height. I also made some shelves for it that could hold some of the smaller equipment safely. You will find that items such as some drum machines, some effects processors and other devices that are designed to be tabletop units do not lend themselves to be mounted effectively in a rack. This support stand shelf idea solves that problem. You can build the shelves yourself easily and simply (this is detailed in the next section). However, even this approach didn't solve all of my equipment mounting problems. What about patch bays, rack mount equipment, and heavy tape decks? One interim solution to this problem is the computer desk, which has worked well for several years in my studio.

You can eyeball a computer desk in a catalog and build one yourself if you're good enough at woodworking, or you can buy one already assembled. I opted for the latter choice, as my woodworking skills are virtually nonexistent. I looked at quite a few desks before I decided on a relatively nice solid oak unit at a cost of about $200 (15 years ago). There were lots of inexpensive units made out of particleboard, but they looked cheap, and their strength and stability was suspect. I didn't want the desk to collapse with all of my equipment on it. I'm reserving that memorable moment for the "big" Southern California earthquake.

The horizontal desk portion of the computer desk worked well as a writing space and as the area to support heavy units such as open reel tape decks and power amps. The shelving structure that sat on the desk held all of my rack mount equipment, small-box electronics, and my patch bay. I used a jigsaw to cut holes in the back panels of the shelves for cable egress. The unit also came with shelves down below that I used for storing tapes, cables and equipment not presently in use. The computer desk I bought offered good functionality at a fair price, and it fulfilled the mounting requirements not provided by tubular support stands or rack mount cabinets. You can see it in the background of Figure 26.

If you only have about $100 to spend on some studio furniture, then you might want to buy some tables and arrange them into a contiguous 90° table surface in a corner of your studio. Another approach would be to buy an inexpensive computer desk, such as the Model 10942 O'Sullivan 2-Tone Corner Computer Workcenter (~$99 at www.bestbuy.com). This is a corner unit with a reasonable horizontal workspace and shelves upon which to stack equipment and a computer monitor.

As you collect more and more equipment in your studio, you will need to give some thoughts to ergonomics (facilitating the man-machine interface) and the work habits or work flow that you have in your studio. Take the time to figure out where you are and what equipment you use when you are performing/recording/tracking, editing, mixing, mastering, writing, etc. This will allow you to figure out what equipment to group together and how to group it for the most effective and efficient flow. (See the section entitled "Locating Equipment In The Studio" for more information on this subject.)

    More recently, I have removed the computer desk
from my studio and sprung for some professional studio
furniture in the form of a mixing desk and two 84" equipment racks. When you get down to it, it really helps to
have a support infrastructure that is specifically designed
for the ergonomics of recording studios. The only nega-
tive thing is that this equipment does not come cheaply.
There are now several companies out there competing for
your studio furniture dollar. Here are some to check out:
* Anthro: http://www.anthro.com
* Argosy Console: http://www.argosyconsole.com/
  home.htm
* Bryco Products: http://www.brycoproducts.com
* Middle Atlantic: http://www.middleatlantic.com
* Nigel B.: http://www.nigelb.com
* Omnirax: http://www.omnirax.com
* Quik-Lok: http://www.quiklok.com
* Raxxess: http://www.raxxess.com
* Spacewise: http://www.spacewise.com
* Ultimate Support: http://www.ultimatesupport.com
* Wenger Corporation: http://www.wengercorp.com/

References:
Rideout, Ernie, "A Place for Everything", *Electronic Musician*, Dec. 1993, p. 53.

Equipment Racks:
A great deal of studio equipment manufactured these days
comes in the 19" rack mount format, and as you amass
more electronic equipment in your studio, you will at some
point be faced with the decision of buying a rack. There
are certain ways you can go here, and some are more expensive than others. One way is to buy your own rack
rails from any reputable music/studio equipment retailer
and build your own rack mount system. Some good online
retailer   sources   are   Musician's   Friend
(www.musiciansfriend.com), Sam Ash (www.samash.com)
and   American   Musical   Supply
(www.americanmusical.com). I've used all of these companies in the past and have found them to be reputable.

The rack rails usually come in lengths of 2U to 45U. (The measurement unit U for racks means Unit, and each 1U in height is 1.75".) You can build your own framework or a simple box out of wood and mount the rack rails to it. I have built small rack-mount boxes for my own equipment, and this is definitely the cheapest way to go. See Figure 7.

Figure 7: Homemade Equipment Rack

When you build the box, be aware that the 19" width dimension is from the outside of one rack rail to the outside of the other rack rail. The centerline screw holes for the rack mount equipment are actually 18.25" apart.

If you don't want to be bothered with building your own box or rack using rack rails, you can buy a fairly cheap rack from a surplus electronics/equipment dealer. You can get used $800-$1000 racks with front and rear mounting rails for about $100. As an example of one such source, see http://www.industrialliquidators.com. To find others, type "industrial liquidators" into the Google search engine. If you want to buy a new low-cost rack frame, a good source is MilesTek (www.milestek.com, 1-800-524-7444). They have 84-inch-high racks capable of holding 45U of equipment for as low as $140. They also have many other rack mount accessories available.

As you plan to install the equipment into your rack, here are some tips you should be aware of. You will want to locate the heaviest equipment (usually power amplifiers) in the bottom of the rack. This will provide a low center of gravity and help prevent the rack from tipping over. A good idea for permanent installations (especially on the earthquake-prone West Coast) is to screw the top of the rack rear to the studs in the wall. With all of the equipment mounted to the front rails of a rack, the rack will tend to be front-heavy and could easily tip over forward. If you are building a rack box to take on the road to gigs and use in your home studio, you should consider adding some rear support for the equipment that goes into the rack. There is a physics concept called the "bending moment" which may damage the front face of your rack mount equipment during bumps, vibrations, and other g-forces on the road. Make sure that you tighten all the rack screws that you use to mount the equipment in the racks. This will help keep the rack angles true and square.

As you mount equipment into any rack, try to take advantage of the concept of natural convection. Natural convection is the process of warm air rising and creating its own upward air current. Blockages inside of the rack will inhibit this free flow of air. Therefore, mount the deepest equipment in the bottom of the rack and the least deep equipment more toward the top. Leave a couple of open rack spaces along the way so that cooler air can be drawn into the rack by the natural convection air current inside the rack.

I have decided to leave the sides off of my racks because I access the equipment inside of the racks so often. This also helps with airflow to the equipment in the racks. If you are going to leave the rack sides on, make sure you leave a large distance between the rack and the wall behind it. Otherwise, accessing the rear jacks on the equipment in the racks is going to be a major pain.

LOCATING EQUIPMENT IN THE STUDIO

Assuming that you have designated one room in your house to be the space for your home studio, the next task is to determine how and where to locate the equipment within that space.

A good place to start is to survey your equipment and determine what equipment is used for each task in the studio. You will be practicing, tracking (recording individual tracks), bouncing tracks, editing tracks (this could be on a computer or a recorder or both), mixing, and creating a final 2-track master. What equipment do you use for each of these tasks? Are certain units used for two or more tasks? Is there a way to physically group these often used units to cut down on the amount of getting up and moving to a different area to complete any task? Are some of the units just set up once and then left alone for long periods? Can any tasks be completed more efficiently if a remote control is purchased or built for one or more pieces of equipment?

Once you have determined which are the most often used units in your studio, and you have the furniture, racks, tables and stands that the equipment will mount in or on, you can take steps to build a scale model of the studio. The simplest way to do this is to measure the dimensions of the whole studio, and then draw a scaled representation of the length and width of the room onto graph paper. You can make an assumption such as 1 foot of studio space equals 4 tiny blocks on the graph paper, or whatever works out to adequately represent the studio space on one whole sheet of paper. Next, measure each major piece of equipment (desks, cabinets, racks, stands, etc.) and draw a scale model of each one on another piece of paper. Once you have the major pieces drawn, cut out each piece with a pair of scissors. You will now place those pieces on the scale model of the room you drew previously. The idea is to take what you learned from the task analysis above and apply it to the layout of the studio space. Instead of physically moving the actual equipment around in your studio, however, let your fingers do all the work by arranging the little cutout models on the layout diagram. I did this in my studio and had the layout finalized even before some of the furniture had arrived at my house. (I used measurements obtained from the manufacturer of the furniture and made scaled cutouts of the pieces.)

You can even apply this concept to the pieces of equipment that will go into a rack, onto a mixing desk, or onto a keyboard stand. Just measure each unit and then cut out a scaled representative piece of paper for each unit. It is much easier to play ergonomic games with little pieces of paper representing units you will mount into a rack than it is swapping actual units into and out of a rack. If all of your equipment is to be tabletop mounted, then this is a great way of determining how best to locate that equipment on the tables to facilitate an efficient flow of work.

References: Elsea, Peter, "Studio Ergonomics", *Electronic Musician*, May 1990, pp 79-80.

SHELVES FOR KEYBOARD SUPPORT STANDS

The tubular types of support stands (such as the products from Ultimate Support Stands) are great for holding keyboards. However, they can get expensive if you have to buy a pair of horizontal support arms for each small equipment box (such as a drum machine or a hardware sequencer) you want to mount on the stand. The easy and inexpensive solution to this problem is to build a shelf for the support stand using 1/4" plywood or pine shelving. You can pursue this option even if you don't own any keyboards!

Figure 8: Shelves for Keyboard Support Stands

One of the shelves I built is 45" wide by 12" deep. I constructed it to run the full width of the support stand.

A lip is required so that the studio equipment doesn't slide off of the shelf. I fashioned the lip out of 1 1/2-inch-high by 3/8-inch-thick molding. I used wood glue and small brads to attach the front lip molding to the full width of the front edge of the shelf. After the glue dried, I spray painted the whole shelf flat black to match the support stand.

The shelf rests on a pair of the horizontal support arms that I mentioned above. A substantial cost savings was realized because I only needed one pair of the horizontal support arms instead of a separate pair for each piece of equipment mounted on the shelf. This arrangement is shown in the photo of Figure 8. I have built two of these shelves and saved over a couple hundred dollars. Also, they are indispensable for mounting small objects on the support stand, such as the Yamaha YMM2 MIDI Merger shown in the figure. Tabletop units such as the YMM2 don't lend themselves to rack mount or horizontal support arms due to their size, but they mount just fine on a homemade shelf. For added stability of the equipment, you can add a strip of Velcro to the underside of the equipment and to the homemade shelf. This will secure the equipment in place. (See the "Pedal Board" section below.)

PEDAL BOARD

The floor in my studio is carpeted. This is great for absorbing reflected sound within the room or for muffling the noise of a foot tapping to the beat. However, I was having a problem with the stability of some of my keyboard pedals and footswitches on the carpet.

The easy solution for me was to use a 1/4-inch-thick sheet of plywood cut to the dimensions of 1 foot deep by 2 1/2 feet wide. This is large enough to accommodate my complement of foot controllers (volume pedal, sustain pedal and multi-track punch-in foot switch) with space left over for future additions. For some foot controllers, this is enough of a solution, because the rubber pads on the bottom of the foot controller will prevent any skidding on the wood.

Some controllers do not have rubber pads and may require a little more work. At your local hardware store or drug store, you can buy small squares of Velcro (or more cost effectively, whole reels of hook and loop Velcro material). Glue a couple of pieces of Velcro to the bottom of the foot controller. In the same pattern, glue the other side of Velcro to the plywood pedal board in the desired locations. Don't use epoxy or white wood glue in this application, or you'll work up a sweat trying to remove the Velcro if you ever want to change locations around on the pedal board.

Figure 9: Pedal Board Before Painting

I recommend using General Electric's Silicone II Household Glue and Seal. This is an excellent adhesive that will adhere to most metals, wood, glass and plastics (without melting them). The silicon-based glue stays flexible, will not dry out and is easy to peel off if you change your mind later. Figure 9 shows my pedal board with one of the footswitches removed to reveal the Velcro squares. After this picture was taken, I painted the pedal board black.

ELECTROMAGNETIC INTERFERENCE & NOISE

How and where you locate or mount your equipment can have a big effect on the amount of noise or electromagentic interference that appears in your audio.

The two most common causes of hum and noise in audio systems are ground loops caused by improper grounding of the electrical equipment and noise induced by the coupling of a magnetic field from one electrical conductor to another conductor.

The problem of ground loops can occur when two or more pieces of electronic equipment are connected together as in Figure 10. Due to the electrically completed loop in the conductors and the ground shields, small electromagnetically induced currents can flow between the electronic equipment. In most cases, this current flow takes place in the ground conductor of a signal cable connected between the pieces of equipment. It is this 60 Hz current flow that causes the annoying hum accompanying ground loops.

One solution to the problem of a ground loop is to remove the offending connection that is completing the ground loop. This isn't much fun, but the process of identifying the connection can be facilitated if you have a patch bay in your system. Monitor the audio signal at each tie point and listen for the offending 60 Hz hum. You should first make sure that all equipment is properly grounded via chassis ground to the third-wire safety ground in the power plug (if there is a safety ground). Be advised that whenever the third-wire ground (the green wire safety ground) is disconnected, lifted or non-existent on a piece of equipment, then that piece of equipment is considered to be "floated," and the chassis and case can assume the potential at which the output ground is connected. Therefore, an electrical shock hazard can exist given certain circumstances.

After the hum-inducing connection is identified, there are several ways to remedy the problem. The one true way to eliminate the hum is to physically eliminate the loop. This involves disconnecting one end of the ground conductor in the signal cable (NOT the power cable) that runs between the two pieces of equipment. Lifting the ground at one end will break the loop, preventing 60 Hz current flow in the conductor. As long as the ground conductor in the signal cable is connected to ground at just one of the pieces of equipment, the circuit will function correctly. The ground connection linking the two pieces of equipment is actually made through the earth connection in the power supplies of the two units.

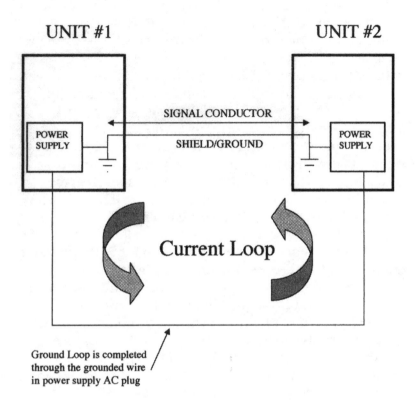

UNIT #1   UNIT #2

SIGNAL CONDUCTOR

POWER SUPPLY   SHIELD/GROUND   POWER SUPPLY

Current Loop

Ground Loop is completed
through the grounded wire
in power supply AC plug

Typical Ground Loop

Figure 10

Signal ground lifting is a fairly involved process. If you don't want to treat the cause, but merely the symptoms, you can employ a parametric EQ to notch out the hum at the offending 60 Hz frequency. You would, of course, want to use a high Q (i.e., narrow the notch as much as possible) to avoid affecting the neighboring frequencies. (The Q is a measure of a filter's "sharpness" or "width.") Another tool at your disposal is the noise gate. The noise gate will allow the signal (and offending hum) to pass through only when a preset sensitivity level is detected to open the gate; otherwise, no signal is allowed to pass through the gate. The idea here is that the audio signal itself will mask the hum during the time that the gate is open. These two fixes above are merely temporary fixes and do not fix the real problem. If you have the money and the inclination, you can employ a ground isolator, such as the Jensen ISO-MAX audio isolators. The ISO-MAX units are fairly expensive (about $100 per channel of isolation). To help combat the ground noise problem, Jensen has a kit to track down and troubleshoot hum and buzz grounding problems (for about $315). Bill Whitlock of Jensen has also written an informative white paper on troubleshooting ground noise in audio systems; you can download a pdf file of that white paper (and use Adobe Acrobat to read it) at http://www.jensen-transformers.com/apps_wp.html.

Another possibility to try if your equipment is rack-mounted is to use isolator (non-conductive) washers and insulating screws to secure your equipment into the rack. This sometimes prevents the return path to ground for pesky ground loop problems. A company called Dana B. Goods markets a product called Humfrees specifically for the purpose of isolating rack equipment from the metal rack. You can check these out at http://www.danabgoods.com/Humfrees. Also, if the offending piece of equipment has a two-prong AC connector that is not keyed (i.e., both prongs are the same size), you can try reversing the AC plug in the AC socket, so that the plugs are in the other holes. Sometimes this can reduce the amount of ground noise in the system.

Another way that noise can be introduced into electrical systems is through the coupling of a magnetic field between two conductors. Any conductor or wire that has an electric current flowing through it has the capability of generating a magnetic field around the conductor. If another conductor (especially an unshielded conductor) comes sufficiently close to this magnetic field, an electric current will be induced in this second conductor.

Typically, you will not encounter magnetically induced noise problems between two shielded preamp level signal cables (such as RCA cables connecting between a digital effects box and a mixer), unless the shields in the cables are faulty. This is because the shield around the center conductor is grounded, thereby insulating the center (signal) conductor from most *low-level* magnetic fields. Also, the current flow in a preamp level signal cable is at such a low level, the magnetic field that surrounds it is negligible, especially considering the grounded shield surrounding the conductor. Therefore, it is acceptable to bundle together preamp level signal cables and route them in parallel with little fear of cross-coupled noise inducement.

An induced-noise problem can occur when preamp level signal cables are routed in parallel with AC power cords and speaker cables. AC power cords and speaker cables exhibit a relatively substantial magnetic field around them due to the size of the current traveling through them and due to the fact that they are not shielded. In order to minimize the effects of noise inducement, route all signal cables at right angles to AC power cords or speaker cables and as far away from them as possible. Get into the habit of routing signal cables down one side of an equipment rack and the power cords down the other side. Be careful to keep the AC power cords away from the speaker cables, too, or you may hear that familiar 60 Hz buzz in your monitor speakers. Another source of induced noise is cables that carry digital signals. Noise can be induced into low-level analog signal cables when the digital signals change state in a rapid manner.

One method you can try to get rid of high frequency

noise induced into a cable is a snap-on ferrite core. The ferrite is a material that "chokes out" the high frequencies induced into a cable from EMI or RFI sources. The ferrite is formed into a shape that looks like a doughnut and is encased in a plastic sheath that snaps over the cable. You can snap these over signal lines or power cords to suppress high frequency noise. I've seen suppliers sell these for $15 to $18 each, which is a ridiculously high price. You can get them for under $1.50 each at Parts Express (www.partsexpress.com). Look for their part numbers 1119-035 and 119-030. This approach will not remove 60 Hz hum.

Other sources of magnetic noise problems can be transformers and relays. In a well-designed transformer, the magnetic field is fairly well confined within the metal core itself. However, there may still be some magnetic fringing effects (field leakage) that can couple into nearby conductors or circuitry. The best rule of thumb is to keep signal cables and even speaker cables well away from transformers. If you stack your equipment, make sure there is a metal (steel, not aluminum) plate between the transformer of one piece of equipment and the circuitry of the next piece of equipment. Most modern rack mount equipment is enclosed in a steel case (you can verify a ferrous metal case using a magnet), but if you use older equipment that is not properly shielded (old wooden analog synthesizers for example!), or if you build your own equipment, or if you remove an electronic unit's case, you should take the proper precautions to prevent magnetic field coupling.

Another nasty source of electromagnetic radiation is a poorly shielded wall wart. Wall warts contain transformers (explained above), and if the transformer is poorly shielded, it can induce noise into poorly shielded cables, analog tape deck heads and even into microphones that employ their own transformers. A good strategy is to find a wall wart with the same output connector and voltage/current output capabilities, and then substitute that for the offending wall wart. If you find a well-shielded wall wart with the correct voltage and current output but the wrong connector, just cut that connector off and buy the right connector at Radio Shack. Solder this new connector on (observe the correct polarity) and use heat shrink tubing to insulate the conductors if required. One last-ditch trick to try once you have identified the offending wall wart is to wrap the top of body of the wall wart in aluminum foil (being extremely careful not to get the foil near the AC prongs of the wall wart). Then use a short length of wire connected to the foil with an alligator clip to connect to earth (3rd wire safety) ground. It would be a good idea to affix a tight balloon over this foil on the wall wart to prevent it from tearing or coming into contact with the AC prongs of the wall wart. Again, this is a last resort.

Relays are even worse than transformers with respect to the magnetic field around the component. In a relay, the magnetic circuit is completed in air (as opposed to the transformer, where the magnetic circuit is completed within the core), therefore the magnetic field emanation is fairly large. If you use relays in your studio or in your electronic projects, make sure you shield them and keep them away from audio circuitry. Also, make sure you use suppressor diodes on the relay's control leads, as the diodes will vent to ground the electrical spike due to the reverse voltage generated from the collapsing magnetic field of the relay as it becomes de-energized.

Avoid the use of fluorescent lights in and around your studio. Not only do the bulbs make audible noise when they are energized, but the components used to make the bulbs glow can induce electrical noise into nearby circuitry.

The last source of electromagnetic energy I will discuss is the CRT found in TVs and video monitors. As these units find their way into more and more studios, the musicians using them need to be aware of the potential problems they can cause. I'm sure everyone knows that a CRT generates a substantial electromagnetic field around it. But a real problem for the unwary can come from the focusing and degaussing coils on the CRT. The degaussing coil (only found on color CRTs) is wrapped around the screen of the CRT and is energized briefly by a large current when the CRT is first turned on. In addition, all video monitors and TVs have focusing coils to direct the electron beam that illuminates the screen. If you store your floppy disks, audio tapes or even video tapes on top of your CRT, you may be surprised one day to find that the data is scrambled on those tapes and disks. It depends on the design of the CRT, but the best prevention is not to store magnetic media on or next to your CRT, or make sure you have a specially shielded video monitor.

SPECTRUM ANALYZER AND RTA

One handy piece of auxilliary equipment I've purchased is the spectrum analyzer. A spectrum analyzer is a device that gives an optical display of the relative amplitudes of certain frequency bands across the entire audio spectrum. This device does not itself alter or modify the audio signal as does the equalizer or digital effects box; it is simply a device that monitors the amount of electrical energy in each frequency band in an effort to let you graphically see what you are hearing. This process is also called Real Time Analysis (RTA).

The first application of the spectrum analyzer is to use it with an equalizer to achieve a flat frequency response on the control room monitors (speakers) in the studio. A flat frequency response here is essential in that you want to be assured that the sound you hear is not colored in any way (or at least the coloring is minimized) by the interaction of the monitors and the studio control room environment. For instance, if the monitor/room interaction results in a large boominess at 250 Hz, you may end up trying to equalize this boominess out of your recording due to what your ears are telling you. However, you will find that playing back your recording in another studio or on a home stereo results in a definite lack of signal at 250 Hz, because you removed it all at a prompting from the colored sound of your studio. This problem can be reduced with the use of a spectrum analyzer.

The spectrum analyzer that I have contains an onboard pink noise generator. Pink noise sounds like hiss. Technically, it is composed of a continuous band of a limitless number of sine waves. In other words, it is the inclusion of all frequencies. Pink noise is a particular kind of noise that contains equal energy per octave (as opposed to white noise which contains equal energy for each frequency present) and is useful in contouring the monitor speakers' response for flatness. This is depicted in Figure 11. Pink noise has a warmer sound than white noise, hence the name pink.

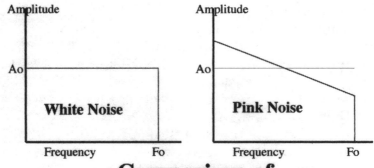

Comparison of
White and Pink Noise

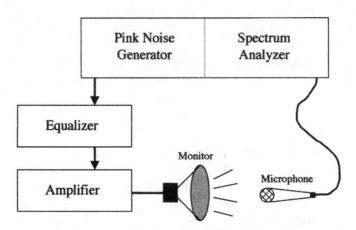

Equalizing the
Monitors for Flatness

Figure 11: Pink Noise & Equalizing for Flatness

To equalize the studio for flatness at your specific monitoring position (i.e., where you put your chair to mix your songs), set up the equipment as shown in Figure 11. Position the microphone at ear level in the location where you normally sit to listen to the monitors (ideally, this is the close field area if you are using close field monitors). Do not try to flatten the response at all locations in the room; it simply won't happen. Set all equalizer controls to the flat position. Turn on the equipment and feed the pink noise through the equalizer to the amplifier. Using the microphone to pick up the audio and send it to the spectrum analyzer, you can view the real-time display of the pink noise. (Note: you will want to use a microphone with an extremely flat frequency response for this application.) Adjust the equalizer controls to give as flat a response as possible on the spectrum analyzer. Do this with one channel at a time. Of course, you may find that moving the monitor speakers around within the studio can radically change the final response of the monitor/ studio interaction. Moving the speaker towards the floor and into the corner increases the apparent low frequency response of the speakers, while moving the speakers up off the floor towards the middle of a wall decreases the low frequency content. Also, sound reflections within the studio can reinforce or cancel out the original sound at certain frequencies, depending on speaker and microphone placement, creating a non-flat frequency response and an unsatisfactory listening environment. (This is why you might want to try the close field monitoring technique that I mentioned earlier.) You should experiment to find the best arrangement.

If you are looking for a microphone that was designed with this specific application in mind, there are several on the market. I recently bought a new Behringer ECM8000 measurement microphone advertised for just $40. (See Figure 12.) It has an electret condenser measurement element with an ultra-linear frequency response. Or, you can buy or rent an Earthworks M30 measurement microphone, which is also optimized for the RTA task.

The other application for which I use the spectrum

analyzer is to monitor the outputs of my synthesizers and drum machine during the multi-tracking process. For instance, I may be recording a synthesized French horn that has an unruly resonance at one particular section of the keyboard that overdrives the audio into distortion and pegs the VU meters. Using the spectrum analyzer, the offending frequencies can be identified and the problem eliminated with a judicious application of a parametric equalizer or even a graphic equalizer. I also monitor the final mixdown to the stereo mastering deck to see the relative amplitude content at all frequencies in the audio bandwidth.

Figure 12: Low-cost Measurement Microphone

You can certainly pay a fair chunk of change for a spectrum analyzer. But what if you don't have a lot of money to spend? You can configure your own calibration system relatively easily. Purchase an equalizer with a fluorescent spectrum analyzer-type display, such as the Radio Shack 31-2030 10-band equalizer (~$130). If you want to build your own, Velleman has a spectrum analyzer kit at http://www.velleman.be/kits/k4300.htm. You can turn your PC into a spectrum analyzer using this DOS software program at http://www.hampubs.com/spec.htm for about $90. If you do a search on Google for "audio spectrum analyzer" you will find many computer-based audio spectrum analyzers, some for free. The analyzers that use the computer CRT for display will most likely give you better frequency resolution.

The pink noise source can be generated by one of your synthesizers (or if you have no synthesizer, you can find a simple pink noise generator circuit in a circuit cookbook and build one yourself). If you want to buy a white/pink noise generator, you can purchase the RDL ST-NG1 for about $100. Go to http://www.rdlnet.com/stng1.htm. Velleman has a kit for a pink noise generator at http://www.velleman.be/kits/k4301.htm. And here is a simple circuit for building your own pink noise generator, if you are so inclined: http://www.discovercircuits.com/P/pinknoise.htm.

Connect the pink noise generator to the input of an equalizer (a different one than the one with the spectrum analyzer display on it, unless the spectrum analyzer section you are using can be used independently of its equalizer section). Connect the output of that equalizer to your amplifier and use that signal to drive your studio speakers. Connect a microphone with a flat frequency response to your mixer and feed the output of it to the spectrum analyzer. Now, you essentially have the same calibration system as described above. Use the same procedure described above to adjust the speakers for flatness in the studio.

There is another technique you can use to help predict some of the normal modes or preferred frequencies at the low end of the audio spectrum. You can calculate the problematic low frequencies in your home studio through some simple mathematics. You can use the simple formula $F = 565/L$. In this formula, F is the frequency of one of the normal modes in the studio. L is the length of one of the room's dimensions. 565 is the speed of sound in air (given in feet/second) divided by two (1130/2). Any dimension in the room can contribute to a normal mode (i.e., floor-to-ceiling, side-to-side, front-to-rear, etc.), and all combinations of dimensions do contribute. In addition, there will be a room mode component at each integer multiple of that fundamental frequency. For example, if there is a room mode at 55 Hz, there will also be other modal resonances at 110 Hz (2 x 55), 165 Hz (3 x 55), 220 Hz (4 x 55), etc.

For my own home studio, the two predominant dimensions are the two wall-to-wall dimensions. I have a cathedral ceiling in my studio, which is actually an advantage in this case. (You can't use this simple formula to calculate the normal mode of a dimension that is constantly changing.) In my studio, I have wall-to-wall dimensions of 9.875 feet and 10.958 feet, which after plugging those figures into the formula yields 57.2 Hz and 51.56 Hz, respectively. Therefore, I would expect to have problems at these frequencies: 51.56 Hz, 57.2 Hz, 103.12 Hz, 114.4 Hz, 154.68 Hz, 171.6 Hz, 206.24 Hz, and 228.8 Hz. The best way to tackle these resonances is with a multiband parametric equalizer, but the equalizer boost or cut settings will depend on where I locate my listening position within the room.

One thing that I would like to touch on while we are talking about frequency spectrums is the Fletcher-Munson curve. Fletcher and Munson discovered that the sensitivity of the human ear is different depending on the frequency of the sound. The human ear is less sensitive to lower (bass) frequencies than to middle or higher (treble) frequencies. This is why when the sound on your stereo is turned down lower, the low frequencies are not so pronounced in relation to the middle and higher frequencies (and it is also why you find a "loudness contour" button on consumer stereos). Be aware of this fact as you are listening at different volume levels to a monitor system that has been tuned "flat" with respect to the speaker performance and room response. The Fletcher-Munson phenomenon is discussed in more detail in the "Nature of Sound" section of this book.

REMOVING AUDIBLE NOISE

There are many things that contribute to audible noise in the home studio. Some are external to the studio (jet and traffic noise, neighborhood kids, dogs barking, the gardener (unless that's you), etc.) and some are internal to the studio (hiss, hum, crackle, pops and clicks generated electronically, heating and ventilation equipment, fans and disk drives on computers and samplers, etc.). How can these unwanted noises be eliminated?

Overview of room treatments and acoustics:
This subject was covered earlier in the section entitled section "Acoustics In Your Studio".

Single-ended noise reduction units:
Even with the fantastic recording specs on the latest digital recorders and DAWs, audio noise in the studio is still going to be one of your main enemies. You will get audio noise from any analog tape decks such as cassette decks and reel-to-reel decks, old electronic musical instruments and amplifiers, and cheap effects boxes. You will also have to battle noise if you do not appropriately set up the fader levels on your mixers or the recording levels on your recorders. (See the section "Gain Structuring" to cure this problem.) Fortunately, there are a number of different devices generally called single-ended noise reduction systems that can help battle these problems.

Single-ended noise reduction systems are basically a black box where you can put a noisy signal in and magically get a cleaner signal out. They are called "single-ended" because they do not require encoding and then decoding in two passes (as the Dolby and dbx noise reduction systems require). The single-ended noise reduction systems are just inserted in-line with the signal flow to remove the noise.

The simplest noise reducer is the noise gate. It has a threshold adjustment on it to set the point where you want the gate to close. When the gate does close, it removes all audio (both good and bad). This type of noise reduction is good for removing noise mixed in with solo instruments. This method depends on the idea of frequency masking or spectral masking when the gate is open. Loud sounds at certain frequencies (the valid audio signal) will mask the softer noise signals of other frequencies. The noise is actually still there, but the human ear tends not to notice it.

Another type of noise reducer is the downward expander. It also has a threshold control to establish the point where the noise reduction kicks in. Unlike the noise gate, however, it merely reduces the overall volume of the signal going through it instead of removing it altogether when the threshold point is reached. The idea with the downward expander is to further reduce the level of the signal when it falls below a certain point to remove (or at least hide) the noise that accompanies the valid audio signal. The noise reduction effect of the downward expander may be less intense than the noise gate effect.

The third type of single-ended noise reduction system is the sliding filter (also called the dynamic filter). This type of noise reducer divides the frequency spectrum up into several bands and then monitors those bands for acoustic energy within each frequency band. Depending on the level of signals within the band, the sliding filter will start to close down a filter starting with the highest frequencies. For example, if the only thing playing is a bass guitar, the sliding filter might close down its bandwidth all the way to reduce high frequency hiss. If a piano and bass are playing together, the sliding filter might open up more to allow some of the higher frequencies of the piano to get through. Then if a drum set is added to the mix with lots of cymbal crashes, the sliding filter will open up all the way to let the audio signal through without any filtering. The idea here is that the high frequency content of the cymbals will mostly mask any high frequency hiss that might also be present. Therefore, sliding filters also make use of the psychoacoustic principle of spectral masking to accomplish noise reduction.

No one single-ended noise reduction system can handle all types of noise. You may need several different types of units in your studio to handle the various types of noise you can encounter. If you are buying equipment, a good place to start is with the noise gate, and then add the sliding filter to your arsenal later.

There are several older units you can buy on the used market these days. My absolute favorite is an analog processor called the Autocorrelator (also know as the Phase Linear 1000). I bought this unit back in the '70s and it still works great! It is a combination of 3 separate functions: a multiband filter set that detects audio within each band and adjusts the filters appropriately, a downward expander and a subsonic filter (which was used to remove turntable rumble around 20 Hz back in the Stone Age of albums). If you can find one of these units, buy it! It is like a Swiss Army Knife for noise reduction, and it does it all without digital signal processing.

Other single-ended noise reduction units you can find on the used market include the Peavey Q-Factor, Rocktron's Hush Super C noise reduction rack system, Rocktron's Hush noise reduction pedal (for guitarists), Rocktron's Hush Elite, Rocktron's Hush IICX, dbx 563x Silencer, Roland SN-550 and Boss NS-50 Noise Suppressor. Older units that were originally designed for stereo buffs include the Pioneer RG-1 Expander, SAE 5000 Impulse Noise Reducer, Burwen 1201 A Sliding Filter, dbx 3BX Expander, the Source Engineering Noise Suppressor sliding filter, and the MXR Compander. You can go to www.google.com and do a search on all the above units to see if you can find someone who is selling one.

Newer units on the market that incorporate noise reduction are the Alesis 3630 Compressor (has dual noise gates) and the BBE 362NR Sonic Maximizer (has a sliding filter). You can even make use of a parametric equalizer for noise reduction. Identify at what point in the frequency spectrum the offending noise resides, then dial in the parametric controls to eliminate the noise. For example, if 60 Hz hum is the problem, dial in the parametric equalizer to cut frequencies around 60 Hz with the highest Q (i.e., narrowest width of filtered frequencies). This should leave sounds in adjacent frequency bands largely unscathed.

There are several plug-ins available for MacIntosh DAW computers such as the Cedar DeClick, Cedar DeCrackle, Cedar DeHiss, Digidesign DINR noise/hum reduction, Steinberg DeClicker, and Steinberg DeNoiser plug-ins. For PC DAWs, some available plug-ins are the Creamware Osiris, the Sonic Foundry Noise Reduction Direct-X, the Steinberg DeNoiser, and the Steinberg DeClicker. These plug-ins have list prices from about $400 up to $5000.

Removing other noises in the studio:
If the offending unit is making audible free-air noise due to physical vibration (due to a vibrating transformer inside the unit, for example), you can buy some stick-on rubber feet to try to dampen out the vibrations. Another technique is to use RTV silicon sealant as a dampening agent. Uninstall the offending piece of equipment, squirt some of the silicon sealant onto the area where the vibration occurs, let the sealant cure, then reinstall the unit into your rig. If it is a vibrating transformer, you can try to isolate the transformer itself inside the unit from its chassis with rubber washers, but this is a fairly involved process.

Removing Mic Popping Noises:
Pop filters are really handy for removing the vocal popping sounds when you record vocals at a close range with microphones. These vocal popping sounds are also called voiced plosives, and they are generated by a closure of the mouth, then a build-up of pressure inside it while the vocal cord vibration continues, until the final sound is suddenly released. This effect is most noticeable with hard P and B sounds. You can make your own pop filter from some panty hose (it is probably best to break down and actually buy some *new* panty hose for this application, folks) stretched on a set of embroidery hoops. However, the mounting of such a homemade device onto the microphone stand can be a fairly clumsy arrangement, so you might want to take the easy route and just buy a commercial pop filter. You can find some fairly low-cost units at

Popless Voice Screens (www.popfilter.com) and Stedman's (www.stedmanpop.com), or any music dealer in your town.

Removing audible computer noise in the studio:
Another technique you can apply to a piece of equipment that is making audible free-air noise that can be picked up by a microphone (e.g., the fan in a computer) is to remotely locate the offending unit to another room or into a closet. If you remotely locate the computer CPU (with the offending fan), you will still need to have access to the keyboard, mouse and monitor in the studio. For PC-type computer keyboards and mice, you can just buy a longer serial cable from a supplier such as CompUSA, Fry's or any other computer parts supplier. Mac-type keyboards and mice use a unique connection scheme called the Apple Desktop Bus (ADB). This scheme uses a S-VHS style cable for connection of the ADB keyboard to the computer. You can get reasonably long lengths of S-VHS cable from any video store or Radio Shack.

To locate the monitor some distance away from the computer CPU, you will need to extend and possibly re-drive the video signals going from the computer to the monitor. You can try using longer very high quality BNC cables (the style of connection most PC-types of computer uses). If you have a fat wallet with at least $595 in it, you can use one of the commercial units on the market made specifically for this purpose, such as the Gefen Systems PCX150S. The PCX150 extends your keyboard, video and mouse up to 500 feet away from the location of your PC computer. It is compatible with all PC computers, monitors, mice and trackball devices. (Go to the Gefen web site at www.gefen.com.) If you are using a Mac computer with the DB-15 style video connector, you will need to use a different unit. The TSE150 (also $595) from Gefen Systems extends your monitor, ADB keyboard and ADB mouse up to 500 feet from your Mac computer. Remember that SCSI cables must have a total length of less than 20 feet, so if you have your SCSI Bus hooked to your sampler or some other device in the studio, this could be a problem.

What if you don't want to go through the hassle of

remotely locating the computer? You can build a little wind tunnel baffle for the fan(s) on the computer like I did. Out of wood, I built a tube shaped like a big squared-off 'S' that looks like one of those toy periscopes. It is about a foot tall and has a square cross-section of about 5" (this dimension will be dictated by the size of the fan opening on your computer). Before I nailed and glued the whole thing together, I lined the inside with open-cell soft foam to absorb as much of the fan noise as possible (just use wood glue to affix the foam in place). Then I mounted the wooden tube to the back of the computer where the fan exhaust is. The wind tunnel baffle can be made cheaply and easily from scrap material in your garage, and it will cut your computer's fan noise substantially (~20 dB).

If you are really serious about eliminating (or at least reducing) the noise emanating from your computer, you can replace the power supply in the computer with the Ultra-Quiet Silencer Series of supplies from PC Power and Cooling (reach them at 800-722-6555 or point your browser to www.pcpowerandcooling.com). PC Power and Cooling is located near me in Southern California. They claim that the high-efficiency fan and low-turbulence circuitry in their power supplies reduce noise by up to 90%. You might also replace the stock cooling fans in your computer with the PC Power and Cooling Silencer® Cooling Fans.

A good friend of mine, Dave MacCormack (formerly the Technical Fellow of Sensormatic Electronics Corporation), also has some excellent advice on quieting down noisy computers in the studio, and I am reproducing his advice in this paragraph with his permission. He suggests first of all that you determine if your computer chassis really needs all of the fans that are in it. I recently bought a computer chassis that had 4 chassis fans in it (2 in the front and 2 in the rear), a processor cooling fan, a power supply cooling fan, and cooling fans on the motherboard, CD/RW drive and DVDROM drive. That's 9 fans total! It sounded like a 747 taking off from the runway. To determine if all of the chassis fans are required, you need to monitor the processor temperature (usually there is some motherboard utility software that does this) and the general ambient temperature inside of the chassis. Remove as many of the fans as you can while maintaining a safe processor and ambient temperature in the computer. The best bet is to remove the fans in the front of the chassis first and see how that affects the overall noise level outside of the box. The theory is that the rear-mounted fans should provide enough negative (exhaust) pressure inside the chassis to pull cool air in through the bottom and the front faceplate holes. Once you have removed the front fan, mount a thin layer of insolite or closed cell foam into the front plastic shell of the computer case. Keep the foam thin so that air can still be drawn into the chassis, but so that the fan noise (especially high frequency component) will be attenuated. You may also try to mount some foam inside of the computer itself. Be careful here— don't create a fire hazard! Keep the foam thin, and glue it securely to the case (and away from any electronics), so that the fan noise bouncing around inside of the case is absorbed.

Pay attention to where and how you place your computer in the studio. If possible, put it on a thick rug or some other suitable substance that will absorb fan sound and chassis vibrations. If the chassis fans are pointing back towards the wall (the most likely arrangement), you can mount a piece of thick carpet or other insulating material behind it, and this will knock several dB off of the radiated and reflected noise. (Or, you can build the wind tunnel baffle as I described above.) Dave also called to my attention the fact that the IEEE802.11a wireless standard now allows you to use a relatively silent computer (i.e., laptop) in your studio and connect it wirelessly to a screaming multi-processor monster computer out in your garage or in an adjacent room. The laptop then acts as a relatively silent man-machine interface while all the computationally intensive tasks are performed on the noisy computer somewhere else in the house. Thanks for the additional studio quieting ideas, Dave!

Balanced versus unbalanced equipment:

It is important to understand the difference between balanced and unbalanced audio equipment. Most consumer and lower-cost semi-pro audio equipment uses unbalanced signal connectors. These are generally the RCA type (also called phono connectors) or 1/4" phone type of connectors. An unbalanced signal has one of its conductors (the shield) connected to ground, and the other conductor carries the signal referenced to ground. This is a cheaper circuit to produce, hence its use in consumer equipment. The problem with unbalanced connections is that they are susceptible to hum and noise because the shielded conductor can allow ground currents to flow between the interconnected pieces of equipment. You always get what you pay for, right? (Well, usually.)

Balanced signal connections solve the ground current problem because they have two opposite-polarity, non-grounded conductors (with equal impedances referenced to ground) to carry the high and low side of the audio signal. Plus, they have a separate third conductor that acts as a shield for the other two conductors. Balanced signals typically appear on XLR type of 3-pin connectors. For balanced signals, ground noise and induced magnetic noise or RF noise should appear on *both* non-ground signal conductors in equal amounts, and when those noises are processed by the electronic circuits downstream, the net effect is that the noises cancel out because they are of opposite polarity. This is called Common Mode Rejection. Of course, the electronic circuits for balanced circuits are generally more expensive (as are the balanced cables that interconnect the equipment), and therefore balanced signals generally only appear in pro or higher-end semi-pro equipment. If you can afford to do it, implementing balanced signals in your home studio is definitely the way to go for increased signal performance and integrity. If you have a mix of balanced and unbalanced equipment, you can connect them together, but you will need to purchase or build special adapters to do so.

Generally, consumer equipment is referenced to what is called −10 dBV, and pro equipment is referenced to what is called +4 dBu. Simply, this means that the unbalanced signal levels are generally between 150mVRMS to 750 mVRMS and the balanced signal levels are around 1.2 VRMS. Therefore, you will need some sort of an adapter to connect these two signal types together. This adapter can be as simple as building your own adapter cable (build one by connecting the center conductor of the unbalanced RCA connector to pin 2 on the balanced XLR connector, and connecting the shield on the unbalanced RCA connector to both pins 1 and 3 on the XLR connector), or as complex as adding impedance matching transformers to truly match the various impedances in the balanced and unbalanced circuits. If you get unacceptable results with the simple cable adapter (noise, distortion or reduced bass response), you will need to buy or build a more sophisticated transformer adapter (go to http://www.jensen-transformers.com for more detailed advice on this).

Direct Boxes:

Direct boxes have an important role in the studio. A direct box is a device that is used to directly plug a guitar or bass into the mixer's line inputs. The reason the direct box is required is that electric guitar and bass pickups generally have a low-voltage/high-impedance output signal. Unbalanced mixer line input channels usually want to see a signal in to 150 mV to 750 mV range with a relatively low impedance value. So, when you plug a guitar or bass directly into the mixer channel, an impedance and signal level mismatch occurs, affecting the volume level and sometimes the amount of distortion in the signal. This can be fixed by adding a direct box to the guitar's output before you plug it into the mixer. The direct box contains some active circuitry that matches the guitar or bass output voltage and impedance to what the mixer channel wants to see.

You won't need to add a direct box to most electronic keyboard outputs, drum machine outputs, or to a guitar which has already been plugged into an effects box or stomp box. Additionally, products exist that will allow you to plug unbalanced signal outputs from electronic musical instruments, line-level sources, film projectors, tape recorders, phonographs and guitar amplifiers into the balanced microphone inputs on your mixer. If this is something you need to be able to do in your studio, then go to http://www.procosound.com/prod02.htm (or do some Internet searches on Active Direct Boxes).

The Control Room vs. The Recording Space:

I'm sure you have seen the pictures of big budget recording studios that have one room (at least) dedicated to recording the instruments and vocalists, and another room called the control room that houses all of the recorders, mixing consoles, rack mount equipment, monitor speakers, etc. Usually, the control room is separated from the recording space by a glass window, so that the people in both rooms can interact visually. The control room usually has a type of an intercom called talkback (which is actually built into the more expensive mixing consoles), so that the individuals in the control room can talk to the individuals in the recording space.

In your home, I doubt that you are going to elect to destroy a wall between two adjacent bedrooms and install a window, so that you can have a separate control room and recording space (but, you never know!). There are some nice advantages to separating the control space from the recording space, chief among them being the isolation of noisy computers, tape decks, fans and other equipment from sensitive microphones. If you want to use an adjacent bedroom to your studio for a microphone recording space, a great idea is to use a set of wireless intercoms to allow communication between you in your studio (the control room) and the person or people recording in the other bedroom (the recording space).

You can buy some relatively inexpensive systems at Radio Shack. One system communicates over an FM wireless link (P/N 43-204, $40 for a pair). Another system communicates over the AC power wiring in your house (P/N 43-486, $40 for a pair). And a third system communicates over the phone lines already installed in your house (P/N 43-483, $50 for a pair). If you really want to go the el cheapo route, you can just buy a pair of battery-operated wired intercoms, and run the wire temporarily between the two rooms when you record (P/N 43-222, $15 for a pair). Of course, if you have children, someone may have given your family one off those wireless baby monitors at a baby shower, and those will work just as well for this application (in one direction only).

PART THREE: MODIFYING YOUR EQUIPMENT

TAPE DECK REMOTE CONTROLLER

If you are the owner of an open reel tape machine such as the Teac 3340 or 3440 (or any other large reel/reel deck), you know that the remote control can be a fairly expensive device, if you can find one. You'll find this to be a mandatory piece of equipment, though, if you perform serious multi-track recording, overdubbing and punch-in editing. If you own one of the Dokorder open reel machines such as the 8100, 8140 or 1140, you can forget about buying a remote control; Dokorder went out of business years ago. However, there is a very inexpensive and easily realized alternative. You can build a remote controller yourself. (Remote controls that incorporate LED position readouts and other features are beyond the scope of this book.)

In general, most lower-end tape machine remote control signals are simply switch contact closures to ground if the tape machine utilizes logic-controlled solenoids for the tape transport mechanism. If your tape machine uses this type of logic-controlled tape transport, you may be able to build the remote controller detailed in this book. If the tape machine uses a manual mechanical linkage to control the tape transport, as is usually the case in older open reel machines and quite a few cassette decks, you're out of luck on this one. On some of the cassette multi-track machines, it just depends on which model you have. For example, the Yamaha MT50, Fostex X-18/XR-3/XR-5, and the Tascam Porta 07 all have mechanical linkages from the function buttons to the cassette mechanism, while the Yamaha MT4X/MT8X, Tascam 424/464/488MKII, Marantz PMD721/PMD740 and the Fostex XR7/280/380S machines have logic-operated control buttons.

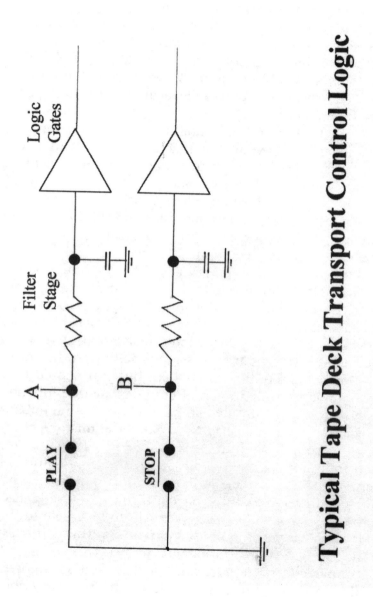

Typical Tape Deck Transport Control Logic

Figure 13: Tape Deck Transport Schematic

Inside the tape machine, the electrical control lines are *normally open* circuit types. Refer to the simplified schematic diagram in Figure 13. When the control buttons are pressed, the particular control lines are shorted to ground, activating the appropriate tape transport functions. For machines that incorporate remote controllers, each control signal is usually picked off before the filter stage (points A and B in Figure 13) and brought out to the remote control connector usually located on the back panel of the tape machine.

The first step in building a remote controller is to find a schematic of your tape machine. These can sometimes be obtained from the manufacturer, repair centers or a parts house that carries Sam's Photofacts equipment manuals. You may also be able to procure the schematic from the original equipment manufacturer (if they are still in business) or get a copy from your local equipment repair shop. (See the section in this book entitled "Finding Schematics for Your Equipment.") The schematic is essential in determining which pin jacks on the back panel remote control connector are connected to the various tape transport functions. You may be able to check each pin jack with a VOM (Volt Ohm Meter) or DMM (Digital Multi Meter) to see which pin jack is grounded when the corresponding control button is pushed, but you should only do this to verify your design after you know the function of each signal pin. In my estimation, there is no substitute for the schematic. Do **NOT** make the mistake of inserting a grounded pin in each connector pin jack to see which tape transport function engages. Some manufacturers put +5VDC on one or more of the pin jacks to drive LEDs in their remote control boxes. If you short the +5VDC to ground, you may have set yourself up for a trip to the repair shop. If you are really industrious, you can trace out the circuitry yourself and figure out the wiring scheme.

After you have determined which functions correspond to which connector pin, you can draw the schematic for your remote controller. In the remote controller I built for my Dokorder 8100 open reel machine, I used momentary action, normally-open pushbuttons (Radio

Shack part number 275-1547). The schematic I generated for my Dokorder 8100 is shown in Figure 14. It would
be difficult to find a remote controller schematic much
simpler than this.

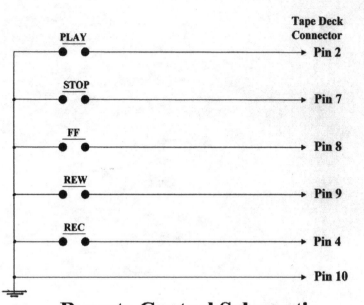

Remote Control Schematic

Figure 14

I used a small plastic box and mounted the
pushbutton switches in it. I bought about ten feet of 8-
conductor jacketed cable and wired one end to the switches
in the remote controller box, as shown in Figure 15. I
recommend using multi-conductor jacketed cable because
it frees you from having to fool around with protecting or
routing each individual wire. Use cable with stranded wire
rather than solid wire to prevent it from breaking as a
result of too much flexing. Now comes the fun part.

You are probably going to have to build your own
connector, because chances are remote (no pun intended)

that you will be able to locate the correct mating connector to the connector on your tape machine. If you can locate one, the remainder of this project is easy. If you can't find the correct connector, then you can try the solution that I used.

Figure 15: Completed Remote Control Box

I cannibalized an old car stereo connector and removed the pins from it. After making sure that these pins fit snugly into the pin jacks of the remote control jack on the tape machine, I soldered the five pins onto the end of each utilized conductor in the jacketed cable. Then I took the lid off of a 35mm film canister, sized it up against the tape machine's connector, marked the location of pins 2, 7, 8, 9 and 10 on the inside of the canister lid and drilled five holes at the marked locations on the lid using a $5/64"$ drill bit. Use a drill bit slightly smaller than the diameter of the pins, so that the pins fit snugly in the lid. Next, I inserted the pins into the lid from the inside of the lid. At this point, you should have something similar to the device shown in Figures 16 and 17.

Figure 16: Side View of Remote Connector

Figure 17: Rear View of Remote Connector

Before continuing with the fabrication effort, you should test the remote control to make sure it works properly with the tape machine. You should be able to plug the unfinished canister lid and connector pins right into the tape machine's connector.

Figure 18: Front View of Remote Connector

To complete the connector, cut the bottom portion off of the film canister to use as the body of the connector. Snap the lid containing the pins onto the canister and add a generous helping of Silicone II Household Glue and Seal to hold the pins in place. The idea is to pot the pins in place. Allow the silicone glue sufficient time to cure before you use the connector. Silicone glue is great stuff, and it is an excellent electrical insulator.

I'll be the first to admit that the finished connector is not exactly a thing of beauty (see Figure 18), but it works fine. Since it connects to the back of the tape machine, no one sees it anyway.

But what do you do if you want to add a remote controller function to a tape deck that has a solenoid- or logic-controlled tape transport, but it doesn't have a remote control connector on the back? You can still build a remote control for the tape deck, but it is a bit more involved and is much more risky. Again, you will want to procure, beg, borrow or steal a schematic for your deck, if at all possible. Also, absolutely don't try this modification on a unit that is still under warranty, unless you don't mind a voided warranty. Since all decks are different, I will give you the general approach to follow rather than the specifics on where to solder and where to mount a connector.

Basically, what you want to do is replicate another set of the same switch functions that are on your deck, but locate them in a remote control box. Most likely, one terminal of each switch that controls functions such as stop, play, rewind, etc. connects to ground. The other terminal connects to downstream circuitry, as was shown in Figure 13. The terminal of interest is the one that connects to the downstream circuitry, since when that terminal is grounded, the deck will perform the desired function. Now here is the trickiest part of this modification: you need to solder a wire onto each of these points (one wire for each switch function you want to replicate in the remote control).

If the transport control switches on the tape deck are panel-mounted with wires running to a circuit board, then soldering another wire to the terminal is relatively easy; just wrap your wire around the terminal of interest and solder it on, being careful not to unsolder or dislodge the original wire going to the terminal. (Use plastic-insulated wire, stranded or solid, 22 gauge, 24 gauge or even 26 gauge.) If the transport control switches on the tape deck are PCB-mounted (printed circuit board-mounted) switches, then it may be next to impossible to solder a wire onto the legs of the switches. In this case, you will probably have to tack solder a wire onto the back side (i.e., the circuit side, as opposed to the component side) of the PCB. This is not easy, and you may want to consider aborting the modification right here. It is easy to accidentally lift a circuit pad or a circuit trace on the PCB when you do a mod like this, so extreme care must be taken. (If you don't have reasonable experience with this sort of soldering operation, I recommend that you NOT experiment with it now.) After you have soldered a wire onto each of the switch terminals or PCB pads, you need to add one more wire for ground. You don't necessarily need to use the ground that connects to the switches themselves, but verify that the point you do take the ground from is the same ground as the one used for the switches (use a DMM to verify continuity close to zero Ohms resistance).

Now, you want to take these wires you soldered onto the switches and bring them out to the back panel. You have three options to do this. I will detail each of the three options here.

Option 1: Mount a connector on the back panel of the deck wherever there is unused panel space. This is certainly the cleanest option for aesthetics and functionality, but it involves drilling out the back panel sheet metal and mounting a connector in the hole. If you do elect to drill the back panel, take great care not to get metal filings into the electronics of your deck, or your deck may become very unhappy at some point in time (and then you, too, will become unhappy). One secret to doing this is to put masking tape on both sides of the panel before you drill it. The masking tape tends to collect the metal filings, and also help prevent the drill bit from slipping and leaving a deep gouge across the face of the back panel.

If you mount a connector on the back panel, here are a couple of tips to make the effort easier. Round connectors are much easier to mount than any other type because you can cut the hole with a drill. Of course, you may have trouble finding a drill bit with the correct diameter for the hole you need to drill. If the hole is fairly large, you may need to drill a series of increasingly larger pilot holes, rather than jumping in with the correct-size drill bit immediately. Non-round types of connectors generally require you to start the hole (or a series of holes) with a drill, and then finish up with an instrument called a nibbling tool. (See Figure 19.) The nibbling tool does just what its name implies; it nibbles away at the sheet metal until it forms the hole to be the size you want. This procedure is generally a pain in the buttocks, but there are few alternatives to the nibbling tool, especially if you are working inside of a completed piece of equipment (like a tape deck) rather than on a blank panel in your workshop. Radio Shack sells a nibbling tool (P/N 64-823) for around $11.

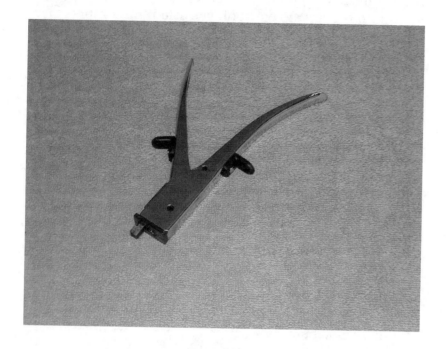

Figure 19: Sheet Metal Nibbling Tool

Another tact you can try is to cut a much bigger square hole than you need, and then mount your connector on a small subpanel that mounts over the bigger square hole. This allows you to work on the actual (weird-shaped) connector on your workshop bench, and then mount that subassembly onto the back panel of your deck with 4 screws/nuts.

Note that the connector that is mounted onto the rear panel of the tape deck should always be the female connector. The reason for this is that on a female connector the pins are not exposed to accidental shorting to external harmful voltages or physical damage. Regardless of what kind of connector you end up using, make sure you find and purchase both sides of the connector, a male (plug) and female (jack) mating pair. This will make things much easier when you attempt to build the remote controller box and interconnect cable. If you can find a locking connector of some sort (i.e., where the male portion locks into the female portion), you will have a much more positive connection of the remote controller to the tape deck.

Option 2: Use a connector on a pigtail. With this option, you avoid drilling a big hole in the back panel of the deck, but the connector is hanging out on a pigtail, which is not the most aesthetic approach. (However, it is on the back of the deck, so who is going to see it?) You will still need to drill a small hole somewhere to get the wire bundle/connector pigtail out of the deck. Perhaps you can nibble out a small channel on the edge of the back panel using the nibbling tool. If you attempt this option, make sure that you strain-relieve the cable at the ingress/egress points on the back panel, and also use a grommet or something to prevent the cable from chafing on the sharp metal edges of the panel.

Option 3: Wire the remote controller directly into the deck with no connector (i.e., it is always connected). This may not be very desirable, but it certainly can be done with no harmful electrical effects. Again, if you attempt this option, make sure that you strain-relieve the cable at the ingress/egress points on the back panel. Make sure that the panel will not cut into the cable or chafe it if the cable is repeatedly moved.

No matter which option you select, you should make sure to document your work. This will allow you to get the correct wires to the proper pins in all of the connectors and inside of the remote control box. It would be frustrating to hit the stop button and have the deck jump into fast forward mode. Draw up a little schematic for yourself and staple it to the tape deck's schematic, or keep it with the tape deck's manual. You may need to refer to it at some later date. Double check your work before applying power, and test the whole system before you close up all the boxes.

ADDING A POWER SWITCH

If you have a piece of equipment that has no power switch, it is a relatively simple matter to add one to it. However, do not attempt to do this if the equipment is still under warranty, as this modification will surely void the warranty. Also, do not ever attempt to modify any equipment while it is plugged into an AC receptacle, or it may void your body's warranty!

In general, the power supply section of most equipment (that has an internal power supply) resembles that shown in the schematic of Figure 20. This circuit shows a two-prong standard AC power plug. Here is a quick review of the functions of the power supply components. The fuse is a protective device that prevents the electronic circuitry from drawing too much current from the 115 VAC, 60 Hz power source. The stepdown transformer reduces the amplitude of the input voltage from 115 VAC to a lesser value on the order of 24 VAC or less. There are other components downstream from the transformer, such as a 4-diode bridge rectifier, which converts the AC to unfiltered DC. The power supply filtering section usually contains one or more capacitors to smooth out and remove any ripple from the DC output voltage. The power supply output section may also contain other components such as Zener diodes to clamp the voltage at a specific value. If your equipment uses a three-prong AC power plug, it will most likely be configured as in Figure 21.

Point A denotes the place in Figures 20 and 21 where the new power switch should be inserted. It should go in the leg of the circuit that contains the fuse; this is the "hot" leg of the circuit. (Note: I have seen equipment that was incorrectly designed with the fuse in the neutral line. Observe and be careful!) The hot leg of the circuit connects to the smaller prong of the power plug (black is the conventional color), while the neutral leg (white is the conventional color) connects to the wider prong. Green is designated as the safety ground (Earth) in a 3-wire system.

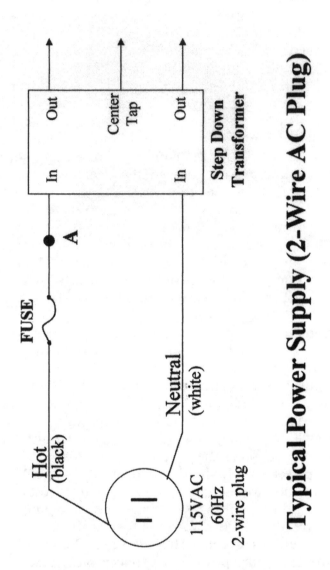

Figure 20: Typical 2-Wire Power Supply

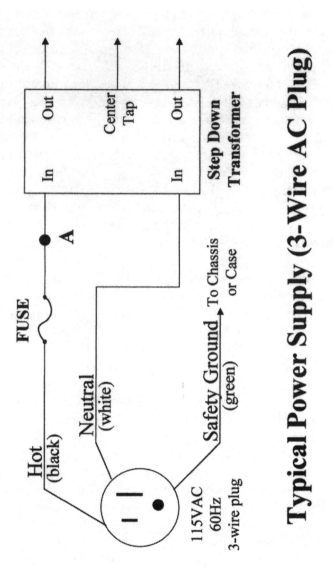

Figure 21: Typical 3-Wire Power Supply

The power switch should be selected with a safety factor of at least two times the maximum current-draw of the unit into which it is installed. To calculate the current-draw of the unit (if it's not given in the owner's manual or on the unit's back panel), divide the power rating of the unit by 115 to give the ampere (current) rating. For example, if the equipment dissipates 86 watts of power, it draws (86/115 = 0.75) 0.75 amps. Therefore, use a switch with a rating of at least 1.5 amps at 115 volts. The type of switch used is not really critical, but thinking ahead to the installation phase can save you some toiling with the power tools. Avoid slide switches, because cutting the rectangular slot in the front panel of your equipment can be a real hassle. I recommend a SPST (single pole single throw) toggle or SPST pushbutton switch that can be mounted in a simple circular hole. Sealed switches generally provide better reliability than non-sealed types. Figure 22 shows a toggle switch (on the left in the photo) that I mounted in a piece of equipment that I use in my studio.

Locate the switch in an area of the front panel that avoids physical interference between the body of the switch and the other internal components. Drill a hole in the front panel. Usually, it's best to drill from the inside of the panel (if you can), so that if the drill bit slips, it doesn't scratch the face of the panel. Sometimes it just isn't possible to drill from the inside due to lack of space within the unit. Be extremely careful to locate and remove all metal filings that are cast off by the drill, as these can wreak havoc in electrical circuits. One helpful tip is to put masking tape over both sides of the panel where you are going to drill. This helps bind up the metal filings and also prevents the drill from slipping across the faceplate of your equipment and leaving a handsome gouge for all to admire. ("Say, nice gouge you've got there, Mr. Handyman!") Remove any burrs around the hole. You can get a deburring bit for your drill for this task, or you can try to file off the burrs. Mount the switch in the panel. Next, locate the wire that runs between the power plug and the one side of the fuse. This is the hot wire. Snip this wire inside the unit at the other end of the fuse (you want the fuse to protect everything downstream, including the new power switch) and solder the two cut ends to the two terminals of the power switch. Use heat shrink tubing to provide insulation for the two bare connection points. That's about all there is to it.

Figure 22: New Power Switch Added

If you really want to do it right, you can add a capacitor across the switch to smooth any voltage spikes generated from opening and closing the switch. Use a ceramic disc type with a capacitance value in the range of 0.001uF to 0.01uF and a voltage rating of at least 250 volts. The altered schematic of the input power section of the equipment now appears as is shown in Figure 23.

Some studio equipment, such as all of the Alesis Midiverb and Microverb types of units and other similar components, use outboard stepdown transformers (commonly called wall warts or bricks) that plug into the wall to provide 9, 10, 15 or even 18 volts AC to the circuitry within the unit. While I think it's good that these manufacturers isolate the transformer in a remote location to avoid magnetic coupling effects to nearby circuitry, I have mixed feelings about this practice. (By the way, the reason that these manufacturers use wall warts is that it makes the compliance and certification process much easier and less costly for these products. It's a financially driven decision.) The problem is that it is so hard (read: impossible) to plug in several of these big transformers next to each other in a wall socket or in a power strip. I have a good tip regarding this later at the end of the book. A better solution (but more expensive to the manufacturer) is the "lump-in-the-middle" power supply, sometimes called the desktop power supply. Regardless, you can still add a power switch to units that employ remote transformers. All the rules and procedures are the same as I outlined previously. The finished schematic should appear as in Figure 24.

Be aware that some outboard transformers are not meant to be plugged into the wall socket 100% of the time when the equipment is turned off; this may limit their over-all operating life. If you see thick smoke emanating from your outboard transformer (not really, but they do tend to run warm to the touch), then you probably own one of these types. To avoid that inconvenience, you should plug all such transformers into a power strip that you can turn off when the studio is not in use. This will isolate the transformer from the 115 VAC power.

Note that the above-mentioned wall warts put out AC voltage, not DC voltage. Some wall warts put out DC voltage, and you need to be keenly aware of which ones are AC output and which ones are DC output. You can usually read right on the wall wart itself what it expects for an input voltage (nominally 115 VAC, 60 Hz in the USA) and what kind of voltage and current it will output. DC wall warts have a polarity associated with them (center conductor positive or center conductor negative). You can use a Digital Multi Meter (DMM) or volt meter to determine if the center conductor is positive or negative. Make sure this jibes with the indication on the piece of electrical equipment into which you are plugging the wall wart! There will usually be some sort of indication right near the power jack on the unit.

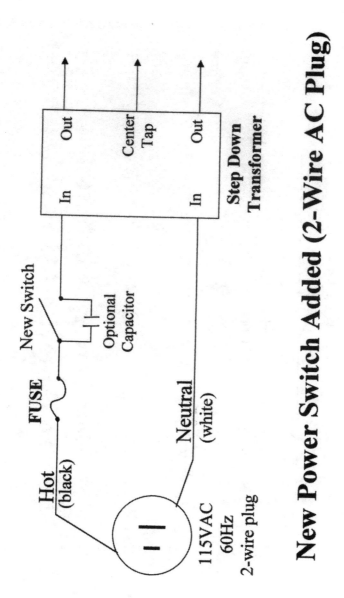

Figure 23: New Power Switch Added (2-Wire)

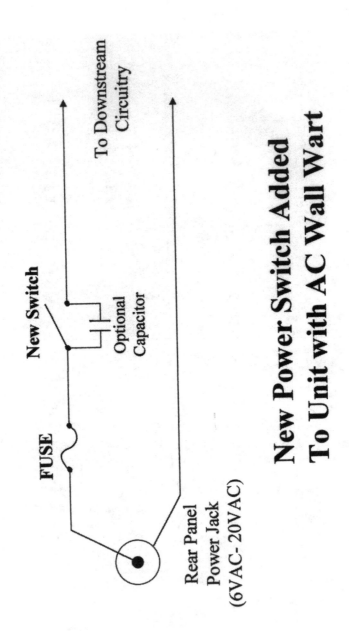

Figure 24: New Power Switch Added (Wall Wart)

If you want to add a power switch to a unit that uses a DC wall wart, first identify the internal wire inside of the unit that attaches to the positive conductor on the power jack. Cut this wire while making sure to leave enough room to insert and solder the wires for the front-panel-mounted power switch. If you don't leave enough room, you will find that it is difficult to cut, strip and solder the wire. You will simply be inserting the power switch in this one wire to interrupt the flow of current from the wall wart to the piece of equipment. Use heat shrink tubing to insulate the soldered connections. Mount the power switch on the front panel as described above for the AC power switch. The power rating on the switch should be such that it is at least twice the power rating of the wall wart. Determine the power by multiplying the wall wart's voltage output by the current output. For example, 12 VDC x 300 mA (milliamps) = 3600 mW (milliwatts) = 3.6 watts. For reference, there are 1000 milliamps in 1 amp, and 1000 milliwatts in 1 watt.

ADDING A HEADPHONE JACK

If you want to add a headphone jack to a piece of audio equipment, you can do it with one of several kits now available on the market. You have a couple of options here. You can build one of these headphone amp kits (especially the small PAiA or Ramsey kits described below) right into the piece of equipment, drilling holes in the front panel of the equipment for the headphone volume pot and the headphone jack. Or you can make a small headphone amplifier box using a metal project box and then add RCA phono jacks to it. This may be more flexible, as it allows you to plug in any line level output and listen to it with headphones. This is a great tool for troubleshooting your system (plug it in to any output at the patch panel to see if a signal is present) or for practicing without disturbing others (plug your guitar effects box output into it and wail away).

If you are going to add a headphone jack inside of an audio power amplifier, you need to find out where to pick off a line level audio signal to feed to the headphone amplifier. For a straight audio power amplifier that has no volume controls, the best place might be at the input jacks for the power amp. For a device that has a volume control on it, the best place might be right at the volume control. For example, the volume control on a guitar amp is the point that separates the preamp section from the amp section. A preamp (or line) level signal appears across the top and bottom of the volume pot. The wiper of the pot them establishes the level of the signal to send on to the next section (which is the power amplifier section that drives the speaker). So, if you are going to add the headphone jack to your guitar amp, pick off the signal from the top side of the volume control pot, and pick off the ground from the bottom side of the volume control pot.

PAiA has a stereo headphone buffer/driver amplifier kit available for about $25. It comes with a small, simple circuit board, the required components, mono volume control and ¼" headphone jack. (See Figure 25.) You will need to tap off the internal bipolar supply in the equipment to which you add the amplifier. The circuit requires +/-5 VDC to +/-18 VDC to operate correctly. If you want to control a stereo source, you will need to add a dual-ganged volume pot. You can see the circuit diagram and order the kit at the PAiA web site (http://www.paia.com/headbuff.htm).

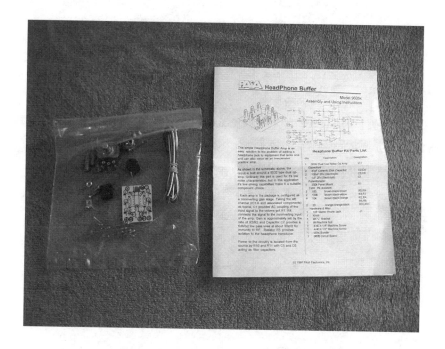

Figure 25: Low-cost Headphone Amp Kit

Ramsey Electronics has a small, inexpensive head-phone amp kit called the SHA1. The basic kit price is $20, but add $15 for a matching case and knob set. This unit uses a single DC supply of 9 VDC to 15 VDC. Check it out and then order it at http://www.testequipmentdepot.com/ramsey/kits/sha1.htm.

Other headphone amplifier kits in which you might be interested are:

- The Gateway Electronics KT-383 Headphone Amp Kit (http://www.gatewayelex.com/kits20.htm#kit383). Price is $20. This is the same as the Ramsey kit.

- The Gateway Electronics Guitar Headphone and Preamp Kit (http://www.gatewayelex.com/kits17.htm#K4102). Price is $35.
- The HeadBanger Headphone Amp (http://www.minidisc.org/headbanger.html)
- The World Audio Design HD83 Headphone Amp (http://www.worldaudiodesign.co.uk/products/hd83destext.html)
- The AVA Versa-Kit Headphone Amp (http://www.avahifi.com/versa2.htm). Price is $250.

If you are looking for a great web site that discusses everything having to do with headphones, then check out the HeadWize site at http://www.headwize.com. Another excellent site devoted to headphones is Head Fidelity at http://www.head-fi.org.

MASTER FADERS

At one point in time, I put together a custom mixer for my home studio using some Teac Model 10 mixer modules. See Figure 26.

Figure 26: Home Studio with Custom Mixer

You can see the mixer I built on the far left of this picture, which was taken about 15 years ago. A warehouse in Los Angeles was selling new, in-the-box mixer modules for $30 each, marked down from list prices of $150 to $525 for each module. For about $200, I put together a 16 x 4 stereo mixer with a cue mix, an effects loop, and 24 monitor channels. This mixer served me well for many years.

One of the shortcomings of this mixer was that it didn't have a pair of linear slide pots to serve as the master output faders. During the final mixdown from multitrack to stereo master, I was forced to use separate rotary input level pots on my stereo master open reel deck to handle the fade out at the end of a song. If you've ever tried to twirl two rotary volume pots to have the audio fade at exactly the same rate in each channel, then you know what a pain this is. Another problem I had was lack of volume control on the send to the power amplifier that drove the monitors in my studio. If your studio also suffers these kinds of shortcomings, or if you just need a set of linear pots that you can insert anywhere in a low-level audio chain, read on.

My solution to this problem was to build a remote box to house two master faders. Ideally, the requirement is to have two long-throw, *audio* taper, linear slide potentiometers situated near each other, so that stereo fadeouts can be accomplished easily with one hand.

The first hurdle is to find some pots that fit those requirements. Apparently, linear slide pots are not a popular item, because few distributors that I know sell them. I ordered some from Mouser Inc. (http://www.mouser.com). To order a catalog, contact them at (800) 346-6873 or fax (817) 804-3899. Be careful to purchase only audio taper potentiometers, not linear taper. Don't be confused here; the slide action of these potentiometers is along a linear track, but the rate of change of the resistance along that track varies logarithmically, as does the perception of loudness by human ears. If you use linear taper pots in this application, you'll find that most of the sensitivity of the pot (as perceived by your ears) occurs over a relatively small range of the pot's excursion, thereby making it unsuitable for use in volume control circuits. Mouser part number 312-619A-10K would be a good choice.

The schematic for this circuit is quite simple. The input signal cable attaches its center/hot conductor to the top of the pot and its ground/shield conductor to the bottom of the pot. The output signal cable attaches its center/hot conductor to the wiper of the pot and its ground/shield conductor to the bottom of the pot. Basically, the master fader allows the audio signal to pass through unaffected when the slider is at the top of its travel (zero resistance) and begins diminishing the amplitude of the signal as the slider is moved to the bottom of its travel (maximum resistance). Also, note that there are no active electronics associated with these pots, therefore impedance matching is not preserved, and there is no gain.

The longer the throw (travel) of the fader, the easier it is to have a smooth fade out. The pots I bought have a 2-inch throw. If you can find a pot with a longer throw, by all means use it. A 3-inch throw is a good length for a mixer fader pot, but they are tough to find. The impedance value of the pot can be any value between 10 kΩ and 100 kΩ, with 10 kΩ being a good target value. I used RCA jacks for the input and output connectors. Radio Shack is a handy source for these connectors, but you can get them at any electronics parts supplier. Radio Shack part number 274-322 contains 4 RCA connectors on one bakelite panel for under $2, or you can use individual RCA jacks as I did. Mounting the individual RCA jacks is easy with a drill.

In order to keep hum and noise to a minimum, proper shielding and proper grounding procedures should be followed. Use a metal case for the project, if you can. The case should be grounded, so that it acts as a shield against magnetic fields radiating from other equipment that can induce hum into your circuit. You may find that the case you have is anodized; this anodizing treatment prevents the metal of the case from conducting electricity. You will need to scrape off the anodizing and use a star washer, if you want to make good metal-to-metal contact with the case. Use a "star" ground approach for all ground connections. That is, there should be a central point to which all ground wires connect within the box. You can bus the 4 ground connections together on the RCA phono jacks. This, then, is the center of the ground star. For the cabling from the pots to the RCA jacks, use sections of shielded cable. I just cannibalized an RCA patch cable and cut it into short sections for this application. Solder the shield of each cable section that runs between the RCA connectors and the slide pots at the ground star end, but not at the potentiometer end; just solder the center conductor of the cable to the pot. Refer to Figure 27 for the locations of the potentiometer connection terminals. Note that if you use a metal case, it's not absolutely mandatory to use shielded cable for inside connections, though I still recommend it. If you use a wooden or plastic case, you should definitely use shielded cable, however. The partially assembled slider pots with shielded cables are shown in Figure 30.

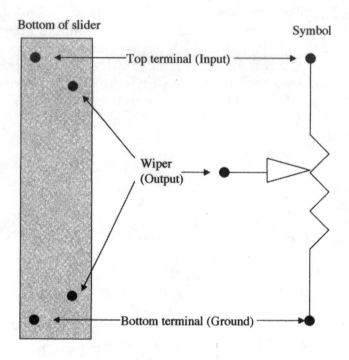

Typical Slide Pot
Terminal Locations

Figure 27

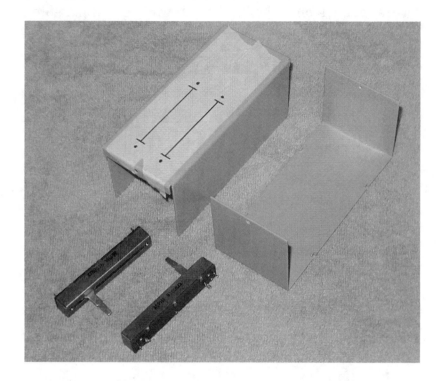

Figure 28: Components Before Assembly

Probably the most difficult part of this project is slotting the case for the wiper handle to slide back and forth. Unfortunately, there doesn't seem to be any easy way to do this, unless you happen to own a sheet metal shop. The method I have generally used involves using a jigsaw to cut a thin slot in the case. I mark off the limits of travel of the wiper handle on the top panel of the case. To do this, use masking tape, as it will also serve to protect the finish on the case. See Figure 28 above. At the top limit of travel of the slider, I drilled a series of small holes that allow the jigsaw blade to be inserted into the panel to cut the slot. Then, I drilled a set of holes for the mounting of the pot. See Figure 29. When you are cutting the slot with the jigsaw, be careful not to run the jigsaw past the two points that mark the maximum wiper travel limits, or you'll run the slot into the mounting holes for the pot, which will cause much wailing and gnashing of teeth. I used a nibbling tool (refer back to Figure 19) to clean up the slot for the wiper travel. The prototype master faders that I built are shown in Figure 31 and Figure 32.

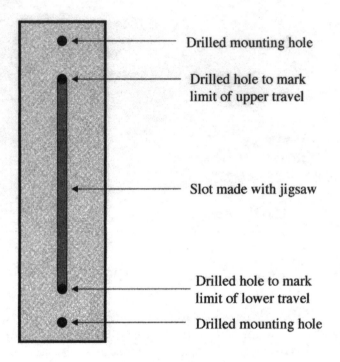

Drilled mounting hole

Drilled hole to mark limit of upper travel

Slot made with jigsaw

Drilled hole to mark limit of lower travel

Drilled mounting hole

Diagram of Slider Hole Patterns

Figure 29

Now that you've got the master faders built, where do they go? Insert them in the signal chain between the master output of the mixer and the input to the mixdown (master) tape machine as shown in Figure 33.

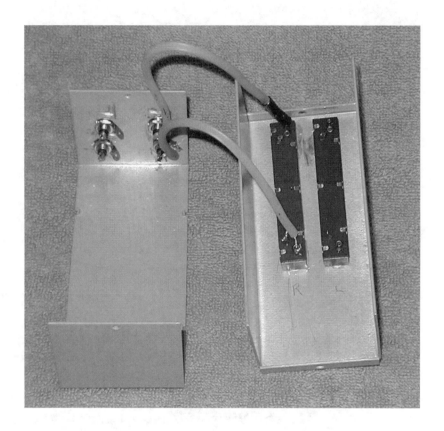

Figure 30: Partially Assembled Faders

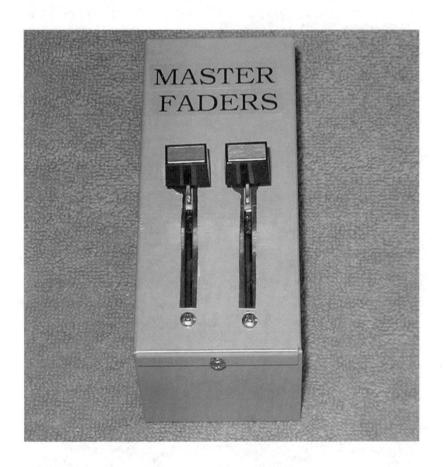

Figure 31: Top View of Master Faders

Remember that these faders can only reduce the signal level; they can't increase it. Typically, the input circuitry of your mastering tape machine will not mind that its inputs are grounded when the master faders are all the way down. If it does react strangely, add a small series resistor in-line with the output signal of each fader; 10Ω should be sufficient. (Usually there is some resistance inline when the faders are all the way down anyway.)

Figure 32: End View of Master Faders

Also, remember to never short the output of a preamp or amplifier circuit directly to ground. (The output transistors of many amplifying circuits are protected from sizzling as a result of the large currents which flow during a direct short to ground, but you may be unhappy to discover that your amp, preamp or mixer is not properly protected to sustain a direct short of this nature.) You can also use the master faders between a CD player (that has no volume control on the preamp output) and a straight power amp.

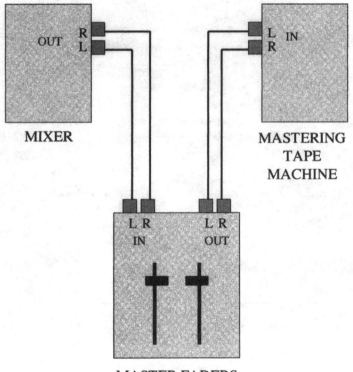

MASTER FADERS

System Interconnection of Master Faders

Figure 33

Another application for the master faders is to use them to regulate the output level of a SMPTE or FSK code generator device that you are using to stripe a synchronization track on a multi-track tape deck. I always try to record the SMPTE track with the lowest (yet still reliably solid) level I possibly can to prevent it from bleeding into the adjacent audio track on an analog multi-track tape deck during subsequent recording or playback. However, don't record it so low that the synchronization becomes unreliable upon playback. I use one channel of the master fader to regulate the record level during a "practice run" while I monitor the output with another SMPTE time code reader. When the signal gets too low, the SMPTE reader will lose lock and drop the sync; I boost the level sufficiently beyond that point, and then go back and stripe the tape for real. This approach has worked every time for me! By the way, always stripe the synchronization time code onto an edge track of the tape (e.g., track 8 of an 8-track machine), as this will minimize the amount of cross talk into adjacent channels (signals bleeding from one track into another track).

SIMPLE PASSIVE AUDIO MIXER FOR $5:

Mixers are used to combine audio signals from two or more separate sources. The reason you can't just tie signals together without buffer or mixer circuits (using a Y-cable, for example) is that the output circuits of each piece of equipment will end up fighting each other, and eventually one or more of them will be ruined. You can use a Y-cable to direct a single output to two or more inputs of other equipment, however.

There is a simple way to make an inexpensive passive mixer that will allow you to combine two separate signals into one mono signal. Passive means that there are no active electronics (transistors, op amps, or ICs requiring DC or AC voltage to operate) in the device. This design uses 3 resistors to combine the two signals and to present a high impedance to the next stage, so that the next stage is not loaded down. A schematic representation of this circuit appears in Figure 34.

The simplest way to build this device is to buy a couple of cables from Radio Shack or some other audio equipment vendor and then cannibalize the cables. You may already have the cables in your collection. At Radio Shack, buy one short cable that has two RCA phono jacks on it and two RCA phono plugs (P/N 42-2353; $3.99). Actually, any RCA cables will work for this project, if you have the right adapters to connect the passive mixer to the equipment. You will also need to buy two 470 Ω, 1/4W, 5% tolerance, carbon film resistors (Radio Shack P/N 271-1317), and one 10 kΩ, 1/4W, 5% tolerance, carbon film resistor (Radio Shack P/N 271-1335). The resistors are sold in packs of five at Radio Shack for about $0.50 per pack. The 470 Ω resistor value is not that critical, but try to stick around the 470 Ω value.

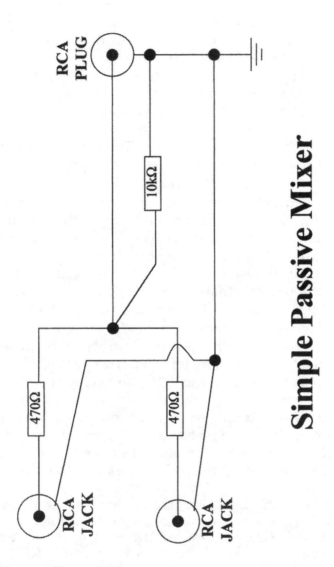

Figure 34: Simple Passive Mixer

Take the cable with the RCA plugs and jacks and cut each of the connectors off 6" from the connector. Strip back the insulation on both cables that go to the RCA jacks and on one of the RCA plugs. Take one end of 470Ω resistor and solder it to the center conductor on one of the stripped RCA jack cables. Keep the length of the resistor lead short. Do the same thing again with the other stripped RCA jack cable (solder a 470Ω resistor to the center conductor). Cut two 2" lengths of heat shrink and slide them over and past each of the resistors on the two cables; you will use these later. Cut two more short pieces of heat shrink tubing (enough to cover the resistor body and bare center conductor wire), and slide these over the resistors as far as they will go. Now, twist the open ends of the 470Ω resistors together. Trim excess length. Next, take the stripped RCA phono plug cable and solder the 10kΩ resistor to the outside shield conductor of the RCA phono plug cable. Again, keep the length of the resistor lead short. Cut a 2" length of heat shrink and slide it over and past each the resistors on the RCA phono plug cable; you will use this later. Take the center conductor of the RCA phono plug cable and the open end of the 10kΩ resistor and solder both of these to the twisted-together ends of the two 470Ω resistors. Finally, you will need to solder both outside shield conductors on the two RCA phono jacks to the outside shield on the RCA phono plug. Cover internal connections with small pieces of electrical tape. Slide the heat shrink tubing on the jack pieces down to the Y and shrink them into place. Slide the remaining piece of heat shrink tubing on the plug piece down and over the other heat shrink tubing, and shrink it into place. You are done!

You have just constructed a simple resistive divider circuit that can mix two line level signals together into one mono signal. Granted, it is not the most aesthetic piece of equipment in the world, but it is functional, highly portable, and it cost you less than $5. If you want to make a more aesthetic version of this circuit, buy a small metal experimenter's project box, panel mount jacks, the same 3 resistors, and build the circuit inside of the metal box.

References:
Howell, Steve, "Splitting a Lead", *Keyboard*, May 1988, p120.

LINE OUTPUT CONVERTER

What if you want to use the output of some speaker-level audio unit (car stereo, boom box, Speak-n-Spell, etc.) as an input audio source to your studio? You can't just connect a speaker-level output into the line-level input of your mixer or recorder, as it will cause severe distortion to the audio and potential damage to the destination equipment (mixer or recorder). You could record the speaker's output with a microphone, but if you want to record the signal directly, you will need some sort of converter to convert the speaker-level signal to a line-level signal (approximately 150 mV to 750 mV). Radio Shack sells their P/N 12-1338 converter for about $20. You can also buy the Pyramid Adjustable Line Output Converter, which is a similar unit, from MCM Electronics (1-800-543-4330). Order MCM P/N 60-480 for $9.59. Parts Express offers two products to convert from speaker level to line level. The non-adjustable P/N 265-025 ($4.20) can convert stereo speaker signals less than 15 watts per channel, while the adjustable P/N 265-023 ($12.90) is rated for speaker levels up to 50 watts per channel.

FINDING SCHEMATICS FOR EQUIPMENT:

Finding a schematic for the equipment you own can be a challenge, especially if the original manufacturer has been out of business for some time. If you are going to tear open your equipment and work on it or modify it in some way, it really helps to have a roadmap of the design in front of you. Without a schematic, you will generally be forced to trace out the circuit yourself on a piece of paper, so you can see what you have and what you need to change or replace.

Just because you have a schematic for a piece of equipment does *not* mean that the circuitry inside the equipment will match that schematic. I have an old ARP Odyssey synthesizer that had the white noise circuit stop working. I have a schematic for the synthesizer, so I opened up the synthesizer to troubleshoot the problem. While most of the synthesizer circuitry did match the schematic, it turns out that the white noise circuit was completely different than what was shown in the schematic. I had to recreate the schematic manually for the white noise circuit by inspection. Only then could I troubleshoot the problem and find suitable replacement parts. You will find that some companies are less than perfect in their document control procedures, so the actual hardware may not match what is written in the documentation. Don't automatically assume that just because it is written on the schematic that it is 100% correct!

The following are sources of schematics that you can access to find documentation on your equipment. If all else fails, try a search on the Google search engine for that specific schematic (e.g., Dokorder 8140 schematic or Tascam 3340 schematic).

- http://www.samswebsite.com/photofact/efact.html
- http://www.compufind.com/schem.html
- http://nanaimo.ark.com/~pat/
- http://www.waltzingbear.com/~audio/Schematics/Schematics.html
- http://www.one-electron.com/FC_ProAudio.html
- http://w3.one.net/~robgrow/circuits/circuits2.html
- http://www.mcp-logics.com/schemlinks.htm
- http://www.sls.lib.il.us/reference/por/features/99/sams.html

LIST OF NEW & SURPLUS ELECTRONICS PARTS SUPPLIERS

The following are various suppliers I have used for my home studio projects and for prototypes in my engineering career. They have all been good suppliers for me.

All Electronics Corporation
905 S. Vermont Ave.
Los Angeles, 90006
213-380-8000
http://www.allcorp.com

Digi-Key Corporation
701 Brooks Ave. South
Thief River Falls, MN 56701-0677
800-344-4539
Fax: 218-681-3380
http://www.digikey.com

Electronics Express
365 Blair Road
Avenel, NJ 07001
800-972-2225
In NJ: 908-381-8020
Fax: 908-381-1572

Gateway Electronics
9222 Chesapeake Dr
San Diego, California 92123
858-279-6802
FAX (858) 279-7294
http://www.gatewayelex.com

MCM Electronics
650 Congress Park Drive
Centerville, OH 45459-4072
800-543-4330
Fax: 937-434-6959
http://www.mcmelectronics.com

M. P. Jones & Associates, Inc.
P.O. Box 12685
Lake Park, FL 33403-0685
800-652-6733
Fax: 1-800-432-9937

Parts Express
340 E. First Street
Dayton, OH 45402-1257
800-338-0531
Fax: 937-222-4644
http://www.parts-express.com

Tech America
P.O. Box 1981
Fort Worth, TX 76101-1981
800-877-0072
Fax: 1-800-813-0087
http://www.techam.com

PART FOUR: CAPTURING SOUND RECORDINGS

THE NATURE OF SOUND

The Physics of Sound:

This section of the book deals with the fundamental nature of sound. If you are going to record sound, it helps to understand a little bit about its nature. Understanding the nature of sound necessarily means understanding the physics of sound. Sorry, but there is no easy way around it.

All sounds in nature are either periodic or aperiodic. Periodic sounds are generally created from some sort of vibration, examples of which are a vibrating column of air in a pipe organ or the vibrating strings of a guitar or piano. This vibration sets up pressure fluctuations that are greater than and less than the ambient atmospheric pressure. These sounds repeat the same basic signal waveform over a discernible period of time, hence the term periodic. The pressure fluctuations in these periodic sounds have certain amplitudes, and these sound waves can propagate from one point to another over time. These cyclical fluctuations in the pressure created by a sound are called compression (greater than ambient pressure) and rarefaction (less than ambient pressure).

Most periodic sounds in nature are complex sounds made up of a fundamental frequency (usually the lowest frequency of the vibrating material or medium) and a series of harmonic frequencies. The harmonic frequencies are mathematically related to the fundamental frequency. For example, the second harmonic is ½ the period (2 times the frequency) of the fundamental, the third harmonic is $1/3$ the period (3 times the frequency) of the fundamental, and so on. The number of periodic cycles of sound in one second defines the frequency of the sound. Each cycle per second is called 1 Hertz, and is abbreviated 1 Hz. So, a signal that cycles or vibrates 200 times per seconds is said to have a frequency of 200 Hz. A signal that vibrates

1000 times per second has a frequency of 1000 Hz, which is also called 1 kiloHertz, or just 1 kHz.

Aperiodic sounds have no fundamental or single discernible frequency associated with them. Noise is an aperiodic sound. Noise is classically defined as a type of sound that is composed of an infinite number of audio signals over a continuous band of frequencies. In other words, noise is composed of every frequency. Since all of these different frequencies add together, there is no dominant single fundamental frequency, and no discernible period can be assigned to the waveform. Hence, the name aperiodic is given.

Sounds produced by musical instruments have a defining quality called timbre (pronounced tam-ber) that allows one to detect the difference between a trumpet playing Middle C and a flute playing Middle C, for example. The difference is the harmonic content contained within the sound of each different musical instrument. This harmonic content shows up as the relative intensity of many different overtones (mathematically-related frequencies) within the sound, giving each sound a different waveform. When all of the many overtones add together in certain combinations, you get the sound of a trumpet, and when they add together in other combinations, you may get a flute, a violin, a trombone, or maybe a tuba— all of this even though the fundamental note frequency is the same. In addition, the timbre of a note can change over the duration of the note. For example, when a piano note is struck, you will initially hear the hammer strike the piano string, and then you will hear the initial timbre of the piano note as it rings. As the note decays, you may hear certain overtones ring louder and longer than other ones. As an example, listen to "the note that never ends" at the end of The Beatles' song "A Day in the Life." As the piano note dies out (actually, it is several pianos all struck at the same time), you can hear tons of overtones ringing out even within the same piano sound.

Many synthesizers are built on the principle of adding or subtracting various overtones to create new, unique sounds. Synthesizers that start with a harmonically rich waveform and then subtract out the overtones that are not wanted are called subtractive synthesizers. Synthesizers that start out with a waveform that has very little harmonic content and then add other waveforms to it to create the desired sound are called additive synthesizers. Of those two types, the subtractive synthesizers dominate the market, at least for analog synthesizers.

Sounds can travel through any medium, such as steel, plastic, water and air. The sound pressure fluctuations that comprise audible sound travel through the air at about 1130 feet per second. As a quick and easy number for estimating purposes, I usually use 1000 f/s (feet per second) or 300 M/s (meters/second). Therefore, it will take sound about 5 seconds to travel one mile (5280 feet) through air. You can use this information to determine how far away a storm's lightning strike was from you; each second of time lapsed between the lightning flash and the thunder represents about 1/5 of a mile. At the other end of the rule-of-thumb spectrum, it will take sound 1 mS (or 1/1000 of a second) to travel 1 foot.

Human hearing consists of many physical elements that work together as a system. The human outer ear is shaped to collect and transmit sound to the middle ear. The middle ear takes these sounds and, via an eardrum and some tiny bones, transforms them into a compression wave in the inner ear fluid. These inner ear fluid compression waves are then turned into electrical impulses that are sent to the brain. The brain is then able to discern the frequency, amplitude and direction of the sound. Humans can hear sounds with frequencies from about 20 Hz to 20,000 Hz (20 kHz). As we get older, the top end of our hearing becomes less sensitive, and we are generally not able to hear the highest frequencies any more. Of course, this condition can be brought on more rapidly due to prolonged exposure to loud noises or from certain bacterial or viral infections that affect the inner ear.

The human ear is an amazingly sensitive device, especially in the way in which it responds to sound intensity. The perceived intensity of a sound is based upon the amount of sound energy that propagates past the ear in a certain amount of time. The ear will hear vibrating sound waves as louder when they have larger vibrations, which excite the molecules of air near the ear in a more vigorous fashion. The quietest sounds that the human ear can detect occur at the limit known as the threshold of hearing (e.g., the rustling of leaves), and the loudest sounds are over a billion times louder, at a point known as the threshold of pain (e.g., a jet aircraft engine). The ability of the ear to detect sounds over this range is so great that we use a logarithmic scale to define the ear's range of sensitivity. This makes the numbers easier to work with, especially when comparing the intensity or sound pressure level of two sounds.

The decibel (dB) scale was developed to compare sounds on a logarithmic scale using a power ratio between them. If you aren't used to working with logarithms and power ratios, then the dB scale can be confusing. Here are a couple easy data points to remember. If Sound A is 2 watts and Sound B is 1 watt, then Sound A has 3 dB more acoustic energy than Sound B. (Determined by 10 times the Log (2/1).) So, any 2:1 ratio of power results in a 3 dB logarithmic ratio. This also means that a 500 watt sound is only 3 dB louder than a 250 watt sound. Other data points to remember are that a 4:1 power ratio is a 6 dB difference, and a 10:1 power ratio is a 10 dB difference.

How does this equate to our perception of a sound's loudness? Even though a 3 dB increase in a sound's acoustic energy results in a doubling of that energy, it doesn't really sound twice as loud to our ears. For a sound to be subjectively perceived as twice as loud to our ears, the acoustic energy of the sound must increase by about 6dB to 10dB. This is an important rule of thumb.

Here is a short table that gives some relative values of sound intensity as perceived by the human ear.

Sound Pressure Level (dB)	Typical Sound Source
130	Threshold of Pain
110-120	Rock Concert
100	Large Orchestra
70	Busy Street Traffic
50	Car Interior- Road Noise
25	Quiet Homes
0	Threshold of Hearing

Of course, the perceived sound intensity is largely a function of your distance from the sound source. The reason for this is because as the sound waves propagate out from the source, their energy is dissipated into heat as they excite the air molecules into compression and rarefaction. Therefore, over a distance from the sound source, the sound intensity decreases. This is called the Inverse Square Law.

The Inverse Square Law states that when the distance from a sound source is doubled, the amount of sound intensity (or sound energy per unit area) reaching that point is divided by 4. It may sound like a ho-hum concept, but this is an important concept in acoustics. Each time we double our distance from the source of a sound, the sound intensity where we are standing drops 6 dB. From the information given above, this 6 dB loss equates to just ¼ of the original power. And the opposite is true also; each time we half the distance to a sound source, it becomes 6 dB louder. This is a good fact to remember for audio recording and microphone placement.

Power levels for sound do not sum linearly. That is, a sound source of say 90 dB when added to another sound source of 90 dB does not produce a total sound intensity of 180 dB. The greatest increase in sound intensity for two sounds added together is when they are both equal in intensity, and that yields an increase of 3 dB for both sounds. So, a 90 dB sound added to a 90 dB sound gives an overall sound intensity of just 93 dB. A 90 dB sound added to a 96 dB sound will only give an increase of 1 dB. So, a 90 dB sound added to a 96 dB sound will give 97 dB. As you can see, if the difference in two sound levels starts to become greater than about 10 dB, the sound with the smaller value of intensity will start to become masked by the louder sound. This is another important point to remember during audio recording, and especially during audio mixing. It is also the reason why you can only hear about 35% to 45% of the instruments in a large orchestra when they are all playing at the same time. Also, single-ended noise reduction systems depend on this fact!

The Inverse Square Law holds true when we are a sufficiently large distance from the sound source. But as we get nearer and nearer to the sound source, the Inverse Square Law starts to not hold true. A halving of the distance to the sound source results in less than a 6 dB increase in the sound intensity. At the point where the Inverse Square Law does not hold true, we enter a region called the close field. This close-field distance from the sound source is on the order of the actual size of the sound source itself. In this book, I advocate the technique of listening to studio monitors in their close field, as the effects of the studio room will be small in comparison to the intensity of the sound from the monitors. Another example of the close field phenomenon is the rise in bass levels when using a close miking technique.

The reverberant field of a sound indoors (in your studio, for instance) is what we observe as the sound decays away. We first hear the initial direct sound from the source. As the sound bounces or echoes off of the first few walls in the room, we hear the early reflections or the early sound field. Then, as the sound continues to bounce around in the room, the echoes turn into a continuous decay of sound; this is called reverberation (reverb for short). The amount of time it takes a sound intensity to decay by 60 dB is called the reverb time. On many signal processors and effects boxes, you will see the reverb time parameter. This is a measure of the time it takes for the sound to decay by 60 dB within the signal processing algorithm of that effects box.

In a small room, such as a bedroom where your studio might be located, the sound that reverberates back and forth off the walls, ceiling and floor will set up what are known as normal modes. The normal modes are dictated by the dimensions of the room, and they are the preferred frequencies at which sounds within the room will resonate. This subject is covered more completely in the "Acoustics in Your Studio" section of this book.

Psychoacoustics:

Psychoacoustics is the study of how we subjectively judge sound in relation to the intensity, frequency, timbre (the quality of the tone), noise and directional cues that we hear. Human hearing is not a linear system, but rather it is non-linear. The judgment of the listener (including the emotional and physical state of the listener) will subjectively alter how he or she perceives the sound, and that makes the system non-linear.

Two researchers named Fletcher and Munson developed a way to compare sound intensities at different frequencies called the Equal Loudness Contours. The important thing to know about these contours (basically, curves on a graph) is that the human ear is much more sensitive to midrange sounds than it is to very low frequency or very high frequency sounds. For example, for a 30 Hz tone to be perceived as having the same loudness as a 40 dB, 1000 Hz tone, the 30 Hz tone would have to have a loudness of about 80 dB, according to their curves. For a 10 kHz tone to be perceived as having the same loudness as a 40 dB, 1000Hz tone, it would have to have a loudness of about 50 dB. It is because of this fact that home stereo receivers have a loudness boost button on them for listening to music at lower volumes. The loudness boost button increases the volume of the low frequencies to compensate for the ear's lack of sensitivity to those frequencies at low volumes.

The other item of note that the Fletcher-Munson curves show us is that the ear's hearing becomes more linear as the signal volume increases. For example, for a 30 Hz tone to be perceived as having the same loudness as an 110 dB, 1000 Hz tone, the 30 Hz tone would have to have a loudness of about 120 dB, according to their curves. This is not much of a relative difference as compared to the example above. The reason for the change is the ear's better sensitivity to low frequency sounds at higher volume levels.

The human ear can discern most of the qualities of a sound (intensity, pitch, timbre) just by using one ear; however, it takes two ears to establish the direction of a sound source (called localization). The reason that it requires two ears for localization is that the human brain can detect even minute delays in the time it takes for a sound to reach one ear in relation to the other. These delays show up as phase changes in the signal. The ear can also determine minute differences in signal intensity. For example, a sound off to the left of the listener will reach the left ear first and then the right ear. It may also be marginally louder in the left ear than in the right ear. The brain will detect these differences and know that the sound is off to the left of the listener.

All stereo audio systems make use of these localization cues. A pair of stereo speakers can be set up in front of a person for listening tests. If a signal is fed to only the right speaker, the brain will detect the time and intensity differences, and it will determine that the sound is to the right side of the speaker array. If the exact same signal is sent to both speakers, then the same signal intensity and phase reach both ears, and a phantom sound image appears directly in front of the listener. This concept of a phantom sound image is powerful, as it is the basis of establishing a sound stage of various instruments during a mixdown session.

The phantom sound image can be steered left or right in one of two ways. If the same signal is sent to both speakers, but the volume of the signal sent to the left speaker is decreased somewhat, the perception of the phantom sound image will move from directly in front of the listener towards the right side. This is the basis of the panpot system on your mixer. The other way to shift the phantom image is to introduce a time delay to the signal going to one of the speakers. For example, if the same signal is sent to both speakers, but a time delay of 5mS is introduced to the signal going to the left speaker, then the perception of the phantom sound image will again move from directly in front of the listener towards the right side. This is called the precedence effect or the Haas effect.

The Haas effect can be overcome (i.e., the phantom sound image can be moved back to directly in front of the listener) if the amplitude of the signal going to the non-delayed speaker is decreased. This fools the brain, because the signal in one ear has less intensity (meaning it is farther away from the other ear), but the signal in the other ear is delayed (meaning it, too, is farther away from the other ear). These two effects cancel out, and the phantom sound image again appears directly in front of us.

I like to use this psychoacoustic fact during mixdown. To really fatten up a sound (e.g., a lead vocal track) and make it sound like two different vocal tracks (or at least a very broad single image), I will take the original dry vocal track and pan it left in the mix. Then I will pick off part of that signal and send it through a delay line set to about 20 mS of delay. I will pan this delayed signal to the right. I will decrease the volume slightly on the original dry vocal track in relation to the delayed track. This makes both tracks sound about the same in volume, but they sound like two different tracks due to the phase differences in the two signals that reach the ears. Try that trick in your next mix. Note that this effect breaks down with delays of greater than 60 mS; the ear perceives these increased delays as discrete echoes of the first sound.

The last area of psychoacoustics I am going to discuss is spectral masking. Spectral masking is the phenomenon of a sound that is at a certain frequency (or band of frequencies) masking (making it difficult to hear) a sound or group of sounds at another nearby frequency. As the masking sound increases in volume level, the wider the band of nearby frequencies it is capable of masking.

References:
Eargle, John, *Sound Recording*, Van Nostrand Reinhold Company, 1976.
Mapp, Peter, "Mind Games", *Sound & Video Contractor*, September 1998, pp 80-82.

Measuring Sound Intensity:
We can't see sound, so how do we measure it in the studio? There are usually two types of meters on studio equipment to help us electrically measure sound levels: one type that reads the average signal level and the other type that reads the peak signal level. The averaging meter type reads the average level of the signal at any instant, and it does not give a true reading of the actual signal peaks (especially quick, loud, transient sounds). The peak meter reads the instantaneous peak level at any instant in time. Your mixer may be equipped with either type of meter, or it may have a meter that can be switched between average and peak reading. Some mixers have averaging meters with peak LEDs that light up when the signal attains a particular high level.

Many of the average-reading meters are of the VU type. VU stands for volume units. These are the type of meters that have a physical needle that moves over an arc, with numbers on the arc representing the volume level. You will find the reading 0 VU right at the point where the meter background changes from white (or black) to red (hence the term 'going into the red'). This is designated as the highest signal level you can have without incurring some sort of distortion in the signal. At this point, the meter is referenced to a standard power level of 1 milliwatt (which corresponds to a 0.775 volt voltage level into a 600Ω standard impedance) for professional equipment. And at this point on professional equipment, 0 VU equals +4 dBm.

For semi-pro and consumer level equipment, the signal to be measured is referenced to 1 volt, so the 0 VU at 0.775 V equals -10 dBV (note the capital V). Unfortunately, this caused too much confusion with the different reference levels (I wonder why?), so engineers devised an additional measurement standard, the dBv (note the small v). With the dBv standard for semi-pro and consumer level equipment, the 0 VU point is referenced to 0.775 Volts (independent of impedance), so 0 VU equals 0dBv (small v). At 600Ω, dBv and dBm are the same. There is also another reference floating around out there called the dBu, and this is the exact same thing as the dBv. Don't you love it? Could it possibly be any more confusing? Just remember that professional gear is referenced to the dBm scale (where 0dB is 0.775V into 600Ω) and semi-professional gear is referenced to the dBV scale (where 0dB = 1Volt and −10dB = 0.775V).

On an average-reading VU meter, it is important to understand that the actual peaks of the signal may be well into the red zone, while the needle is just barely registering at 0 dB. On an analog recorder, this might not be so much of a problem, since the onset of distortion happens gradually. However, on a digital recorder, this could be a big problem due to the way audio signals are digitized and recorded. There is no gradual onset of distortion on a digital recorder; all of a sudden it is there in full force, and it is ugly!

Another tool that is commonly used to measure a sound's intensity in the studio is the sound level meter. The sound level meter has a calibrated microphone built into it that picks up the audio through the air and converts it to electrical signals. The sound level meter takes into account the hearing response of the human ear as it calculates the relative intensity of the sound. The sound level meter then displays the sound intensity in dB on a VU-type of meter or via an LCD or LED display. Most sound level meters allow you to choose the type of weighting to give the measured sound. A-weighting is the most often used, and you sometimes see A-weighting quoted in high-end audiophile equipment specifications. The A-weighting most closely resembles the ear's frequency response at lower volume levels. The B-weighting factor most closely resembles the ear's frequency response at mid volume levels, and the C-weighting factor most closely resembles the ear's frequency response at high volume levels (where the ear is more sensitive to low frequency sounds).

References:
Lanser, Bryan & Milano, Dominic, "Tech Talk", *Keyboard*, June 1986, pp 46-48.

MIKING/TRACKING INSTRUMENTS & VOCALS

Tracking in General:

The first and most important step to achieving an excellent recorded song is to capture each of the individual performances that are the elements of the song. This is called tracking, as you are capturing each performance to a track on the recorder. The ability to set up a recording chain properly, including the miking of individual instruments, is truly an art that is learned over time. It is just like any other complex learned task. You will make mistakes and eventually learn what does and does not work well. The key is to learn from your mistakes.

There are some good habits to learn when tracking. Adopt an attitude of immediately fixing problems that you encounter during the tracking process; don't adopt the "I'll just fix it later on in the mix" attitude. Problems with timing and musical performance are especially critical during this phase, as they can't easily be fixed later on in the mix.

When laying down tracks, try to record the hottest (i.e., highest in amplitude) volume level you can on each track, without distorting the audio. The reason for this is to maximize the signal to noise ratio (SNR). The noise on the track is always going to be there as a given, especially with analog tape. As you increase the signal amplitude in relation to that fixed noise level, you are increasing the effective signal to noise ratio. On an analog recorder, it is permissible to occasionally "go into the red" on the level meter. This is because when most analog recorders distort, they do so gradually, and they produce distortion that is harmonically related to the original signal. This distortion effect can actually fatten up a sound or give a needed edge to a sound (for instance on a kick drum or snare) that otherwise might be missing.

Digital recorders are an entirely different story. When they distort due to signal overload, the resulting distortion is not harmonically related to the original audio signal, and the distortion is not at all pleasing to the ear. On a digital recorder, 0dB is usually the maximum signal that can be recorded without distortion. Check the owner's manual to see what recording levels the manufacturer recommends for your particular recorder. It is not a bad idea to RTFM (Read The Friggin' Manual). It is also not a bad idea to have the musician play through the part he or she is going to play before you record it. While they are playing the part, you should be monitoring the sound arriving at the recorder, checking your levels and making sure you are going to capture an optimum recording.

When recording the initial tracks to my digital and analog recorders one track at a time, I rarely use my mixer. If I am using a microphone to capture an instrument's sound, then I use a standalone microphone preamp to boost the level and go directly into the recorder with it. I may patch a compressor or some other effects box in series with the preamp output, if the track needs it. For devices such as drum machines and synthesizers, I go directly into the recorder with them and bypass the mixer entirely. There is no point in adding all the mixer's electronics into the signal path if it is not warranted.

Miking Vocals:

Capturing a clean, clear and powerful vocal performance is probably one of the most difficult things to do in recording. All singers are different, and each individual signer can have much variation in tone, dynamics and technique throughout his or her range.

Mic selection for vocal recording is very important. Various microphones are optimized for different tasks, and buying, renting or borrowing a microphone that is optimized for vocal recording can only help. In general, the cardioid and hypercardioid condenser microphones are sensitive enough to pickup the nuances of vocal performances, and these are the types generally used for this purpose.

There are a couple of things you can do to tilt the odds in your favor right from the beginning. First of all, use a microphone stand in the studio. This will prevent handling noise from a vocalist holding the microphone body. The best approach is to use a shock mount for the microphone, which suspends the microphone in a rubber or elastic web, and decouples the microphone from vibrations through its body. Make sure the microphone cable is out of the way of the vocalist, because physical vibrations can travel up the cable and couple into the microphone body also. I usually wrap the cable around the microphone stand to keep it out of the way. I like to have some thick carpeting under the vocalist. This will prevent reflections coming back up to the microphone from the floor, and it will deaden any foot tapping noise from the vocalist. Use a pop filter on the microphone if the vocalist is having a problem with popping the P and B sounds at the beginning of words. This will prevent the voiced plosives from ruining an otherwise acceptable recording.

Room acoustics play an important role in how your vocal recording will ultimately sound. If you are going to be recording in a bedroom of your house, then it is best to try to minimize the acoustical effects of the room and rely on the artificial reverb environment you will create later within your mixer. Of course, you might want to make use of the "live" natural acoustic environment in a bathroom or kitchen to achieve a certain effect. If the room is much too live, you might want to take steps to deaden it with baffles (homemade or purchased). Position the baffles behind the vocalist in a semi-circle. The distance of the baffle from the back of the singer will affect the amount of deadening that the baffles contribute. An inexpensive way to achieve this effect is to hang some thick drapes or carpeting behind the vocalist to absorb the reflected acoustic energy in the room. This will work for mid and higher frequencies only.

When I mount the microphone for myself to sing, I usually mount it up a little high (about nose height) and then point it down slightly. I find this helps me hit the higher notes, rather than if the microphone is down lower and my neck is compressed with my head looking down. It also helps me minimize the problems associated with plosives. This is a personal preference though. If you record in a room with a low ceiling (I don't), this technique might result in reflections from the ceiling. Those reflections can result in phase cancellations, and certain frequencies will then be affected adversely in the recording. The best place to start is to position the microphone directly in front of the vocalist at mouth height and see what results you get.

The microphone's distance from the vocalist's mouth is determined by experimentation. If the microphone is extremely close, the microphone will exhibit the proximity effect, which gives a bump in the mid bass region. This may be the effect you are looking for to warm up a vocal, or it may be the effect that is muddying up the vocal performance. It really depends on the vocalist and the microphone used. Some microphones have a bass roll-off switch that allows you to compensate for this proximity effect when close miking the vocalist (or any instrument for that matter). Remember that close miking will reduce the effects of the room acoustics, while far miking will accentuate the effect of the room acoustics. In either case, make sure you have adequate level at your microphone preamplifier when you record the vocals.

How do you assure an adequate level output from the microphone? The vocalist may be moving around and changing the distance from his or her mouth to the microphone at any instant. This is where the compressor comes in. Using a compressor for vocal recordings will help assure that a constant signal amplitude level goes to the recorder. The compressor acts like a very quick volume control that tries to adjust the gain or cut in the signal amplitude to maintain a constant volume level. Don't overcompress the signal because it is difficult to overcome this later, plus it adds more background noise to the recording. If the vocal track really needs more compression, you can add more to it later during the mix down. A good place to start with vocal compression settings is a 3:1 compression ratio and a −10 dB threshold.

My personal preference is to use as little EQ as possible on a vocal when I record it. Mostly, I use no EQ at all. If the vocal needs to stand out a little more from the rest of the instruments, I use my Aural Exciter or BBE Sonic Maximizer to give it more spectral sparkle. If you don't have those kinds of effects, then you can make the vocal stand out a little more by adding some EQ in the 2 kHz to 4 kHz range with an equalizer, but be careful not to over do it. I recommend doing this when you mix down, that way you can experiment with what is really needed for the mix when all the other instruments are present. If you commit any effect to tape (or disk), then you are permanently stuck with it.

When recording the vocal, it is best not to put reverb on the signal and commit it to tape (or disk). Once the reverb is added to the signal, it is nearly impossible to get rid of it. Of course, if you only have a 4-track cassette deck, you might want to do so because of the constraints of the system.

The vocalist is going to need to monitor his or her performance with headphones, particularly if they want to stay in sync with tracks that have already been recorded. This usually presents several problems. The first problem is the mix that the vocalist wants to hear in his or her headphones is probably going to be different than the mix that the person recording the vocal track wants to monitor. The person recording the vocal track (that's you) generally wants to monitor many or all of the tracks already recorded to see how the vocal performance is going to sit within the rough mix. The vocalist probably wants to monitor just some of the tracks to provide a guide for what he or she should be singing.

A second problem is bleed through from the vocalist's headphones into the microphone. If the bleed through is bad enough, it can lead to howling feedback in the headphones. This can be minimized by using closed-ear headphones for vocal monitoring and by moving the microphone farther away from the vocalist's headphones. If the problem can't be solved physically, then solve it electrically with a noise gate. The noise gate should close (i.e., prevent any sounds from passing through) when the vocalist stops singing, and it should open up as soon as the vocalist starts singing again. (Here is an idea I have for you if you are getting excessive bleed from the singer's headphones into the microphone. Try using the small in-the-ear type of headphones that come with portable CD and tape players (e.g., Sony MDR-A34 or similar). Since they fit right into the ear, you might be able to reduce the monitor level to the point where there is very little bleed from the headphones into the microphone. In addition, you can modify those cheap headphones to install a switch inline with one of the drivers, which will allow you to accommodate singers who only use one side of the headphones while they sing.)

The third problem that arises is the inability of the vocalist to sing in tune because of a bad headphone mix. It could be that the instruments that are defining the proper key and pitch are not being heard clearly in the headphones by the vocalist. If the vocalist's problem is an inability to keep time with the song, then the instruments that define the rhythm and timing of the song may not be able to be heard clearly in the headphones. Inability to hear one's self in the headphones can also lead to vocal strain, which can ruin a vocal performance. Make sure each vocalist has a good mix (as defined by the vocalist!) in his or her own headphones. If you simply can't capture an on-pitch vocal performance, then see the recommendation at the end of the book on the Antares ATR-1a Autotune Processor.

I mentioned using a pop filter to help minimize vocalized plosives. Another common problem with recording vocals is too much sibilance. Sibilance is the high frequency sssssssss sound that sometimes becomes too exaggerated through the microphone. A device called a de-esser can be used to reduce the sibilance effect. Before you use the de-esser, see if you have boosted the high frequency EQ too much in the 6 kHz to 8 kHz range on the mixer. It is usually better to cut the highs than to boost them and then try to remove sibilance with a de-esser.

One trick to fatten up a thin vocal line is to double-track it. When double tracking a vocal line, the vocalist sings the line once on one track of the recorder. Then the vocalist listens to the first performance in the headphones and sings the same line exactly in the same way again while recording it to a separate track on the recorder. When these two tracks are mixed together later, a blending occurs that fattens up the overall vocal due to minor timing and pitch differences between the two recordings. You can simulate this double tracking effect by running the vocal through a digital (or analog) delay device and delaying the vocal by 15 mS to 35 mS. Add this delayed vocal back to the mix while panning it to the side opposite the non-delayed vocal track for a nice wide vocal effect, or pan both vocals to the center.

References:
Ziffer, Amy, "Recording Vocals", *Home & Studio Recording*, March 1988, pp 14-16.
Bartlett, Bruce, "Microphone Recording Techniques Part IV: Lead Vocals", *Pro Audio Review*, Sept. 1997, p 52.
Swanson, Leanne, "Better Vocals", *Home & Studio Recording*, Sept. 1991, pp 57-60.

Miking Instruments:
Musical instruments excite a column of air, a string or a surface to produce sound waves that eventually impinge on our eardrums. Each different instrument has peculiar characteristics that require unique approaches to successfully capturing its sound. Here are some suggested ways to microphone individual instruments for best results. Keep in mind that these are just suggested starting places for your experimentation. The final decision on how to record the instrument needs to come from you and your ears.

Brass:
Most all brass instruments are highly directional instruments. Most all of the bright sound comes out of the bell of the instrument, and very little of the sound is distributed to the sides of the instrument. Consequently, miking the brass instrument directly in front of and close to the bell will produce a bright sound with a great deal of high frequency content. However, miking the brass instrument slightly off-axis will produce a less edgy sound. The close-miked, on-axis brass sound has sharp audio

spikes associated with it that can overload a sensitive condenser microphone. The way to combat these problems is to use a dynamic microphone, and then experiment with the sound you get by changing the miking distance and the amount of on-axis content you pick up. If possible, monitor the recording with peak-reading meters, or else reduce the recording level about 10 dB from what you would normally record.

Woodwinds:

Woodwinds are different from brass instruments in that most of the sound emanates from the finger holes in the instrument, and not from the bell. The best place to microphone these instruments is right in front of the person playing the instrument. The woodwind musician usually points the instrument at the ground (clarinet), to the side (flute), or the ceiling (bassoon). Experiment with placing the microphone (a condenser would be a good choice here) above the holes in the instrument and possibly more towards the mouthpiece. See how the character of the sound changes as you move the microphone from near the mouthpiece to over the holes at a distance of 18" to 24". Be aware of breath noise (especially on the flute), and don't get too close to the instrument.

Sax:

Sometimes a saxophone is grouped in the brass category, but it has many characteristics of the woodwind family. A sax can get fairly loud in the close field, as compared to the other woodwind instruments. If you position the mic on the sax down near the bell of the instrument, you will get more of a bright and hard sound. If you position the mic on the instrument half way along the length of the instrument and about 18" away, the sound is more mellow and natural.

Harmonica:

You can use a microphone specifically made for harmonicas, such as the Shure 520DX Green Bullet microphone. This microphone is meant to be used in the very near field of the harmonica. This will give a hard, gritty sound. For a more mellow or natural sound, try a condenser microphone about 12" to 18" away.

Piano:

The piano is also a very difficult instrument to mic due to its size and the way it disperses sound. You will find that there is no one sure-fire way to mic the piano that always works. Your best bet is to try some of the techniques listed here and see which one works out best based on the piano, the microphones, where the piano is located in the room, and the overall acoustic environment that you have.

One thing to realize is that the location of the piano within the room will affect its sound. Just like a speaker, the closer you move the piano to a wall, the more pronounced the bass response is going to be. Walls can also set up multiple reflection paths for sound emanating from the piano, which may lead to phase cancellation problems depending on where the microphones are located. Before you even start recording, a smart thing to do is to get the piano to sound good to your ears. This can be done by changing the location of the piano (especially its distance from the walls) or possibly changing what is on the walls to reflect or absorb the sound from the piano. Is the sound you are attempting to capture a mellow piano sound to blend into the song or a hard and bright piano sound to cut through the mix? Is there a problem with noise interference from other sources within the room? If you are having trouble with the pianist tapping his or her foot, put a thick rug under the piano to deaden the foot tapping noise.

For a grand piano, one approach is to use a pair of cardioid condenser microphones positioned about 2' or 3' away, so that they are looking down into the instrument along the line of the piano's lid. Have the lid open as high as possible. This will minimize the number of multiple reflections coming off of the lid, which can smear the clarity of the sound. One microphone should be positioned toward the front of the instrument, and the other microphone towards the rear. This approach is good for classical music.

If you want to close mic the instrument with a mic inside the case, remove the lid entirely to minimize reflections off of it. Stick your head into the piano case, cover your outside ear, and find the sweet spot that gives a tonal balance for all of the keys above Middle C. Position a cardioid condenser microphone here. Do the same thing to locate the sweet spot for all of the keys below Middle C. Position a second cardioid condenser microphone there. You can adjust the timbre that the microphones pick up by moving them closer or farther away from the strings and soundboard. As you move the microphones closer, you will get a harder, brighter sound with more hammer attack noise. As you move the microphones farther away, you will get a richer and mellower tone. This approach is good for classical or jazz piano.

A different approach is to position a cardioid condenser microphone in the middle about 6" above where the hammers sit. Position a second microphone down near the lower strings above the hammers. This is a good approach for rock piano that needs to cut through a mix.

To get a good stereo piano sound without any phase cancellation problems, take a pair of cardioid condenser microphones and mount them in an X-Y position over the hammers in the middle of the piano but pointing down into the strings (one pointing at the low strings and one pointing at the high strings). An X-Y configuration means that the microphone bodies are together forming an X or a cross. The angle between the two is variable, with 90° being the nominal value.

In any of these miking suggestions, work with microphone placement before you start to add any EQ on your mixer. The tone of the instrument can be changed quite a bit just by shifting the microphone position around. The dynamic range of the piano is very large. This can be reduced with application of compression to the signal. If you want a more of a honky-tonk sound without the hassle of retuning the piano, try a detuning program on a digital effects box.

One thing to remember if you are miking a piano (or any instrument or sound source) in stereo is to make sure that it still sounds OK when the image is collapsed to mono. If it doesn't, it means you are having phase cancellation problems, and some frequencies (notes) will not sound correctly. Phase cancellation will occur with two (or more) microphones when the peak of one sound wave from an instrument hits one of the microphones at the same time that the sound wave trough from that same instrument hits another microphone. Then, when the signals from the two microphones are combined at the mixer, the resultant signal amplitude at some (or all) frequencies is near zero because the two out-of-phase signals have cancelled each other at those frequencies. The best rule of thumb to combat the phase cancellation problem is to use the 3:1 rule. This rule states that if you are miking a sound source with one microphone from a certain distance, then you should not have another microphone within 3 times that distance of the sound source. For example, if I am miking a sax from a distance of 1 foot, then I should not have any other microphone within 3 feet of the sax.

Solo Violin:

For classical recordings, the objective is to capture a smooth violin sound. The best way to do this is to back off of the instrument a distance so that some of the unevenness of the sound falls away, and some of the room ambience is picked up in the microphone. Use a condenser microphone positioned about 4 feet in front of and then just above the horizontal plane of instrument's strings. Try different pickup patterns on the microphone (if so equipped) to find the right mix between direct violin sound and ambient room sound. Applying a light compression can help smooth out changing dynamics in bowing technique. For rock or country music, try a close miking approach, so that the violin is better able to cut through the mix. Move in to about 1 foot in front of the bridge of the violin and then just above it with a cardioid condenser microphone.

Solo Cello:

Try a cardioid condenser microphone about 1.5 to 2 feet from the front of the cello. Experiment with the height of the microphone anywhere from even with the bridge of the instrument to a foot above it.

Electric Bass Guitar:

There are 3 basic options to recording the bass guitar. The first option is to record the bass as a direct inject (DI) into the mixer. This is done with a direct box (described elsewhere in the book), or possibly with a bass stomp box pedal of some sort. Boss, Zoom and Ibanez make different types of bass stomp boxes that can be used for recording a bass directly into the mixer. The second option is to use the bass head (amplifier) to preamplify the bass guitar signal. Most bass heads have a preamp output signal that can be plugged directly into the mixer. The third method of recording bass guitar is to mic a bass speaker cabinet and play the bass guitar through the speaker.

For any method of recording bass, it is always best when the bass sounds as good as it can before you ever start to record it. Replacing the old strings on the bass with new strings will give a better tone than old strings filled with sweat, dirt and grime. Use a high quality guitar cord to connect the bass.

For the option of miking the bass cabinet speaker, use a dynamic microphone that can handle high sound pressure levels. If you have a Shure SM-57, an Electro-Voice RE20, a Sennheiser MD421, or an AKG D-112, then these are good places to start. Locate the microphone about 3 inches from the front of the speaker and a couple of inches off to the side of the center of the speaker cone. As you move the microphone from the center to the edge of the speaker, the tone will change. Make sure you have enough volume from the speaker to get the real bass tone of the complete bass system (guitar, amplifier, and speaker cabinet).

You will most likely need to add compression to the bass signal once it gets into the mixer. If your mixer has an insert on the channel used for the bass guitar, use the insert to effect compression on the bass guitar signal. Adjust the compressor for a crisp and punchy sound (as opposed to boomy and mushy) with a reasonably constant volume level. The compressor should be able to level out the changing volume levels that occur due to the bass player's technique or the different strings that are played. Start with a 3:1 ratio setting, a fast attack setting, and a medium decay setting, and then see how that works with the mix. As you increase the amount of compression on the bass signal, the overall effect will produce more level dynamics, but possibly also a smaller or thinner sound.

A problem that can creep into bass tracks is RF (radio frequency) noise induced into the pickups on the bass guitar. The bass pickups are actually coils of wire that can act as little RF antennas if they don't have adequate shielding. One saving grace is that even if they aren't shielded well, they are at least somewhat directional, so moving the orientation of the bass around in the studio may temporarily cure the RF buzz while you record the bass. Sometimes the RF buzz disappears when the bass player touches the strings. A temporary cure you can try is to buy an ESD (electro-static discharge) bracelet at a computer store or some other electronics store. Have the bass player wear the bracelet on the picking hand and attach the alligator clip of the ESD bracelet to the metal bridge cover of the bass guitar or some other metal connection point that may result in a grounding of the induced RF signal.

One new option that has recently come on the scene is to use a bass amp/cabinet modeling processor when recording bass guitar. This option is attractive because it allows you to have the convenience of DI recording without the thin sound usually associated with DI bass recordings. The bass amp/cabinet modeling processor has digital signal processing (DSP) algorithms in it that impart the effects of an emulated bass amp and the bass speaker cabinet onto the bass guitar signal. Most processors have several different combinations of amps and cabinets from which to choose. In this way, you can get all of the fat and ballsy bass sound from a bass guitar without having to mic a speaker cabinet and blow away your neighbors. Examples of bass amp/cabinet modeling processors are the Korg AX1B ($120), Zoom BFX708 ($139), Digitech BP-200 (~$150), Sans Amp Tech 21 Bass Driver (~$180), Line 6 Bass Pod (~$350), and Line 6 Bass Pod Pro (~$600).

Electric Guitar:

Many of the miking and recording concepts discussed under the bass guitar section above also hold true for electric guitar. This is mainly because the bass is also an electric guitar; it is just playing in a lower octave.

The electric guitar can be recorded in several different ways, just like the bass. A stomp box or DI box can be used to play the guitar directly into the mixer. The guitar head amplifier can be used to send a preamp level signal directly into the mixer. The classic method of course is to mic the guitar speaker cabinet.

Many people are under the misconception that you need a powerful speaker amp and a monster speaker cabinet with four 12" drivers in it to get a big guitar sound in the studio. This might be a requirement for an awesome live stage presence, but in the studio you can get a huge sound from a small 20W or 50W guitar amp/speaker if you set the controls intelligently and mic it properly.

When miking a guitar speaker cabinet, you need to be aware of whether the amp/speaker cabinet has an open back or a closed back. On an open back cabinet, much of the lower frequency tone will come out of the back of the cabinet, and the rest will come out of the front of it. On a closed back cabinet, all of the sound comes directly out of the front of the cabinet. Therefore, you may need to mic both the front and rear of an open back cabinet, but just the front of a closed back cabinet.

Due to the relatively high sound pressure levels right next to the speaker, it is best to use a dynamic cardioid microphone when miking the front of the cabinet. Good choices are the Shure SM-57, the Electro-Voice RE20, and the Sennheiser MD421. The SM-57 is easily the classic choice for this application. (If you are going to use a large-diaphragm condenser microphone for this application, make sure that it can withstand the sound pressure levels right in front of the speaker without overloading the microphone preamp, or move the microphone away from the speaker cone a distance.) Locate the dynamic microphone about 3 inches from the front of the speaker and a couple of inches off to the side of the center of the speaker cone. As you move the microphone from the center to the edge of the speaker, the tone will change. The higher frequencies emanate from the center of the speaker cone. You may be able to dial in the tone you want just by moving the microphone around. Don't reach for the EQ knob first!

If you are miking the back of an open back cabinet and the front of the same cabinet, make sure you change the phase of the signal coming from the microphone at the rear of the cabinet. The reason is that as the speaker cone is pushing forward, the front microphone sees a positive pressure wave, but at the same time the rear microphone sees a negative pressure wave. If these two signals are combined in the mixer, phase cancellation will result. Therefore, reverse the phase of the rear microphone signal by 180 degrees, so that both signals are now adding in phase.

As with the bass guitar, there are now many guitar amp/cabinet modeling processors available for recording electric guitar. Most of these processors have several different combinations of amps and cabinets from which to choose. If you are interested in picking up one of these processors, you can choose from many different models: DigiTech Genesis 1 (~$100), DigiTech Genesis 3 (~$300), DigiTech GNX1 (~$300), DigiTech GNX2 (~$400), Zoom 606 (~$100), Zoom GFX707 (~$140), Zoom GFX8 (~$260), Zoom GFX4 (~$300), Johnson J Station (~$150), Korg AX1G (~$100), Korg AX100G (~$170), Korg AX1500G (~$300), Boss ME-33 (~$240), Boss GT-6 (~$400), Yamaha DG Stomp (~$300), Yamaha AG Stomp (~$400), Line 6 Pod 2.0 (~$300), and Line 6 Pod Pro (~$600).

Acoustic Guitar:
The acoustic guitar is one instrument where mic

position plays a very key role in how the guitar will eventually sound when recorded. But before you ever set up the microphone, take a look at the guitar itself.

It is very difficult to get a world-class recording out of an el cheapo acoustic guitar. No amount of processing afterwards can save the recording of a lame acoustic guitar. Also, if the strings on your acoustic guitar are buzzy, then you might be playing too hard or not fingering the notes cleanly, the action might be too low on your guitar, or possibly the frets on your guitar are worn unevenly. Using one of the string lubricants on the market can help to reduce finger squeaks. If all else fails, borrow a high quality acoustic (e.g., Martin, Taylor, or Gibson) from a friend for the recording.

The microphone position that I use most often is about 6" to 12" from the face of the guitar. I position the cardioid condenser microphone just over the very end of the fret board (near the sound hole). I usually point the microphone towards the sound hole at an angle of about 45°. This seems to give the best overall balance of a natural acoustic guitar sound. It will pick up plenty of the low frequency content from the sound hole. If it is picking up too much low frequency content, back the microphone away from the sound hole, or move it to be more off-axis from the sound hole. If it is not picking up enough low frequency content, move the microphone closer to the sound hole. If you position the microphone right in front of and too close to the sound hole, you might get a sound that is very boomy.

If you position the microphone about 18" or farther from the front of the guitar, you will start to capture the natural guitar sound combined with the effects of the acoustic environment of the room. From this distance, the microphone will pick up all parts of the guitar that are radiating sound. If the room is dead, there might not be much contribution from it, but if the room is live, you might get some bright reflections that can add to the sound (or perhaps not!).

One way to find a sweet spot for setting up the microphone is to plug your left ear and then turn your head so that your right ear listens directly at the guitar. You are simulating the pickup pattern of a cardioid microphone. Move your head around and listen while the guitarist plays. You will hear thin tones, natural tones, rich and bassy tones, boomy tones, and mellow or muted tones at various locations. Note the spot that gives you the tone you want, and then locate your microphone at that exact position.

An alternate way to record acoustic guitar is with a contact microphone. The contact microphone is small transducer that picks up the guitar's vibrations through physical contact with the guitar body and changes those vibrations into an electrical signal that can be amplified and recorded. You can experiment with a mix between the sound coming from a contact microphone and the sound from a condenser microphone for some interesting timbres. Usually, the contact microphone is located under the strings on the guitar body between the sound hole and the bridge. There are tons of links on the web about how to build your own contact mic out of a piezo transducer disk. This one is well-documented, with color pictures taken of every step in the process: http:// www.silcom.com/~planet5/erinys/contactmic.html. And the price is right at under $5!

If you want to capture a wide stereo recording of an acoustic guitar, try using an X-Y pair of condenser microphones. Position the microphones so that they form an angle with each other of between 90° and 120°. The microphones should be touching right where the diaphragms are located. Point the X-Y pair at the guitar. The optimum distance of the microphones from the guitar can be determined by using your own stereo pickups (your ears) to find the sweet spot for the sound. Pan the microphones left and right during the mix. Another method is to just record the same part twice in separate takes. Or if you have a digital recorder, you can copy and paste the first track onto a second track and delay it from 15mS to 35mS. Pan the two tracks hard left and right.

If you are going to record an acoustic guitarist who also sings, the best approach is to record the voice and the guitar at separate times to different tracks of the recorder. If this is not possible for some reason, make sure you adhere to the 3:1 rule when setting up the microphones for the guitar and the vocals. If the guitar microphone is 1 foot from the guitar, then the vocal microphone must be at least 3 feet from the guitar to prevent phase cancellations. The same holds true with the relationship of the vocal microphone and guitar microphone from the vocalist's mouth.

While recording the acoustic guitar, I usually put some mild compression on the sound to allow it to cut through the mix and to level out some of the playing unevenness. The acoustic guitar sounds good with some reverb on it, but too much reverb will ruin the texture of the sound.

Drums:

The two most important drums in the modern drum kit are the kick drum and the snare drum. The kick is the lowest pitched drum in the kit, and it is the key instrument upon which all the other drums and the rhythm section are based.

Before you start the miking process, make sure the drums are in good shape and ready for recording. Chances are higher that you will capture a good drum sound if you tune the drums correctly before the recording session. The drums should be tuned to complement the type of music you will be recording. If you have a spectrum analyzer (real time analyzer), you can use it to determine the approximate frequency of each tuned drum. Replacing the drumheads can have a profound effect on the sound also. New drumheads will sound tight and crisp, as opposed to the mushy and dull sound of old drumheads. Many people remove the bottom head of the drums for better projection and increased tuning control. For the kick drum, try removing the front drum head. Put a pillow or blanket inside the drum with a weight to hold it down and against the beater head. This will dampen the drumhead and provide a tighter sound. The type of beater you use on the kick drum will affect the tone of the drum. Also, a hard beater will give the kick a sharper attack transient. If the sound of any drum rings excessively, tape pieces of cloth onto the edges of the drumhead. If any tuning keys or other hardware rattle when the drums are struck, tape them down to prevent vibration.

If you want to mic a small drum kit with just two microphones, you will want to capture the kick by itself, and then try to capture the rest of the kit with the remaining microphone. For the kick drum, use a cardioid dynamic microphone with sufficient sensitivity to handle the extremely high sound pressure levels and sufficient low frequency response to capture the deep lows from the kick. The AKG D112 (~$220) is one microphone that was developed especially for this application. Locate the microphone inside the drum with the capsule pointed at the beater. Make sure the microphone you are using for the kick drum is not overloading with distortion from the proximity to the beater. A good way to get the microphone into the correct position without actually touching the kick drum is to use a boom microphone stand. For the rest of the kit, use an omnidirectional microphone located centrally within the kit. The idea is to locate it so that it picks up the rest of the kit, with an emphasis on the snare. Move the microphone around until you get a reasonable balance of the various drums and cymbals.

Another way to mic the drum kit with just two microphones is to use a pair of matched condenser microphones suspended over the drum kit. Point them down on the kit and angle them across it to get a stereo spread. You will want to adjust the physical mic positions so that you get a balanced sound from all drums in the kit, since you will not be able to adjust individual drum sounds at the mixing console. That is the tradeoff with this approach.

Problems that can occur with the spaced-apart pair of microphones are potential imaging problems when both signals are combined and collapsed to mono or the hole-in-the-middle sound when both microphones are panned left and right. There are two ways to combat these problems. One is to use the X-Y pair of cardioid microphones. For the X-Y approach, take two matched cardioid microphones, mount them such that their capsules are touching (one above the other) and their bodies are forming an angle of between 90° and 120°. As the physical angle between microphones increases, so too does the apparent stereo spread between them. Point the bisection of their angle at the center of the drum kit.

The second way to cure the problem is to use what is called the M-S (for Middle-Side) miking technique. This is what is known as a coincident technique, combining two microphones that pick up the middle of the stereo image and the sides of the image. When the two microphone signals arrive at the mixer, there is no hole in the middle of the stereo image, nor is there a monophonic compatibility problem if the signals are both panned to center. You can buy M-S stereo microphones such as the $1200 Shure VP88 and the $1400 Sony ECM-MS5 (or even the $54 PAiA M-S Microphone) that have both capsules built into one body. The downside of the M-S technique for home studio owners is that the M-S microphone does not directly put out left and right signals; it puts out mid and side signals. A decoder is required to convert the mid and side signals to left and right signals. PAiA sells a kit to accomplish this conversion for about $34 (read more about it at http://www.paia.com/msdecode.htm). Also, Mike Sokol, writing in the March 1995 issue of *Computer Video Magazine*, details an extremely inexpensive cable that you can build to decode M-S signals using only passive components (for the required signal phase reversal) and three XLR connectors. View his write-up at http://www.modernrecording.com/articles/soundav/link2.html.

Miking the drum kit with three microphones is the classical method, especially for jazz recordings. It gives a very natural overall sound. Use one microphone for the kick drum as explained above. The other two microphones should be a matched stereo pair of cardioid condensers that are mounted above the kit. I like to have the microphones above each end of the kit and angled, so that each one plays across the drum kit from opposite directions. This gives a nice stereo spread during mixing.

The above approaches to miking the drums are

minimalistic. You can certainly go the other extreme also, if you have enough microphones to accomplish the task. The advantage to miking every drum and cymbal is the excellent control it gives you over panoramic placement, tone and volume of the kit during mixdown. The disadvantages are that it is expensive (lots of microphones required!), there is leakage from the other drums into each microphone, the chances are high for phase cancellations among the various microphones, and it uses up a lot of tracks on your recorder if you give each drum its own track.

When recording the snare drum, many people use a cardioid dynamic microphone, but you can certainly also use a cardioid condenser microphone if it doesn't distort during the attack transients. The best approach is to use a boom stand (or a straight stand if you can fit it in there) and mic the snare from the front of the kit. Position the mic so that it is an inch or two from the edge of the snare drum and an inch or two above it. Point the mic down so it captures the area where the stick hits the surface of the drum. If you find that you are picking up too much bleed from adjacent drums or cymbals, try to position the mic so that the natural rejection zones of the mic are aligned with the offending sound sources. You can also use blocks of foam to try to isolate the snare microphone from the direct sound of a nearby drum or cymbal. If the microphone has a low frequency filter to roll off the lows, try using the microphone with the filter switched off in order to pick up the natural low frequencies of the snare. Make sure that the snare microphone does not pop with the puff of air from a closing high hat cymbal.

Miking the tom-toms (or toms) is similar to miking the snare. The toms may be mounted up high or floor-mounted. Use a cardioid dynamic or cardioid condenser microphone mounted about one or two inches above and one or two inches away from the tom head. Angle the microphone down to pick up where the stick hits the tom head. You can mic each tom separately, or you can use an omnidirectional or bi-directional microphone between 2 toms to pick up both of them at once. In this fashion, you could mic 4 toms with just 2 microphones.

To pick up a good individual signal on a high hat, mic it about 4" to 6" above the top rim of the upper cymbal with a cardioid condenser microphone. Aim it down towards the cymbal edge. Be sure to position the mic so that it does not pick up the jet of air that is squeezed out when the high hat closes.

To pick up a good signal on individual cymbals, use a technique similar to the high hat procedure. Use a good cardioid condenser with excellent high frequency response. Position the mic about 2' above the cymbal and pointing down to the cymbal edge. Make sure that when the cymbal is struck by the stick, it does not fly up and hit the mic.

If you are starting your own home studio, you may want to purchase a set of electronic drums or a drum machine. An electronic drum set generally consists of pressure sensitive pads that can be struck with real drum sticks to trigger sampled drum sounds. These are great for the home studio, because the only external sounds generated are the tapping sounds of the drum sticks hitting the rubber drum head sensors (no neighbor complaints). Any pad can be configured to trigger any sound from the electronic drum set or from any other external module via MIDI. A drum machine is a rack-mount or desktop module that contains samples of various drum and percussion instruments. Usually, drum machines are configured with a set of small rubber buttons that can be played with your fingers, or the internal sounds can be trigggered via MIDI signals from a keyboard or an electronic drum set. Drum machines and electronic drum sets usually have high-quality, 16-bit sampled sounds of real drum and percussion instruments, and they can sound fantastic. If you want to buy a low-end, used drum machine, look for the Alesis HR-16. A much better used machine is the Roland R-8 (desktop) or R-8M (rack-mount) drum machine. New drum machines on the market are the Alesis SR-16 and the Boss DR-770. If you already have a drum machine but you want to play it using real sticks, buy a used Roland Octapad or some other percussion pad. Using the percussion pad (a device with 6, 8 or more individual rubber pads that can send MIDI signals), you can trigger the sampled sounds in the drum machine (or any other MIDI sound module) using the MIDI control signals.

More on Microphones:

I have just scratched the surface on using microphones to record music. The info I have presented here is enough to get you started; however, if you want to research the subject in more depth, check out these *free* publications:

- "Microphone Techniques for Music Studio Recording": http://www.shure.com/pdf/booklets/studio.pdf
- "Microphones and Multi-tracks": http://www.shure.com/pdf/booklets/mics_and_multitracks.pdf
- All of Shure's technical bulletins and booklets can be found at http://www.shure.com/support/technotes/default.htm
- "The ABC's of AKG: Microphone Basics and Fundamentals of Usage"; "AKG Microphones in the Home Studio"; "Micing the Drum Set". These PDF files can all be downloaded for free at http://www.akgusa.com/.

References:

Bartlett, Bruce, "Miking Vocals and Horns", *Recording Magazine*, Dec. 1995, pp 16-18.

Hodges, Ralph, "Instruments I Have Miked", *Popular Electronics*, July 1977, pp 22-25.

White, Paul, "Recording Wind Instruments", *Home & Studio Recording*, Feb. 1989, pp 24-26.

McGaughey, Rob, "Recording Grand Piano", *Keyboard*, Feb. 2000, pp 86-88.

Greenwald, Ted, "Recording Piano & Synthesizers", *Keyboard*, June 1996, p 109.

Nathan, Bobby, "Miking Acoustic Pianos", *Keyboard*, Oct. 1985, p 96.

Parsons, Mark, "Bass Recording Workshop", *Home & Studio Recording*, Feb. 1994, pp 53-54.

Graydon, Jay and Anderton, Craig, "Compressing Electric Bass", *Keyboard*, May 1999, p 84.

James, Ethan, "Recording Unique Guitar Sounds", *Rock It*, Winter 1987, p 17.
Molenda, Michael, "Acoustic Alchemy", *Electronic Musician*, Feb. 1995, pp130-132.
Bartlett, Bruce, "String Theory", *Recording Magazine*, Nov. 1995, p77.
Bartlett, Bruce, "Recording Drums and Other Percussion", *Recording Magazine*, Oct. 1995, pp 25-28.

BOUNCING TRACKS

Track bouncing is the technique of combining several previously recorded tracks onto one or more open tracks on your recorder. The procedure of bouncing tracks is a key aspect of multi-track recording, but it has both positive and negative aspects associated with it. The positive aspect is that you can record the multiple previously recorded tracks onto the open track, and then erase the previously recorded tracks, thereby freeing up those tracks to record more audio. The negative aspect is that once you combine the previously recorded tracks onto an open track and then erase those previous tracks, you are stuck with whatever you recorded to that new track. Any combinations of timbre, volume, timing, effects and panning among the previous tracks are frozen forever on the new track (or tracks).

As an example of track bouncing, let's assume that you have a 4-track cassette multi-track deck. Let's further assume you used two microphones to record your drum set in the first pass of recording. On track 1 you recorded the kick drum, and on track 2 you recorded an omnidirectional mic located in the center of the drum kit. On the second pass of recording, you recorded your bass guitar directly to track 3 using a DI box. Now, you only have one track (track 4) left open for new audio. Using the track bouncing technique, you can combine tracks 1, 2 and 3 in a monophonic (one channel) mix and record that onto track 4. The way to do this is to monitor tracks 1, 2 and 3 in playback mode while arming track 4 for recording. Once you think you have achieved the proper balance of volume, tone and effects on the three tracks, you can then record them all at once to track 4. After you have recorded the tracks to track 4, go back and listen to track 4 all the way through. Make sure it is exactly what you want because you will not be able to change the relationship among those three audio feeds once they are recorded. If you are satisfied that track 4 is OK, then you can go back and erase tracks 1, 2, and 3. Be sure not to also erase track 4 in the process! Now, you can put new information onto tracks 1, 2 and 3 (such as guitar, keyboard and vocal) and essentially get 6 tracks out of your 4-track recorder.

In the above example, we just mixed 3 prerecorded tracks to an open track. However, if your mixer can accommodate it, there is no reason you can't combine a live performance or virtual tracks from a sequencer with the 3 prerecorded tracks when you bounce them to track 4. In the above example, you could play a tambourine into a microphone while you listen to the three previously recorded tracks. In this fashion, you could record 4 separate sound sources (e.g., two tracks of drums, one track of bass and live tambourine) to track 4 during the first bounce. After you erase the first 3 tracks to free them up for more audio recording, you could repeat a similar process. For example, you could record a piano accompaniment on track 1 and a synthesizer background string sound on track 2. Then, when you go to bounce these two tracks to track 3, you could add a live acoustic guitar. Now, you have 4 tracks recorded on track 4 (two drum tracks, bass and tambourine) and 3 tracks recorded on track 3 (piano, strings and acoustic guitar). If you put a lead guitar on track 2 and the lead vocal on track 1, then you have used your 4-track cassette multi-tracker to record 9 separate tracks!

The concept of track bouncing will work with any multi-track recorder that allows you to monitor some of the tracks in playback mode while one or more other tracks is able to record new material. For tape-based recorders, the tracks being played back must be able to be monitored at the same physical point where the new tracks are being recorded, otherwise a time delay is introduced between the record head and the play head. For digital recorders, this is usually not a problem, since there is no physical tape head involved. In fact, many digital recorders let you cut, copy, paste and combine audio in the digital domain which results in fantastic editing capabilities.

For 4-track cassette multi-tracks, there is a variation on this theme that allows you to record a 4-to-2 stereo mix as part of the bounce. If you have a stereo cassette recorder in addition to your 4-track multi-tracker, and the multi-tracker records at $1^7/8$ IPS, you can bounce all 4 tracks from the multi-tracker to tracks 1 and 3 on the stereo cassette deck. After you have done this, take the tape out of the stereo recorder and put it in the multi-tracker. Now you have a stereo mix of 4 tracks on tracks 1 and 3, and tracks 2 and 4 are available for more audio tracks. This method is good if you want to preserve a stereo image during the bounce.

This bouncing technique will work on the simplest 4-trackers and also on recorders with many more tracks. I used to record up to 29 or 30 tracks on my 8-track reel/reel just by bouncing tracks. The key to successful bouncing is to completely plan out the production of the song before you ever start to record the first track. It is like determining all the pieces of the puzzle before you start to put the puzzle together.

One question that usually comes up is when to put effects on the instrument. Should you put effects like reverb or echo on the tracks as you record them, or should you record the tracks "dry" (i.e., no effects added)? The answer to the question depends on the equipment you have, how many tracks you have on which to record, and what the song really requires. If you have enough tracks so that each instrument has its own track, and you have a mixer with one or more effects send and return buses, then you can record the tracks dry and put the effects on the tracks later when you mix them down to stereo. If you only have a limited number of tracks on which to record, and you will be bouncing tracks around, you may need to add an effect to an instrument as you record it. For example, if you have a 4-track multi-tracker, you are bouncing 3 tracks that contain the bass guitar, the kick drum and the rest of the drum kit, and you only want reverb on the rest of the drum kit, then you can't put reverb on the whole submix, or the bass guitar and kick drum will end up with reverb on them also. (Usually you want the bass and kick to be dry or mostly dry in a mix.) So, you will have had to put the reverb separately on the track that contains the rest of the drum kit when it was recorded, or you will need to put it only on that track somehow as you combine the 3 tracks to the 4th open track. This is why you must plan out the tracking assignments and overall game plan ahead of time. After you mix those tracks together, it is too late to try to apply effects to just one sound in the track.

If you buy any multi-track analog recorder, you should check the owner's manual to determine if you can record to an open track while trying to bounce an adjacent track to it. Some analog machines will not let you accomplish this trick. Instead, you will get howling feedback or some other noise from the adjacent track. If this is the case, you will need to leave what is known as a guard track (basically just an empty or unmonitored track) between the track you are recording and the track you are bouncing over to it. I have never heard of this problem on any digital recorders, especially PC workstations.

Here is some other advice that might help when bouncing tracks on an analog recorder. If you know a track is going to be bounced later, it might be good to add some brightness to the sound when you first record it, because some of the brightness will be lost when the sound is bounced over to another track. You can add the brightness with a mixer EQ, outboard EQ or an exciter. Note that if you add the brightness when you go to bounce the tracks, you might be boosting the high frequency noise level. Also, be aware that analog decks tend to boost the bass a little when a sound is recorded to one track and then bounced over to another. This is especially true with cassette multi-trackers. This can have an effect on your bass and drum tracks.

In general, the tracks that are bounced the most on an analog recorder will have the lowest fidelity in the final mix. This is because noise and distortion are added to the signal during every bounce. You may want to keep this in mind when planning the track assignments and bouncing of the tracks for your song. Tracks bounced in the analog domain on a digital recorder are also subject to increased distortion and noise, but usually not to the same degree as on an analog recorder.

For all my recording sessions, I usually generate a track sheet that shows what instruments are going onto which tracks on which recorders, what MIDI channels are used, where the instruments are panned, which effects will be used on which instruments, and which tracks will be bounced to other tracks. It is really imperative to write all this information down, because when you come back to the song a week later (or a year later), you will be able to easily reconstruct where you were in the song and what you were thinking. You may decide to pull out an old song and remix it or add a new lead vocalist, and knowing how you mixed the song before really helps.

References:
Anderton, Craig, "Multitrack Magic for the Budget Studio", *Electronic Musician*, Jan. 1989, p 46.

MIXING

Mixing is the process of combining various individual tracks that have already been recorded (tracked), along with sequenced virtual tracks or live performance audio feeds (if available), while manipulating the individual sounds and the overall sound in the time and frequency domain, to achieve an artistic result.

One key element to mixing multiple tracks on a mixer is to maintain proper levels and gain structure throughout the signal path and the recording process. Within the studio, just about every piece of equipment has some sort of volume level adjustment on it, and many pieces of equipment have multiple volume controls. Most all mixers and recorders have meters on them that measure the electrical signal and give a visual indication of the signal's amplitude.   It is important that you know what types of meters you have on your equipment because these will help you maintain proper signal levels. Consult your owner's manuals for this information. See also the description of the peak and average meters in the "Nature of Sound" section of this book. As a general rule of thumb, VU analog meters are generally average-reading meters and LED meters are generally peak-reading meters. However, this is not always the case. I've seen VU meters that can read peak signals, and I've seen LED meters that can be switched to give an average reading.

Setting Gain Structure:

Detailed in the paragraphs that follow is a good basic way of setting the proper gain structure and signal levels on your mixer. This will allow you to mix signals without having to worry about too much noise (because the signal levels are too low) or too much distortion (because the signal levels are too high). The goal is to maximize the headroom in the signal (where headroom is the amount of signal amplitude still remaining before a distortion level is reached) without incurring too much noise. It is a fine line to walk.

The first step in achieving this goal is to make sure

that the input and output levels on all of your equipment are set to the same input sensitivity level, either the –10 dB (semi-pro level) or the +4 dB (pro-level) standard. If you have both types of equipment, choose one standard and use level converters for the equipment that does not comply with the standard you chose. For examples of level converters, see the Match-Maker and Disk-Patcher from Audio Technologies (www.atiguys.com) or the Match-box and Patchbox from Henry Engineering (www.henryeng.com).

The next step is to set the trim pot on each individual channel of the mixer. The trim pot (usually located at the top of a channel strip) sets the initial gain or loss for that channel. The trim pot is a variable volume control connected to a line level amplifier used to accommodate the different levels it might see from equipment plugged into that channel (microphones, synthesizers, guitar stomp boxes, DI boxes, tape decks, D/A converter outputs from a computer, etc.). Apply the signal at the input connector of channel 1.

If your mixer has a solo button for each channel, start with selecting the solo button (i.e., push it in) for the first channel. The solo function will route the output of the trim amplifier directly to the mixer's meters, to the exclusion of all other sounds. Listen for the loudest passages from the instrument plugged into channel 1. Adjust the trim pot so that the loudest signals coming into channel 1 just light the first red LED on the meter for a peak-reading LED meter (usually +1dB). For an analog VU meter, evaluate the type of instrument coming into channel 1. If it is a relatively non-dynamic instrument (e.g., synthesizer pad), then set the trim pot so that the loudest peaks are right around 0dB. If it is a transient, highly dynamic instrument like a snare drum or a crash cymbal, set the average level down about –10dB, because the peaks will not be registering on the meter. In turn, set the rest of the initial gain structure on the mixer by soloing each individual channel and setting each channel's trim pots appropriately. Note that these levels will be different for each different mixer you encounter. Do not try to adjust the levels by ear, but rather follow the correct method of setting the input gain stage levels.

If your mixer has no solo button and you can adjust the output signal of the instrument (e.g., synthesizer, mic preamp, guitar effects box, etc.), then you will need to modify the gain staging procedure slightly. Set the fader for mixer channel 1 to the optimized level (also called the 0 dB level). There is usually an area that is colored or defined by some other method such a heavy line about 75% of the way up the fader travel, and that is the optimized level for that fader. Next, also set the master faders to their optimized (or 0 dB) level. If you are using submaster channels, then set them for their optimized level also. (A submaster is another bus structure within the mixer that can carry an alternate mix of the instruments, so that the volume of all of the submaster channels can be adjusted independently of the master faders. This is handy if you put, say, all of the drum channels or all of the background vocals on submaster channels, so the overall drum volume or the overall background vocals volume can be adjusted without adjusting each individual fader. Then, you could assign that submaster output to mix into the master output.) Now, listen for the loudest passages from the instrument plugged into channel 1 while observing the mixer's meters. Adjust the instrument's output volume so that the meters just barely peak into the red zone on the loudest passages. Similarly, adjust each of the other mixer channels and the instruments plugged into them for proper gain structuring. Be aware that if you substantially change the character of a sound with either large boosts or cuts in EQ, you may need to go back and establish the correct gain structure for that channel.

You have now set the proper gain values for the main signal path through the mixer. Next, you need to set the proper gain values for the effects send and return loop (i.e., the aux send and aux return). The aux send circuit picks off some of the audio signal flowing through the mixer channel and makes it available at the aux send jacks, depending on how each channel's aux send pot and the aux send master pot are set. This signal is then patched to an outboard effects device, such as a reverb unit, and effects are added to the signal. This effected signal is patched back into the mixer at the aux return jacks. Then, depending on how the aux return pot is set, the effected signal is added back into the overall mix. To set up the proper gain structure of all these gain stages in the effects loop, start by setting the aux return fully off (or counterclockwise). This is to protect your ears and equipment as you get the proper levels dialed in. Next, set the aux send pot at about $2/3$ of the travel (or at about the 2 o'clock position) for the specific channel to which you are adding the effects. If your mixer has a way to monitor the internal aux send bus(es), play the instrument through the mixer channel and set the aux send master pot so that the signal just lights up the first red LED on the meter (or moves the VU meter into the red zone on an analog meter). If there is no aux meter on your mixer, then just set the aux send master pot to the 2 o'clock position. Now, start to bring up the input volume control on the outboard effects processor while continuing to play the instrument through the mixer channel. (Make sure that the effects processor's mix or balance control is set to 100% effects or 100% wet.) Increase the volume on the effects processor input pot until the signal peaks start to just barely trigger the first red LED on the processor's meter.

Now, you are ready to adjust the amount of effects in your mix for that instrument by adjusting the level of the aux return pot. The more level you give via the aux return pot, the more effects you will have in the mix for that channel/instrument. If you are adding effects for multiple channels on the mixer, then you will need to adjust the relative mix of the signals being sent to the effects processor using the individual aux send pots on each channel. The idea is to keep these pots as near to their optimum levels as you can, so as to avoid adding noise into the effects loop. Do not adjust the amount of effects in the mix with the aux send master pot; use the aux return pot for this purpose.

Mixing the Song:

Now you are ready to start the mix of the individually recorded tracks, any virtual instruments, and any live instruments. But first, here is a little advice to make things go easier. As a reference point for your mix, keep a CD of a similar genre of music that you admire nearby and compare your work in progress to it. Be aware of ear fatigue. If you have been working in the studio all day long, it is doubtful that your ears are going to be up for the task of serious mixing. You ears can and will play tricks on you when they get tired. The problem is that you won't know it at the time. A good way to avoid (or at least delay) ear fatigue is to monitor at reasonable levels through headphones and speakers. Be prepared to take plenty of short breaks.

The best way I have found to begin the mixing process is to start with the foundation of the song, which is usually rhythm section. First, set the Master Faders to their optimum (75%) level, and bring up the monitor speakers or headphones to a reasonable monitoring level. The monitoring does not have to be mind-numbingly loud to get a good mix. In fact, the opposite is usually true. Keeping the monitoring levels under control allows you to listen to the nuances of the song and see how the instruments are sitting within the mix. Bring up the faders for the kick drum first (say to –10 dB on the mixer meters) and then the bass. For now, set them at approximately the same level by ear, and pan them both to center. Leave some headroom for yourself on the mixer meters when listening to both instruments mixed together, because you still have to add in all the rest of the instruments. You want to have the individual faders set to somewhere near their optimum (75%) level as much as possible. This gives the best signal/noise ratio for that mixer channel and instrument. Usually the bass and the kick have the most low frequency energy in the mix, and the standard approach is to mix them to center, so that both stereo speakers can share the sonic load. Also, the bass and the kick usually receive little if any reverb. Next, bring up the snare. Make sure it sits right in with the bass and kick, and give it the proper effects type and level for the song you are mixing. The snare should be balanced with the kick sound in intensity. Then bring up the rest of the drum kit. Pan the toms so that they move across the stereo field (from the audience's perspective) when they are played in succession. Pan the high hat just off to the side, and pan the cymbals farther left and right as appropriate. The overall mix should give the effect that each drum instrument is basically at the same distance from the listener. If the kick or the bass are unruly or uneven in the mix, tame them with some compression on a channel insert. Make sure that you leave room at the higher frequencies for the lead instruments that will be added later. Compare that mix to your reference CD.

Once the main rhythm instruments sound good, then you can start to add in the accompaniment or background instruments. These are synthesizers, rhythm guitars, pianos, strings, etc. Keep their levels relatively low, since they are not the main or lead instruments. You can control their front-to-back orientation within the mix via the amount of reverb they receive. More reverb tends to make an instrument sound farther away from the listener, while no reverb at all tends to make the instrument sound like it is right up in front of the listener. You also want to think in terms of frequency stacking. Try to get each instrument to have its own frequency section, so they do not have to fight with other instruments to be heard. If the lead guitar, synthesizer, rhythm guitar and strings all occupy the same band of frequencies, it is going to be tough to pick them out of the mix as separate instruments, and the mix will start to sound cluttered. You may need to use EQ and panning to achieve this separation. It is best to leave the low frequencies to the bass and kick drum to avoid clutter in the low end. Compare your mix to the sound of your reference CD.

Now you are at the point where all of the instruments are in the mix except for the vocals and the lead instruments. Bring the main vocals into the mix. Usually, it is important to have them loud enough to be understandable, especially for a mainstream pop song. If you find that the vocal amplitude level is varying, use more compression on it via channel inserts. Listen to the vocal and see if it is too thin, too tubby, or too dry. You can correct these problems with a judicious application of EQ and reverb. Sometimes, you can make the vocals jump out of a mix without increasing the amplitude of the signal simply by running the vocal through an exciter (e.g., BBE Sonic Maximizer or Aural Exciter). Once the vocal is sitting in the mix reasonably well, you can add in the other lead instruments. Make sure that they have a prominent space in terms of panning, level, EQ, and effects, but not an overwhelming presence. Don't let them overwhelm the main vocal. You now have a basic mix of the song. How does this compare to your reference CD?

The above scenario was an example of how to mix a song with standard popular instruments in it. But, what if you are mixing a song with a completely different structure? For example, what would be a good approach to mix a ballad that has two acoustic guitars and two vocalists? Perhaps the best approach would be to start with the two acoustic guitars. Bring them both up in volume and pan them to 10 o'clock and 2 o'clock. You might want to take the aux send from the guitar panned to 10 o'clock, send it to an outboard reverb unit and then bring it back into the mix, but pan it hard right. Similarly, take the aux send from the guitar panned to 2 o'clock, send it to the outboard reverb unit and then bring it back into the mix, but pan it hard left. This should really widen the sound stage, especially if you apply some pre-delay to the reverb effect. Next, bring up the two vocals and experiment with them. Try to pan them to 11'oclock and 1 o'clock and see how that sounds. Put some stereo reverb on each of them. This should give you a nice full soundstage using only 4 sound sources. If in doubt on how to proceed with a mix, you can always bring up the level of all tracks to be the same, then start reducing the level of background tracks and increasing the level of lead or solo tracks. The point here is that the approach to the mix depends entirely on the structure of the song, the musicians, the equipment you have and the artistic results you are trying to achieve.

Now that CD-R media is so cheap, I find myself making multiple versions of my mixes. After I finish all the tracks for a song, I will record a final mix to CD-R, then turn everything off and let it sit for a day or two. I will listen to the mix on various speaker systems (studio, living room, car, portables) to see how the mix sounds. Invariably, I will come back and change the mix around and record a new master to CD-R. Since I leave everything hooked up in the studio, it is usually easy for me to go back in and change the mix around. I also make a separate mix with no vocals or with other things changed around in the mix. Why not? Once you tear down the setup for that song, it will be difficult to ever recreate exactly the groove you were in. (Or, maybe that's a good thing.)

Tricks of the Mix:

Here are various tricks you can try in your mixes to achieve different results and correct certain problems.

Not Enough Mixer Inputs: With the ability to synchronize multiple recorders, a sequencer and virtual MIDI tracks, you can rapidly run out of mixer input channels during the mixdown process. This is where you need to get creative with your mixer. The obvious inputs on the mixer are the main channel inputs. However, you can also use effects return inputs, bus or sub inputs, and even the tape monitor section as additional inputs. If you plug external MIDI modules (using virtual tracks with a sequencer) into these inputs, you can control the volume of these tracks during the mix with either the MIDI volume control or the volume control on the external MIDI module. You can also use a submixer to premix certain channels to stereo before you connect them to the main mixer.

Applying EQ to Elements of the Mix: Most novices in the studio go overboard with EQ. The best approach is to use EQ as little as possible, because it is so easy to get out of control with it. Adding EQ to a signal produces phase shift in the signal, which is usually an undesirable side effect. It is always better to try to adjust the relative EQ of a sound in other ways. For instruments or vocals recorded with microphones, adjust the microphone position to alter the sound. Changing the mic position even slightly can result in large changes in the sound. For synthesizers, try changing elements within the patch (e.g., open a filter a little more, etc.) to achieve a different spectral result. However, sometimes you just have to use EQ on the mix. When this is the case, try to cut the opposite frequencies rather than boosting the problematic frequencies. For example, if an instrument doesn't have enough low frequencies in the mix, try cutting the high frequency content with EQ and then boosting slightly the volume of that instrument in the mix. This actually has the same effect as boosting the low frequencies, but you end up with more signal headroom than if you had just boosted the low frequencies. The chart below should give you a starting point for boosting or cutting certain ranges of frequencies in the sound. It gives some of the descriptive words that audio engineers use to describe the sounds for various frequency ranges. For example, if the sound does not have enough energy in the bottom octaves, you would boost the EQ somewhere in the 20 Hz to 200 Hz region. If the sound appears to be too boomy, you would cut the EQ somewhere in the 20 Hz to 200 Hz region.

EQ Frequency	Boost Effect	Cut Effect
20Hz to 200Hz	bottom octaves	boom, rumble
200Hz to 500Hz	warmth	mud
500Hz to 1.5kHz	midrange	honk
1.5kHz to 4kHz	1st oct. presence	stridence
4kHz to 10kHz	brightness	sibilance
10kHz to 20kHz	high end sheen	hiss, thinness

Removing Noise and Hiss: Noise and hiss have been the bane to audio recording since the first wire recorder. The sources of noise and hiss are many, including improper gain staging, noisy electronics, tape hiss, ambient noises picked up by microphones, ground loops and many others. The best solution is always to track down the real source of the problem and solve it directly. However, once you have already recorded the noise or hiss, then you are in a compromise position, and you must take action to remove the noise or the hiss from the recording if it is audible. If the rest of the audio in the mix does not mask the noise or hiss, then you can try a single-ended noise reduction system.

Single-ended noise reduction systems have been designed as "black boxes" to remove high frequency hiss and noise. A single-ended noise reduction system can be patched into the channel insert on a mixer channel that has a hissy tape track on it. Adjust the filter control on the single-ended noise reduction system so that it eliminates the hiss but leaves the real audio content as untouched as possible. If the noise is really bad, try using a noise gate to remove it. A noise gate allows the audio to pass through when it is above a certain amplitude level, but the gate closes down and allows no audio to pass through when the amplitude is below that certain sensitivity level. The sensitivity level to open and close the gate can be set based on when valid audio is present or not present. For example, for a noisy vocal recording, set the sensitivity control to close the noise gate when the vocal signal disappears, thereby filtering out all the noise. The gate would open again when it detects the beginning of the vocal signal. The premise behind the noise gate is that when the gate is open, the valid audio signal (the vocal in this case) will be there to mask the noise. As a last resort, use an outboard EQ or even the EQ on your mixer channel to cut the high frequencies (or the lows, if that is where the noise is).

Fattening a Vocal or Lead: One way to fatten up a wimpy vocal or lead instrument is to double track it. Double tracking involves recording the exact same performance again on a separate track and then combining it with the original performance. If the performer does it right, the second performance sounds identical to the first, but with enough minor variances in timing, timbre and pitch to add a pleasing doubling effect when the two performances are combined in the mix. Of course, this presupposes that the performer can give the exact same performance over again and that you have additional empty tracks to use for this purpose. If the performer isn't up to the real-time doubling task, or you don't have extra empty tracks on your recorder, the doubling effect can be simulated rather easily. Send a clean, pre-reverb copy of the original signal to a digital or analog delay box. Use the delay box to delay the signal anywhere from 15 mS to 40 mS. Bring this delayed signal back into the mixer (perhaps using an aux input channel) and pan it to the opposite side of the original signal. You can modify this procedure by adding a slight modulation to the delay line, which will enhance the doubling effect. You can also play other tricks such as changing the EQ on the delayed signal to further separate it from the original signal.

Another way to fatten up a vocal or lead is to pan the original signal to the center, and then send a copy of the signal out to an outboard digital signal processing (DSP) box that can perform pitch shifting. Set one output on the DSP box to pitch shift the signal up by a slight amount (~7 or 8 cents where 1 cent is $1/100$th of a semitone), and then set up the other output on the DSP box to shift the pitch down by the same amount. Now bring these two pitch-shifted signals back into the mix and pan them hard left and hard right. Adjust the levels of the pitch-shifted signals so that they just fatten and widen the original signal image.

An even simpler fattening method (if you have a digital multi-track recorder with empty tracks) is to copy the vocal performance to the clipboard and then paste it to an empty track, but offset it slightly in time (try a 20 mS delay). You can also add different effects to that doubled track, such as EQ, echo, flanging, or chorusing for dramatic effect.

Highlighting a Vocal or Lead: Many people often reach for the EQ or fader when they want to highlight a certain track to make it stand out in the mix. That is certainly one way to do it. A better way is to pick off some of the signal with aux send and send it to an external exciter such as the Aphex Aural Exciter or the BBE Sonic Maximizer. Use these devices to add more high frequency information or spectral sparkle to the signal without increasing the volume of the signal. Then bring the signal back into the aux returns. When you want that particular instrument or vocal to stand out, just increase the level of the aux returns. Another way to highlight an important signal is to compress it slightly, even if only at a 2:1 or 3:1 ratio. This will help the signal stand out in a crowded mix, and it will also solve performance-related dynamics problems.

"Pumping" Volume Problems: If you find that the overall volume level of the song seems to be pumping (i.e., alternately becoming louder then softer), it is a good indication that you are having compression problems with the mix. If you run the whole mix through a compressor (or even parts of the mix (or just parts) through a compressor), the highly dynamic elements of the mix (usually the drums) may be affecting the volume levels of the other instruments, especially the bass guitar. You may be able correct this by changing the attack of the compressor so that it does not react so quickly to the transient sounds. You can also try reducing the amount of compression you are applying to the mix. If you own the FMR RNC Compressor (and I highly recommend that you buy at least one for your studio!), then you know that the Super Nice mode on that compressor virtually eliminates the noise and volume-pumping problem. The Super Nice mode, which combines three separate compressors in series, serves to eliminate the pumping effects and provides an

awesome, smooth compression effect. When you use a compressor in a chain of effects devices, put the compressor first in the chain, so that it does not over emphasize the noise and effects from the earlier effects devices.

Adding Punch and Bottom to Drums: Most modern dance music craves low frequency, punchy drums. You can compress the drums, especially the kick, snare and toms, to make the drums more immediate in the mix. One way to add punch to the drums is to route some of the snare, kick or tom sound out of the aux sends to an external distortion box or even a tube preamplifier. Use these kinds of devices to add bite, edge and punchiness to the drum sound. Then, bring the effected sound back into the mixer via the aux return jacks, and mix the effected sound into the mix to suit.

One way to add a huge bottom octave to the drums and bass line is to use a dbx Subharmonic Synthesizer (or possibly the new Peavey Kosmos Sub Harmonic Generator). The dbx device analyzes the input signal between 50 and 120 Hz and synthesizes a signal that is one half the frequency of the original signal (i.e., a signal from 25 to 60 Hz). When you add this half-harmonic signal back into mix, you can get a physical vibration that will shake your house. You need to be careful with this device for several reasons. You can easily distort a recording by trying to record too much low frequency information. It will quickly use up any available headroom in your mix, and you will be forced to lower the overall level of the mix. You can fry the woofers on your stereo system or studio monitor system if they aren't equipped to handle such low frequency information at high volume levels. Also, if your music is going to be played on cheap AM or FM radios, this low frequency information will never show up.

Better Use of the Solo Button: The solo button on a mixer is great to isolate a track and see what is going on without disturbing the rest of the mix, especially if it is of the solo-in-place type (which preserves the panned position of the sound). However, one mistake that some people make is to only adjust the sound of the track while listening to it in solo mode. The problem with this is that you are not adjusting the sound of the track in relation to the other tracks or how it fits in the mix; you are adjusting it in relation to itself, which is not optimum. For example, a certain guitar part may sound thin when it is in solo mode by itself, but it may fit just perfectly in the frequency band allotted for it in the mix, without stepping on other instruments.

Eliminating Resonance Peaks: You may have recorded an instrument or several instruments that give an annoying resonant peak during mixdown. An example of this might be an acoustic guitar that really resonates on one string with one or two notes. A cure for this is to use a parametric equalizer to tame that particular acoustic guitar resonant peak. A parametric EQ allows you to select a particular frequency of interest and cut or boost it. You can also select how much you want to affect adjacent frequencies. If you want to affect a wide swath of frequencies surrounding the frequency of interest, it is called a low Q setting. If you just want to affect the frequency of interest and not any others surrounding it, it is called a high Q setting. The parametric EQ differs from the graphic EQ in that the parametric EQ allows you to select the frequency to adjust and the Q of that adjustment. On a graphic EQ, all of the adjustment frequencies are permanently preselected for you.

Eliminating 60 Hz Hum: You can also use the parametric EQ to eliminate hum or noise at a particular frequency or band of frequencies. Dial in the parametric EQ to cut the signal at 60 Hz, and set it for the highest Q (narrowest notch of cut). This should get rid of the 60 Hz hum without destroying the rest of the signal. You can also do this with a graphic EQ, but it won't be nearly as effective as the parametric EQ, since you can't select the frequency or the Q setting on the graphic EQ.

Fixing Pre-mixed Tracks: Once you mix several tracks together and bounce them to an empty track, you are generally stuck with the end result forever. However, there are a couple of little tricks you can pull to fix problems after the bounce. If the bounced track has too much of a reverb tail on it, you can try running that track through a noise gate and setting the sensitivity of the gate so it closes down at the appropriate time. This will cut off the end of the reverb tail and possibly fix the problem. If the bounced track has too much bass or kick drum in it, you may be able to isolate those instruments with a parametric EQ and reduce them just enough to save the track.

Making a Sound Appear to be in the Distance: In real life, a sound from the distance has less high frequency energy (this is the energy that is most quickly dissipated into heat), and it has more reverberation, since the sound has had a chance to bounce off of many objects before it reaches you. So, to simulate this in the studio, use an equalizer to remove some of the high frequency content of a sound, and then use a reverb effects device to add a fair amount of reverb.

References:
Anderton, Craig, "The FX Files", *Keyboard*, March 1998, pp 56-60.
Anderton, Craig, "Mixing: Beyond Level Changes", *Keyboard*, Jan. 1996, p130.
Anderton, Craig, "Sonic Tonic", *Electronic Musician*, March 1989, pp 34-35.
"Keyboard Project Studio Guide and Fact-Finder", *Keyboard Magazine*.
Medelsohn, Phil, "Mastering EQ", *Recording Magazine*, April 1997, p54.
Molenda, Michael, "All Mixed Up", Feb. 1995, *Electronic Musician*, pp 90-92.
Nathan, Bobby, "Looking at Levels", *Keyboard*, May 1987, p104.
White, Paul, "Guidelines to the Mix", *Home & Studio recording*, Jan. 1989, pp 64-66.

MASTERING

Mastering is the process of assembling into one complete collection all of the individual songs you have already mixed for a certain project, and then making that collection sound as good as it possibly can. Mastering is a separate and distinct process from mixing. The songs are arranged in the correct order (for the best "flow") with the desired amount of silence between them and then written to the mastering media. One goal of the mastering process is to give all of the songs a uniform sound.   During this process, an overall program level is defined and set for all of the songs.   The songs are further refined with additional EQ, sweetening or compression as required.   This master is then sent out to have CDs, cassettes, or vinyl records manufactured.

What format should you use for the mastering media? If you use analog (reel/reel or cassette) as the choice, you will suffer another generation loss as you record the songs over to the master.   This is a drawback with the analog format, because the extra generation loss can result in additional tape hiss and dropouts (sections where the sound just disappears or drops in level due to problems with the magnetic material on the tape). These problems can be mitigated somewhat with wider tapes, faster tape speeds and noise reduction encoding (such as Dolby SR).   If you use a digital format, you can avoid those problems.   The two most popular formats for digital masters are DAT tape and CD-R.

Digital Audio Workstations (DAWs) have become very popular to use for mastering because everything can be done inside of them entirely within the digital domain without ever committing a sound to tape.   DAWs are able to host plug-in software packages that are optimized for certain tasks, including final mastering.   Editing audio on a DAW is another reason they are so popular.   Extremely precise edits can be done in software, and if you don't like the results, the edits can be undone and changed easily. The DAWs will allow you to apply any sweetening, EQ or compression required, and collect the songs into a queue that will represent the final master. You can play back the songs in the appropriate order just as they will appear on the final product. This allows you to judge the overall product before ever permanently committing anything. When everything is set perfectly, then you can write the results out to DAT tape or CD-R and send that to the manufacturing facility.

If you are going to use the above process to make a master, then you need to be aware that these digital formats give you exactly what you recorded onto them and nothing more. When mastering (or recording in general) to an analog tape, the tape can be pushed into saturation with high signal levels. This can result in a pleasing distortion, especially on bass and drums. You will not encounter this phenomenon when recording to DAT or CD-R.

As you are mastering your songs, again use the technique of listening to a favorite CD or album as a reference point. As you master the recordings, make sure you use a good set of flat-response monitor speakers with which you are familiar. Again, listen to the end result on several different speaker systems (car, living room, headphones, etc.). During mastering, using an excellent compressor such as the FMR Really Nice Compressor can help the overall sonic result. This compressor has a mode called Super Nice that connects three separate internal compressors in series. This mode gives a nice smooth compression without compression artifacts. It can give power and edge to your overall mix without overdoing the effect.

Before you send your music anywhere, absolutely make sure to generate a safety copy first. Murphy's Law dictates that your master will be lost, stolen or destroyed; so err on the side of too much precaution.

A small book could easily be written about mastering techniques, problems and solutions. In fact, someone did write one, and it is free. I highly recommend that you send for the free 36-page booklet entitled *Making a Great Master* by Disc Makers. You can get it by calling 1-800-468-9353, going to their website www.discmakers.com, or sending an email to info@discmakers.com. At the same time, you can request one of their catalogs for pricing of

CDs, cassettes, vinyl, posters, etc.

References:
Making a Great Master, Disc Makers, 2001.

PART FIVE: TOOLS, ADVICE & MISCELLANEOUS

WALL WART ADAPTERS

Most studio users don't like wall warts because they eat up more than one socket in a multi-outlet power strip. However, many manufacturers use them because it results in lower costs in product development, product compliance and certification testing. Here is a tip on dealing with wall warts. One way to get around the wall-wart/power-strip problem is to buy several cheap, short AC power extension cables (the 2-conductor variety). You can buy 6' power extension cables at a home improvement center such as Home Depot for just a couple of dollars each. Cut about 5'6" of wire from the middle of the 6 foot extension cord and then reassemble the extension cord using solder and heat shrink tubing for insulation between the conductors. Make sure that you get the wires hooked back up correctly; one conductor usually has a ribbed plastic insulator on it while the other one is smooth. (See Figure 35.) You can leave each extension cord unmodified if you want, but that is just 5'6" more of unshielded 115VAC power cable hanging around in your rack. Regardless, now you have an adapter that allows you to connect at least two, and more likely three, wall warts to one outlet on the power strip. If you are worried about the wall warts falling out of the modified extension cord, put a tie wrap around all three wall warts and cinch it up. This will keep them firmly in place if you move your equipment for gigs or whatever. You can then tie wrap that set of three wall warts to the side of your rack or right to the power strip. If you want to spend a lot more money, you can buy the Furman Pluglock, which is a 2 lb device that has 5 outlets with adjustable tabs that hold the wall warts in place. It also has a built-in 15A circuit breaker.

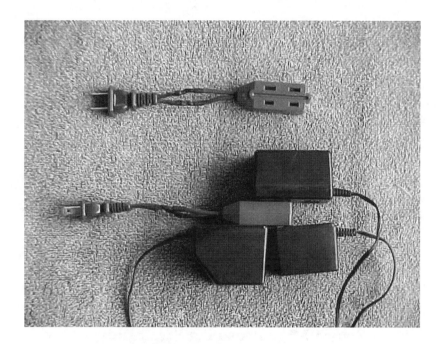

Figure 35: Inexpensive Wall Wart Adapter

Here is another good tip concerning wall wart power supplies. If you are using a wall wart power supply, then you have the potential problem of the power plug being yanked out (or for some reason falling out) of the rear panel power jack. A solution for this is to buy a cable clip with adhesive backing (such as Radio Shack P/N 278-1639) and stick it on next to the power jack on the unit's rear panel. Then thread the power cable through the cable clip and cinch it down (the clip is adjustable and removable). Now you have a ready-made strain relief for the power cable, and it won't pull out of the power jack so easily. (See Figure 36.) I highly recommend that you do this for any equipment you take on the road from your studio. It might save you time in troubleshooting the inside of an equipment rack in the dark, or prevent you from suffering a frustrating loss of power during your recording session.

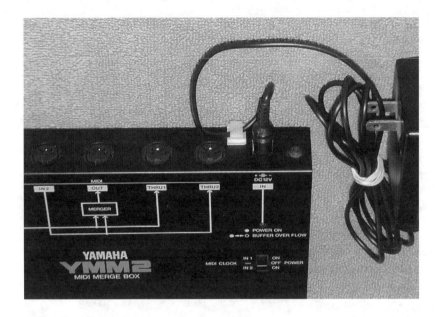

Figure 36: Power Plug Strain Relief

RUBBER CLEANER/REVITALIZER

Take a look at the pinch roller on your cassette or open reel tape deck. Is it caked with a brownish substance? That's a by-product of passing miles of tape between it and the capstan. The tape particles flake off of the tape and collect on the pinch roller. Another phenomenon with pinch rollers is that they dry out, crack and lose their elastic properties. Both of these problems can lead to flutter in your tape machine's audio recording and playback capabilities. It can also result in the tape machine munching your tape, especially in cassette machines.

The quick and inexpensive solution is to purchase a bottle of rubber cleaner/revitalizer and apply the chemical to the pinch roller. The rubber cleaner/revitalizer will clean the tape oxide particles off of the pinch roller and return the roller to its original supple condition (unless you've waited too long and the pinch roller is beyond help).

Don't use chemicals that will aggravate the poor condition of the pinch roller. Some chemicals will melt the rubber; others, such as alcohol, will tend to dry it out. I use the rubber cleaner/revitalizer every two or three months on my open reel machines and cassette decks, and it makes a noticeable difference. By the way, if your equipment has rubber drive belts and pulleys that tend to slip, the rubber cleaner/revitalizer will restore their gripping surfaces. The rubber cleaner/revitalizer also makes the pads on my Roland Octapad (a device that has 8 rubber pressure-sensitive pads that can be played with actual drum sticks to control a drum machine via MIDI) look and feel almost like new.

You may have some difficulty locating rubber cleaner/revitalizer. I certainly did. Radio Shack doesn't sell it, and neither do most of the music stores. I did some research by phone and found a store that distributes it in my area. Projector-Recorder Belt makes the product that I purchased. It is distributed by Russell Industries (3000 Lawsom Blvd, Oceanside, NY 11572). You can call them toll free at 1-800-558-9572 to order their product (part number MS-21A). Retail price is $19.95 for 8 ounces.

Russell Industries also offers the unique service of removing and replacing the old, brittle and cracked rubber on pinch rollers with a new rubber surface. If you send them your tape machine's old pinch roller, they will install a new rubber surface on it much like the retreading of an automobile tire. This is great if you own a tape machine whose manufacturer has gone out of business. It sure beats most other alternatives.

Another source for rubber cleaner/revitalizer is Caig (www.caig.com). They have a product called CaiKleen RBR for rubber rollers, parts and platens.

HEAT SHRINK, COLD SHRINK AND VELCRO

Heat shrink tubing, cold shrink tape and Velcro rate right up there with silicone glue as some of the handiest items around. Too many people still use black electrical tape in various insulation applications, when heat shrink tubing is infinitely more suitable. Heat shrink tubing has the physical property of shrinking from 25% to 75% of its original diameter after heat is applied to it. If you find yourself attempting to make or repair an electrical cable, heat shrink tubing is the perfect insulator for avoiding electrical short circuits between conductors. If you buy white heat shrink tubing, you can write on it or stamp an identifying number on it; this is then shrunken onto the particular cable to make a permanent cable tag. Need to remove the tag? Simply slit the tubing with an razor knife or scissors.

My favorite application for heat shrink tubing is in the role of strain relief for cables. Guitar cables and headphone cables are notorious for developing intermittent open circuits right at the spot where the cable goes into its connector plug. Do you ever find yourself jiggling the cable around until it makes electrical contact and then not moving so that you can get 10 seconds of crackle-free music? Me too, and that's why I now use heat shrink tubing at the normal bend point on all of my heavy use cables. I shrink a sufficient length of tubing to cover half of the connector case and about 2" of the cable, as is shown in the photo in Figure 37.

You can buy a bag of assorted heat shrink tubing at Radio Shack for less than $2 (P/N 278-1627). Heat guns are available for the purpose of shrinking the tubing, or you can use a match or lighter to shrink the tubing. However, beware of getting the flame too close to the tubing, or the tubing will melt.

Cold shrink tape is a great item to have around the studio. It is applied without the need for a heat gun, torch, lighter or match. You just wrap it around the items you want to bind together or repair. By stretching the cold shrink tape as you apply it, the tape forms a molded rubber sleeve in a few short minutes. It is great for bundling loose wires after they are routed within a cabinet or rack. To remove the cold shrink tape, just slit it with an X-acto knife or razor blade, and peel it off. You can order some from Parts Express (www.partsexpress.com) in 10' lengths of 1" wide tape in black (P/N 350-040) or white (P/N 350-042) for about $4 for each roll.

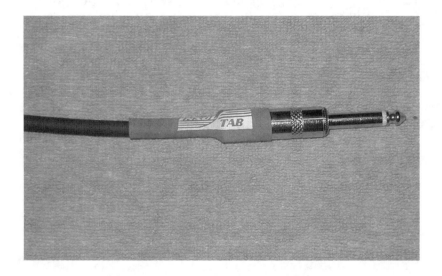

Figure 37: Cable Strain Relief

Another handy item for organizing and securing all of your studio's audio and MIDI cables is Velcro. You can get strips that have the "hooks" on one side and the "loops" on the other side of the same piece. Just wrap a short strip of this around a bundle of cables to secure them. Unlike locking cable ties, these Velcro strips are reusable. A less expensive approach is to buy some separate reels of hook and loop material at the home improvement store, then join them together using the peal and stick adhesive on their back sides. Cut these into useful lengths for re-usable cable ties.

ANTI-SKID RUBBER FEET

I've found that a fair portion of studio equipment enclosures do not have rubber feet or any way to prevent the scratching of the surface that equipment rests on. Rack mount equipment usually falls into this category, since it is meant to be held in a rack by its front panel flanges. Therefore, a problem exists if you use rack mount equipment without a rack, since it tends to slide on the table or the other equipment it rests on.

The quick and inexpensive solution to this problem is to purchase a package of small, self-adhesive rubber feet to affix to the bottom of the equipment enclosures. Radio Shack sells a package of 12 for a dollar (P/N 64-2346), or you can probably find some at your local drug store. These are particularly useful for small boxes, such as remote controls, that you don't want to slide around. I put them on the master fader and remote controller boxes that I built, and I also put them on all stacked equipment that didn't originally come with suitable anti-skid feet. Again, silicone glue is a useful alternative; just put a small dab on each corner of the bottom plate and presto— instant anti-skid feet.

MEDIA BACKUP

Hey, I don't have to mention this, do I? Apparently, I do, because not everyone makes backup copies of their media, be it floppy disk, quick disk or data cassette. After you write new software or edit your old software, make a backup copy of it. It is amazing how many people don't do this. It's all too easy to inadvertently erase a file from your computer or hit the record button of your data cassette machine, and you can kiss that data goodbye. As Murphy's Law warns, catastrophes are bound to happen, such as the tape machine mangling the data cassette, the disk drive head crashing onto the disk and wiping out both the head and the disk, magnetic particles flaking off the media leading to data drop outs, magnets and motors in proximity to the magnetic media, or.....does anyone out there have a frisky puppy? I lost a VCR remote control and a 35mm camera to my pair of Great Dane pups that mistook the remote and camera for chew toys; there's no reason why your (or my) media couldn't suffer a similar fate. The moral is this: back up that data often, and keep the backup copy in a different physical location than the original (preferably off-site). Murphy's Law always takes precedence.

TROUBLESHOOTING AND TOOLS

This section deals with basic troubleshooting, tools and techniques. You should have some low-cost tools on hand to help you solve simple home studio technical problems. There is no escape— you *will* have technical problems, because it is just the nature of the beast!

Basic Tools:

The first thing you will want to buy is a basic multimeter. This is an electronic device that can measure voltage, resistance and current. You can pick up a cheap one at Radio Shack for as little as $10. They become more sophisticated as the price goes up, adding digital readout, auto-ranging, increased accuracy, continuity beeper, diode check, capacitance and inductance measurements and more. You can use the multimeter to measure the remaining life in your batteries, continuity in your cables, and the presence of a signal on a cable.

Another item that might come in handy is a small portable amplifier with speaker. You can use this to trace a signal around your studio to see where it drops out, becomes distorted or noisy. Radio Shack sells a small 9VDC audio amp with speaker for about $12 (P/N 277-1008). This little monophonic amp has $1/8$" input and earphone jacks on it.

You will definitely want to buy a power screwdriver. Mounting and unmounting equipment in an equipment rack is a major bite without a power screwdriver.

Soldering connections is a must if you want an airtight, anti-corrosive connection. You can get soldering irons in various wattages and with various power sources (battery, AC and butane). For the electrical irons, it is good to have a switchable output (say 15 watts and 30 watts) or an adjustable tip temperature, so that you don't melt some of the more delicate connections. As usual, you will get what you pay for. Important: Do NOT use acid core solder for any electrical equipment soldered connections. Always use a 60/40 Lead/Tin Alloy rosin core solder.

A mini-flashlight and dental inspection mirror are also required items for the home studio. I bought a small dental mirror and a mini-flashlight to help in eyeballing hard to see places in and around the studio equipment. I use them to inspect the tape heads on my open reel decks, as it is easier to use the mirror than to stand on my head to view the tape heads. The dental mirror is also very useful in guiding me when I plug a cable into the rear panel of a piece of equipment that's not in direct view. After I plug in the cable, I can verify that the correct connection has been made by using the dental mirror (and the mini-flashlight if it is dark back there). You can buy an inspection mirror and a mini-flashlight at the drug store, swap meet (flea market), or at an auto supply store. If you can find an inspection mirror with an extendable shaft, then this is a better buy. The extendable inspection mirror I have has a magnet at the end of it. This is a handy addition, but I need to be sure to keep the magnet away from magnetic media and tape heads!

If you want to be able to test cables without messing with a DMM (digital multimeter), you can buy a cable tester. I've seen several different types on the market, and I own one. The reason you want to use a cable tester and not just a DMM to test cables is that it allows you to spot intermittent cables that might test OK with a DMM. With the cable tester, it is much easier to wiggle the cable around to see if the connection drops out than it is while holding DMM test leads to pins on a connector.

A good, low-cost cable tester that I recommend is the Behringer CT100 Cable Tester. (See Figure 38.) This unit runs about $35 on the street (well worth this amount) and is able to test XLR cables, RCA cables, MIDI cables, and TRS phone cables (which means Tip/Ring/Sleeve) in 1/4", 1/8" and TT types. It is able to test for continuity, intermittent connections, phantom power in microphone cables, and ground shield integrity. You can even test cables that are installed without removing the cable from service (although it requires a shorting plug at the far end of the cable). The unit also has integral 440 Hz and 1 kHz test tone generators on it with output levels of +4 dbu, -10dbV or –50dbV. This unit is very sophisticated for $35 (it has its own microprocessor inside), and I am impressed by the quality of the heavy-duty construction. If you can't find one locally, you can order one online from www.bswusa.com, which is where I bought mine.

Figure 38: Inexpensive Cable Tester

Another cable tester you might want to check out is the Rolls CT1 Cable Tester (~$45). It can test ¼" TS, ¼" TRS, RCA, XLR and MIDI cables. The Whirlwind Tester can test cables with any combination of XLR, ¼" or RCA phono plugs for shorts, opens or phase reversals. It costs about $65. You can find these items online at American Musical Supply (www.americanmusical.com) and other places.

You can buy cheap portable CD players now for about $25. These make great portable test generators! You can buy a test CD, or you can record your own test CD-R using tones from a synthesizer. To track down potential problems, you can patch in the CD player at various places in your studio. This is where a patch panel comes in handy!

Troubleshooting Techniques:

Now that you have some of the basic tools required for troubleshooting, let's look at some troubleshooting techniques. But before we start, let's learn a couple of basic safety rules. If you are going to take the cover off of a unit and poke around inside of it, make sure it is unplugged from the AC power. Let the unit sit unplugged for at least 5 minutes, so that dangerous voltages can dissipate or discharge within the unit. If you are going to take voltage measurements inside of a unit that is plugged in and powered up, keep one hand in your pocket to prevent the accidental formation of a short circuit path across your heart. Make sure you have adequate lighting to see exactly what is going on. All experienced technicians and electrical engineers follow these simple rules, and you should also.

There is an electrical engineer named Bob Pease who works for National Semiconductor and writes a technical column for *Electronic Design* magazine. He has many years of troubleshooting experience, and he recommends some basic questions you should ask yourself when you first start troubleshooting a piece of equipment or a system. Did the unit or system ever work properly? If it did, what was it doing just before it stopped working? What was it doing while it failed? What are the symptoms that have appeared to tell you the unit is not working properly? Determining the answers to these questions can help point you down an informed path to successful troubleshooting.

There are also some simple and obvious things to check out right away. Are all the units in the signal path plugged into AC power? Are the power strips energized that are supplying power to those units? Are any of the circuit breakers on the power strips tripped? Are all of the appropriate equipment power switches on? One handy item that I use to check for the presence of AC power is the wireless AC Voltage Sensor (Radio Shack P/N 22-103), which is pictured in the center of Figure 1. This is a wireless device that you can hold near power cables, power strips, power switches, and fuses to detect the presence of 70 V to 440 V without any direct electrical contact to the circuit. Very handy!

One other thing you can check regarding power is the fuse on the equipment. Most power amplifiers, larger electronic units such as rack-mount samplers, and even some speakers have fuses on them. To check the fuse, first unplug the AC power cord from the wall, unscrew the cap that holds the fuse, remove the fuse, and test the fuse itself for continuity. Sometimes a fuse will look OK to the naked eye, but it will not have electrical continuity. To check for electrical continuity, select the "Continuity" setting on your DMM (if it has one), touch both ends of the fuse with the two probes, and listen for the buzz that indicates continuity. You can also check for continuity by selecting "Ohms" or "Resistance" on your DMM and looking for a reading near zero ohms. Be sure the replacement fuse you buy is the exact kind of fuse that originally failed. Be aware that there are slow-blow fuses (protecting the circuit until a sustained overload condition exists) and quick-acting fuses (protecting the circuit until a large transient goes through the fuse). Never bypass the fuse, as this could cause a fire in the equipment. In general, fuses just don't blow for the heck of it. There may be a serious fault condition on that piece of equipment, and the fuse is interrupting power to the unit to prevent damage to other circuitry within the device. If you replace the fuse, and it immediately blows again (or if a circuit breaker keeps tripping after you reset it), then you may have a serious problem that requires professional technical service help.

If it looks like everything has power to it, then try pushing the reset switch (if the unit has one) or cycling the power on and off. If the unit has batteries associated with it, take the batteries out and test them with your DMM. If they are weak, replace them. Be aware that some processor-based equipment (especially synthesizers, drum machines and samplers) have internally mounted batteries that keep the contents of memory backed-up. These batteries will become discharged over time, although for Lithium-type batteries this could take years. You will need to open the unit up and replace the battery or take the unit in for service. A clue that this has happened is that all of your presets have disappeared, or anything you save to memory starts to act flaky. See the recommendation on battery-backed RAM in the last chapter of this book.

Other obvious things to check are disconnected cables in the signal path. Some cables may look connected, but have actually been pulled partly out due to stresses and strains from gravity, vibration, moving equipment around, etc.

If the power and the cables seem to be in good operational order, then you are going to have to dig in and perform some signal tracing to see which specific unit is the culprit. In the electrical engineering field, we call this the divide and conquer approach. For the sake of argument, let's say you have an awful crackling noise in the final audio signal you are monitoring. And let's also say that you have a microphone connected to an outboard microphone preamp, then to a compressor, then to a mixer which has a couple of outboard effects devices connected to it, then finally to a multi-track cassette recorder. You are listening to the audio at the cassette headphone jack and you are getting a crackling noise. Now what?

The best thing to do is divide the system interconnection in half and pick a point to monitor. Let's pick the output of the compressor. You need to listen to the output of the compressor directly to see if there is noise in the signal at that point. You can use the small 9VDC-operated audio amp with speaker from Radio Shack (see the "Basic Tools" section) to listen to the signal output to see if it has noise in it. You could also patch directly to that point with a headphone amplifier, if you have one. You could even plug the output of your compressor directly into one input channel of your cassette multi-track and listen to the headphones there. If the noise does not appear at the output of your compressor, then you know the noise is entering the system after that point, so the compressor and all of the equipment connected before the compressor should be OK. Therefore, the noise must be coming from the mixer, one of the outboard effects devices, or the cassette multi-track.

Next, check the output of the mixer. Is the noise there? If not, then it is being generated in the multi-track cassette deck. A possible culprit is a noisy volume control (also called a pot or potentiometer). If the noise is at the output of the mixer, then check one of the Effects Sends to one of the outboard effects devices. If there is no noise there, then it is possible that one of the effects devices is causing the noise. You can make sure by disconnecting the outboard effects device entirely from the mixer and see if the noise disappears from the mixer output. If it does, then the outboard effects device is the culprit. Again, check for a noisy volume control on the outboard effects device. In this divide and conquer manner, you can narrow the search down to finally one component in the system and then take action to rectify that problem. This is one more reason why a patch panel can be such a handy device in the studio!

Noisy Volume Controls:

To solve the noisy volume control or noisy switch problem, you will need to purchase a spray can of contact cleaner and also a lubricant. Start out by removing any dust and dirt from the slider, pot or switch with a high pressure blast of dry air from an air duster can (such as Caig's DustALL). Next clean the fader or pot with Caig's MCL 5% solution spray. This will remove the rest of the oxidation and contaminants. The way this chemical works is that the spray loosens the dirt or oxidation from the contacts, and the evaporative action of the chemical then carries the contaminants away from the electrical contacts. As you spray it into the volume control, twist or slide the pot through its full range of motion several times to help loosen the contaminants. Finally, you will need to apply Caig's CailLube MCL 100% solution. Apply the CailLube MCL 100% solution the day after you apply the 5% solution. The CailLube MCL 100% solution is specifically made to improve conductivity within the fader, pot or switch and to lubricate conductive plastic or carbon strips of material. Using the wrong product here will deteriorate the materials inside the fader or pot, and your troubles will actually increase. For cleaning the contacts of a connector, try Caig's DeoxIT. DeoxIT is made for metal materials (not plastic), so don't use it in a fader or pot. You can get these products directly from Caig on their website (www.caig.com), and search their extensive database of electrical cleaning information. You also can order these chemicals from www.mcmelectonics.com or www.partsexpress.com, among other places.

Intermittent Signal Connection Problems:

Oxidation is the bane of the home studio owner. You will find that many noise and intermittent signal problems are caused simply by oxidation on signal connection points. The best way to fix this problem (temporarily at least) is to unplug the connector and then re-seat it again. One company (D.W. Electrochemicals LTD., www.stabilant.com or (905) 508-7500) markets a clear polymer liquid called Stabilant 22 (or, if you insist, it's a Modified Polyoxypropylene-Polyoxyethylene Block Polymer of the Polyglycol family), which when applied to connectors, switches, and pots will help prevent oxidation and enhance metal to metal contact. The actual description of the chemical action is complicated, but in their own marketing words, "Stabilant 22 is an initially non-conductive amorphous-semiconductive block polymer that when used in thin films within contacts acts under the effect of the electrical field and switches to a conductive state. The electric field gradient at which this occurs is established is (sic) during its manufacture so that the material will remain non-conductive. Thus, when applied to electromechanical contacts, Stabilant 22 provides the connection reliability of a soldered joint without bonding the contacting surfaces together!" I have used this chemical in my studio, and it definitely does help. A little bit of it goes a long way. This product was originally marketed under the name Tweek many years ago. If you visit their web site, you will find a ton of different very interesting application notes. This Stabilant 22 is really a useful chemical for home studios, computer systems, automotive electronics, and even ROM chips or other electrical chips in chip sockets.

Tape Deck Drive Problems:

If you have tape decks of any sort (reel/reel, cassette, VCR, and even the old 8-Track Cartridge format!), you will eventually run into a problem with the tape drive not operating correctly. These types of problems manifest themselves as excessive wow/flutter, inability to hold a constant tape speed, or just plain, old refusal to move the tape at all. The reason for these types of problems could be one or more of several reasons. The drive motor may have burned up or become unstable. You will need to replace the motor or have a trained technician replace it for you. Another potential cause of problems is that the pinch roller may not be making proper contact with the capstan. The pinch roller is the small round rubber puck that presses the tape up against the capstan to provide a constant velocity drive for the tape. This is an adjustment best left for the technician.

However, the problem could also be that the drive belt that connects the drive motor to the flywheel has become old and stretched. (Hey, it happens to the best of us.) Usually, this is something you can fix yourself. If your deck is out of warranty, remove the screws that hold on the case cover. Try to play a tape while you observe the drive motor, the rubber pulley belt and the flywheel. If the motor is turning, but the rubber pulley belt and/or the flywheel is not turning correctly (slipping or not turning at all), the problem is most likely that the belt has become too stretched to make proper pulley contact under the flywheel load. By jove, you need a new drive belt! The best approach is to buy yourself a belt gauge (now!), so that you know what kind of replacement belt to buy (later when you actually need it!). You can get a belt gauge at either MCM Electronics (www.mcmelectronics.com) or Parts Express (www.partsexpress.com) for less than six dollars. With the belt gauge, you can figure out what type of belt to order (in terms of belt width, thickness and inside circumference). You can then order a replacement belt at either MCM Electronics or Parts Express. Most are less than a buck. (Hint: at that price, buy two or more, so you have one for next time!) I just went through this procedure to replace the drive belt in my Teac V770 cassette deck. If this procedure doesn't work for you, then take your deck to a repair technician, but at least you tried the low-cost, DIY approach first.

HOME STUDIO SECURITY

As you start amassing the equipment in your home studio, you will rapidly get to the point where you need to start thinking about security of your studio and the equipment in it. You can spend a relatively small amount on home security and get reasonable results. You can also easily spend a boatload of money on security without too much effort. Probably the best approach is to get a system that is easy to install yourself, simple to maintain yourself, and easy to operate. A good place to start the search is at www.smarthome.com.

Smarthome sells a wireless starter security system for $179.99 (P/N 7301), and I recommend this one, as it is easy to install yourself, simple to maintain yourself, and easy to operate. Plus it gives very good results. You can see it (and order it) online at http://www.smarthome.com/7301.html. The unit is a 7-piece 16-zone wireless security system includes a dialer and control console, one wireless PIR motion detector, two wireless door or window sensors, a handheld wireless remote control, a key chain remote control, batteries, phone cable, and security warning stickers. When this unit detects a break-in, this system will sound a built-in 85dB siren, optional extra-loud sirens inside or outside, and flash X10-controlled lights. In addition, it can call up to 4 different telephone numbers and play back a previously recorded message to warn you (or whomever) that a break-in has occurred. You can have it call your cell phone, your work phone, and a couple of neighbors, if you want. On top of that, after the security dialer calls you, you can push a button on your phone and listen in on a sensitive microphone from wherever you are to hear what is going on in your house. The system is incredibly easy to install with only a screwdriver required. The system also supports the X-10 protocol. (X-10 is a signaling protocol that travels over your power lines to control up to 256 remotely located modules to do what you want them to do.) You can add on to the system as required (the PIR motion detectors are very nice), and all of the accessories are basically plug and play. This is probably the best value-for-money security system available anywhere.

You can go beyond the cost-effective security system mentioned above and add surveillance cameras to your home and studio, but now we are talking increased cost. I elected to do this, but I used to be an engineering manager at a company that designed and developed video surveillance equipment, so it is a professional interest of mine. You can get some low-cost, wireless, color or black-and-white cameras at www.x10.com. You can easily set up these wireless cameras to be remotely switched on and off via X-10 commands. You can record the surveillance video on your VCR or computer, or you can digitize the video on your computer and send it off-site somewhere via the Internet. In fact, if you have a day job somewhere else, you can send the digitized surveillance video to your computer at work and monitor it in a little window on your computer's desktop display. Truly, you can spend as much for security and surveillance as you want.

Here is my big warning regarding low-cost wireless video cameras: Unscrambled wireless video is easily intercepted and eavesdropped by anyone in the near vicinity with the proper receiver. This holds true for wireless audio, also. So, if you are sending the audio from your studio around your house wirelessly, or if you have a wireless camera pointed at areas inside of your house, be aware that you may not be the only person receiving the signal. If you are worried about privacy issues, then video signals within your house should be sent over RG-58 video coax cable, and not broadcast through the air.

Another step you can take is to engrave your name and driver's license number on the back or bottom of your studio equipment. This will help you recover your item if the police find it. Be advised that this may reduce the resale value of the equipment in some cases, especially for a collector's musical instrument. You should also take pictures of your equipment and keep the pictures with the original equipment sales receipts off-site somewhere. This will help with insurance claims resulting from fire or burglary loss, and it will also give the police something to go on to recover stolen equipment.

Here are some additional vendors of security-related equipment. If you want to assemble your own security or video system, you can check out these web sites.

- CCTV Outlet (www.cctvoutlet.com)
- Home Security Store (http://www.norcoalarms.com/)
- Matco (www.matco.com)
- Polaris Industries (www.polarisusa.com)
- Resources Unlimited (www.resunltd4u.com)
- You Do It Security (http://www.youdoitsecurity.com/)

HOME STUDIO INSURANCE

There are several different kinds of problems that might befall you and your studio that insurance should be able to cover. For the home studio, these are problems such as fire, theft, casualty, liability and (if you use your personal home studio as a project studio business to make money) loss of business.

If you want to protect the equipment in your studio, then fire insurance, casualty insurance and theft insurance are the particular types you will need. If you want to protect yourself against others who will sue you for personal or property damage they suffer in your studio, then you will need liability insurance. If you want to protect your studio's stream of financial income against loss when your studio is down (due to fire or whatever), then you will want business interruption loss insurance.

You will need to take an inventory of the equipment in your studio and be aware of the value of that equipment. The overall value of your equipment can change as time progresses. Vintage studio equipment (Moog Minimoog Synthesizer, Gibson Les Paul, etc.) can appreciate in value. Other equipment will depreciate in value. Plus, you may have purchased additional equipment during the year to add to the overall total studio value. Make sure you have the proper insurance policy amount that covers the real value (replacement value) of your equipment. It may require an additional insurance rider to make sure this happens. To be safe, contact your insurance agent.

Make sure that you read specifically what *is* covered and what is *not* covered in any given policy. Insurance companies are very specific about what they do and do not cover. If you live in areas where there are hurricanes, floods, or earthquakes, make sure your policy calls out those specific disasters and defines what constitutes a valid claim regarding them.

Equipment that has been stolen might be covered under burglary, theft or robbery insurance. There is a difference in the definitions among the three, so make sure that you understand what is and is not being covered. Burglary occurs when someone breaks into your house and steals an item. Robbery occurs when you are put in some sort of danger (or perceived danger) and property is taken from you. Theft can be as simple as your "buddy" grabbing a microphone and sticking it in his jacket when you aren't looking.

If something is stolen out of your studio, will the police ever recover it? Maybe, but don't hold your breath. In an effort to substantiate any insurance claims or police actions, I always take pictures of all of my equipment, keep a copy of all purchase receipts and invoices, and record all serial numbers. I then keep all of this information off of the premises of my home studio in a safe place. I update the list once a year.

References:
Dieguez, Richard, "Insuring Your Studio", *Home & Studio Recording*, May, 1989, pp 57-59.

BEST PRACTICES IN THE STUDIO

There are many good practices to acquire in the studio that just make things go better in the long run. I will discuss some of these in no particular order of importance. Does it take more time or involve discipline to do some of these things? Unfortunately, it does. However, I have found them to be worth the effort.

Keep all of the cables in your studio (analog audio signal, digital data, speaker, power) as short as possible. Generally, this reduces the possibility of inducing noise into the cable or of signals radiating out of the cable and interfering with other electronic circuits. Also, it a good idea to leave uncoiled the extra lengths of the cable that you do use. Better to let it fall in a random fashion, which reduces the chance of noise coupling.

Label all of the cables in your studio. In my studio, I label both ends of the cable at the connector. Generally, I use Maco Color Coding Labels (MS828-RG or similar). These sticky-back labels are pre-cut to be 0.5" x 1.75", and they come 21 to a sheet. I use a fine-point Sharpie pen to write the signal name on the label (e.g., 8-track Input 1), then I fold the label over the cable and press the two sticky surfaces together. I have found that over time, the adhesive on these labels can release on a hot and humid day. That is why I also fold a 3/4" wide piece of Scotch tape over the label (sticky back -to- sticky back) to fix it in place. The Scotch tape also gives the label strength, so it can't be torn off as I pull cables around. If you are really a stickler for organization, you can buy some laser printer labels that are specifically made for desktop printers. Then you can use a word processing application to type out the signal names that go on each label and automatically print them.

Keep your food and drinks off of the equipment. This is just common sense. I once built a Stingz-n-Thingz Synthesizer kit from PAiA. After a few years, I sold it to some guy who accidentally spilled a Coke into it about a month later. It permanently ceased operation after that. The acids and sugars in some drinks can physically damage circuit boards and cause electrical failure in energized circuits.

Use dust covers on all your equipment, especially desktop units with exposed slider pots and switches. Dust will find its way into these pots and switches causing intermittent operation, crackling, noise, dropouts, distortion, etc.

Never pull on a cord or cable to unplug it. This will most definitely ruin your cables and result in intermittent operation or complete failure of the cable. Always grasp the connector body to unplug a cable.

You will find that keeping detailed tracking sheets for each song is must, especially if you do multi-track recording. There is simply no way to remember all that information in your head from multiple recording sessions, especially if you come back a week, a month or a year later to finish the recordings. (In fact, it is best to have a written tracking plan before you ever start to record, so you have some sort of roadmap to follow.) The tracking sheets can hold information such as date and time, song name, key and time signature (or beats/minute), musicians, instruments used, microphones used, effects/equalization programs and settings, level settings, pan settings, and any other notes to help you figure out just what it was you recorded and how you did it. Track sheets are a left-brain tool to help offload information so you can focus on the right-brain creative aspects of music and recording.

Label and mark your tapes, disks, floppies, and any other media you use to record. Clearly designate whether they are masters or safety copies or practice tapes or whatever. This can save time and heartache later.

Keep all magnetic recording media away from magnets, unshielded speakers, headphones, transformers, CRTs, TVs and even speaker cables. All of these devices have an electric or magnetic field associated with them that can degrade or outright destroy the information contained on magnetic media.

Bundle together audio cables, and keep those bundles physically separated from AC power cabling, speaker cabling, fluorescent lights, and AC magnetic fields (motors, etc.).

If you are recording to a tape-based medium (reel-to-reel, cassette, PCM video, DAT, etc.), then fast forward to the end of the tape and then back to the beginning again before you ever record on the tape. This will help relieve tape packing strains on the spool and will generally result in a more even flow of tape off the spool when you record.

After several hours of intensive listening in the studio, your ears will become tired. They will start lying to you! First of all, try not to crank the audio to 11 all the time. I know it sounds and feels good, but not everyone is going to listen to it at that volume. A better strategy is to crank it up only when you need to check the mix or verify certain aspects of the mix at high sound pressure levels. You should generally monitor the ongoing activities at a reasonable volume. Be ready to give your ears a quiet break every so often, so they can relax and rejuvenate. Take a look around at all the musicians over 40 who are suffering from permanent hearing loss and learn from their mistakes.

Speaking of hearing loss, you can get a free hearing test over the telephone on any weekday. The phone number to call is 1-800-222-EARS any Monday through Friday between the hours of 9AM and 5PM Eastern Time. If you are not concerned about hearing loss or continually hearing sounds that aren't actually there (called tinnitus), you should be!

Keep a fire extinguisher on hand in your studio. It should be of the type that can extinguish electrical fires (Type C). It would be a shame to have your equipment burn up while you dance around wishing you had a Type C fire extinguisher nearby.

OTHER MISCELLANEOUS TIPS

Tips for Burning CD-Rs and CD-RWs:

If you have a standalone CD-R/RW recorder, then you generally will not have too much trouble burning quality audio disks. Remember to record with the highest signal level while being careful NOT to run the signal into the distortion zone above 0dB. Also, some standalone recorders are picky about what kind of disk type you use in them. Consult your owner's manual for the preferred disk type. You can buy *data* CD-R disks, and you can also buy *audio* CD-R disks. My standalone recorder uses both equally well, but some recorders only work with audio CD-R disks. The data disks are usually much less expensive because they don't have the additional royalty fee to record companies that audio disks have.

If you use a CD-R or CD-RW burner in your computer to make digital audio disks, you can generally use any type of disk (data or audio) with successful results. The most prevalent problem with burning digital disks on a computer is the buffer underrun error. Basically, this means that the digital data was held up for some reason when the computer was expecting it to be available to write onto the disk with the laser. The CD-R and CD-RW writing operation is a continuous process that can't tolerate any interruptions in the data flow to the disk. When this happens, the disk is typically ruined (especially for Disk-at-Once writing formats). To avoid this problem, there are certain precautions you can take in the way you set up and operate your computer.

- To hold the audio data files, use the fastest hard drive you have available on the computer. When you buy a hard drive for your computer, but the fastest one you can find.
- Consider creating what is known as an image on the hard drive. The disk burning program will first write all of the CD-R tracks onto the hard drive, thus creating the image. Then when the disk is to be burned, the computer can more

easily read the target files off of the hard drive image rather than trying to grab the data from various points on the hard drive and assemble them in the proper order. Your disk burning software manual should discuss this.

- Turn off any screen saver software. Turn off any software that tends to go out to the Internet on its own and look for software updates (anti-virus programs are notorious for this).

- When my computer is in the process of burning an audio CD-R or CD-RW, I do not launch any other programs or even type on the keyboard until the disk is done and the TOC (table of contenets) is written. I make fewer drink coasters that way. I suggest you do the same.

Keeping a Notebook:

As you gain more and more experience at miking, tracking, bouncing, monitoring, mixing, mastering, and other studio activities, it helps to keep a logbook or notebook. In the notebook, keep notes as to what settings worked in certain instances, how you were able to effectively use your various microphones in certain situations, complicated procedures for editing tracks, types of audio tape that work well in your machine, outside resources and phone numbers or web site URLs that were of help, etc. The idea is to have a ready reference that you can access one or more years downstream, when there is no way you are going to remember those certain little details that made life in the studio easier last time. And you thought you were done with notebooks when you left high school?

Another big reason for the notebook is that home studio recording can get complex. Figuring out how to operate effects processors, digital recorders, synchronizers, computer-based recording programs, sequencers, MIDI-related commands, large mixers, and the myriad other devices in the studio is largely a left brain exercise. It takes logic, reason and a fair amount of studying the owner's manuals. Unfortunately, the creative aspects associated with writing and performing music are largely a right brain function. If you are doing everything by yourself in the studio, you will be jumping back and forth between left brain and right brain activities. This can easily kill the spontaneity of a musical recording session. If you have made notes in a notebook (or in the blank pages at the end of this book) on complex funtions that you must execute or recreate every time you are in the studio, you can spend less time scratching your head in left brain mode and more time creating music in right brain mode. Believe me, it makes a difference when you don't have to take a 1 hour break to page through a technical manual in the middle of a recording session.

Listening to Your Mix on Other Speakers:
You may have monitor speakers and headphones in your studio, but it helps to listen to your mixes on several different sets of speakers (especially speakers with which you are already familiar). One way to do this is to record the mix onto cassette or some other media, then go into your living room and play it on that system. A more elegant solution is to use a wireless transmitter/receiver pair to transmit the mix wirelessly to your stereo in the living room. There are a couple of products out on the market that will let you accomplish this. The folks at X10 have a system that can transmit video in addition to stereo audio over a 2.4 GHz wireless link for up to 100 feet. This system costs $70 (http://www.x10.com/products/x10 vk57a.htm). Another competing system is the Kima KS-110 Wireless Audio System (http://store.yahoo.com/ourstore-2000/kimkswirauds.html). This 900 MHz wireless system also sells for around $70, and Kima claims that it has a range of up to 1000 feet.

Tips For Better Noise Reduction:
If your recordings are suffering bleed from sync noise on an adjacent track on your tape recorder, try decreasing some of the low frequencies in the sync signal before recording it to tape. If you have an effects box in the signal line but are not currently using it, either physically re-

move it from the signal flow path or electrically remove it with the bypass switch on the unit. Replace cables that create crackle or signal dropouts. If you have a cable tester, use the tester to verify that the cables are really bad (i.e., the cable could be OK, but the audio jack is coated with oxidation). Use good cables with adequate shielding. Don't buy cables just because they are inexpensive. (I started out this way, and believe me, it's not worth it.) See the sources I have listed in this book for low-cost, high-quality cables. Strive to set your volume pots around the 7 level (on a scale from 0 to 10). This will prevent too much noise from inadequate signal levels or too much distortion from excessive signal levels. See the section entitled "Setting Gain Structure" in this book.

Automatic Key Depresser:

One problem I always had when playing my keyboards in the studio was trying to hold down a key on the keyboard while simultaneously adjusting knobs of other equipment in the rack or on the mixer. If the keyboard is not near the equipment to be adjusted, then there is a physics problem! My solution to this was to use a roll of pennies to hold down the key on the keyboard while I adjusted the other downstream electronics for the perfect levels and sound. Of course, this requires a keyboard sound with sustain and 50 cents in pennies. You can use a roll of quarters if you want, but this book is supposed to be about low-cost problem solvers!

Low-cost Light Show Controller:

As some of you will no doubt travel with your equipment to perform gigs, I will throw in this idea for a super low-cost light show controller. This simple idea will allow you to turn on, turn off or dim up to eight spot or flood lights (or any other kind of incandescent light up to 500 watts) from a remote location. This is especially handy if you are a solo performer who controls his or her own lights and sound mix. Basically, this idea uses an X-10 Mini Controller to send commands over the AC power line to up to eight separate X-10 receivers. X-10 is a signaling protocol that travels over your power lines to control up to

256 remotely located modules to do what you want them to do. (These X-10 modules are just excellent and low cost, and I highly recommend you go to www.x10.com or www.smarthome.com to explore them further.) The X-10 protocol is configured as 16 different house codes (A through P) with each house code able to control 16 different module codes (1 through 16). To set up this system, plug up to 500 watts of lighting into each one of 8 receiver modules (Radio Shack P/N 61-2684 at $13.99 each or buy from X-10 or Smarthome). Set all of the receiver modules to the same house code (e.g., K). Now set each receiver module to a *different* module code from 1 through 8. Plug up to 500 watts of (non-fluorescent) lighting into each receiver module and configure them on a light stand or whatever you use to hold and aim them. Now, set the house code on the Mini Controller to the same house code you used on the receiver modules (K in this example). After you plug in the Mini Controller, you can now turn on, off or dim each of the 8 lights independently. Note that for this signaling scheme to operate correctly, all of the receiver modules and the Mini Controller must be on the same branch of power after the transformer (i.e., the same winding of 115VAC power off of the transformer). You will not be able to control the receiver modules if they are on a different branch of 115VAC power than the Mini Controller.

Pertaining to Analog Tapes and Recorders:

I purposely did not go into things pertaining to analog tape and analog tape recorders (reel-to-reel and cassette) such as the basics of analog recording, how an analog tape deck operates, cleaning the tape heads, mastering, editing, splicing analog tape, tape loops, and tape echo. That is because someone at UCSC has already done an excellent job of explaining all that information in easily understandable terms. And the cost is just right; it is free! Go to this web site and print out a copy of the text for yourself: http://arts.ucsc.edu/ems/music/equipment/ analog_recorders/Analog_Recorders.html.

Pertaining to Recording Music to Tape:

There is a free magazine you can get called the *Tape Op* magazine. Go to www.tapeop.com and sign up for it. *Tape Op* bills itself as the Creative Music Recording Web Site. They have some excellent articles in their magazines, and more unpublished articles online. This is another good way for you to learn more about recording in general. They also have links to manufacturers, recording resources and information, duplication services, recording studios and mastering studios. Plus, they are solidly behind the DIY (Do-It-Yourself) philosophy, which I wholeheartedly agree with. You don't often get something good for free, but here is an opportunity.

Keeping Track of Signals on Mixer Channels:

A cheap and foolproof way to help during mixdown is to cut a 1/2" or 3/4" strip of paper and tape it to the bottom of the mixer just under the faders (linear potentiometers). Write the name of the signals on that strip of paper under each fader (e.g., Bkgnd Vocals, 12 string, Bass, Kick drum, Snare, etc.). This helps to make adjusting the faders a breeze during mixdown.

Getting Convincing Guitar Sound from a Keyboard:

One thing that has always been hard to do is to get a convincing electric guitar sound from a synthesizer or sampler. This is especially difficult when playing (or trying to play) guitar chords on the keyboard. Here is an approach that has worked well for me.

First of all, you have to approach this idea with a guitarist's mentality. When guitarists strum a chord, they don't hit all of the strings at the same time, so playing a chord on the keyboard where you strike all of the keys at the same time is not going to simulate real guitar strumming. Also, an up strum hits the strings in a reverse order than a down strum, and the two techniques sound differently. Oberheim made a device called the Strummer. It is a MIDI processor that takes in chords played on a piano-like MIDI keyboard and then restructures them to mimic an up or down strum on a 6-string or 12-string guitar. The Strummer is no longer being manufactured, but you can pick up used units using the sources I've given elsewhere in this book. The Strummer is a great little programmable MIDI processor.

The Strummer is not the full answer, though, to getting a convincing guitar sound from your synthesizer or sampler. On a sampler, it certainly helps to start out with a sampled electric guitar sound. On a synthesizer, you will need to program it to simulate an electric guitar sound, even if it is just a clean guitar sound (no distortion or effects on it). Next, you will need one of the little guitar amp/cabinet modeling processor boxes (e.g., DigiTech Genesis 1, DigiTech Genesis 3, DigiTech GNX1, DigiTech GNX2, Zoom 606, Zoom GFX707, Zoom GFX8, Zoom GFX4, Johnson J Station, Korg AX1G, Korg AX100G, Korg AX1500G, Boss ME-33, Boss GT-6, Yamaha DG Stomp, Yamaha AG Stomp, Line 6 Pod 2.0, or Line 6 Pod Pro). These digital effects boxes contain algorithms that simulate how a guitar amp and speaker transform the clean guitar sound before you hear it. Most of them also have other slick effects such as wah-wah pedals and various distortion effects. Now, you can make some sounds that start to approach what you hear when a Stratocaster plays through an amp and speaker. Play the MIDI keyboard into the Strummer. Program the Strummer to restructure the chords to mimic guitar strumming. Then, connect the Strummer's MIDI output to the sampler or synthesizer that is providing the basic guitar sound. Run the output of that synthesizer or sampler into the guitar amp/cabinet modeling processor. The output of that processor should sound like a real guitar rig. This setup has provided hours and hours of enjoyment and experimentation for me, especially since I am not a guitar player. You aren't going to put Eric Clapton out of business, but you will now be able to play convincing guitar progressions.

Understanding Guitar Effects:

If you are new to the world of guitars or you are trying to make your keyboard samples sound more guitar-like, there is a good web site that explains much of this in relatively easy to understand terms. To start, the Guitar Effects Web Page (www.geofex.com) has some great information pertaining to guitars. Plus, they have tons of DIY projects, circuits, schematics, PCB layouts, and wiring diagrams for the brave musician or audio engineer who wants to dig in and build things for themselves. If you dig a little bit deeper into their site, you come to www.geofex.com/efffxfaq/fzorder.htm. This page gives some descriptions of what effects, such as distortion, equalization, time delays, phasers, chorus, reverb and echo will do to the audio signal. In addition, they discuss what happens when you put one particular effect in front of another one (e.g., putting the compressor before the distortion, or the distortion before the compressor).

Large Keyboard Support Stand:

I have a large 88-key keyboard controller that is almost 5' long. I finally found a great way to support it in my studio. I purchased two of the little oak ice chest stands (they were used before electric refrigerators to hold ice to keep food cold) at a nearby furniture store. These oak ice chests are about 24"H x 22"W x 17"D, and have a front access door. I positioned them about 3' apart and set the keyboard across the top of them. They hold the keyboard at the perfect height for me to play it while seated. As an added bonus, I now have a place to store all of my owner's manuals and studio documentation inside of each latching compartment in the ice chests.

Free Mastering Booklet:

Disc Makers (www.discmakers.com) offers a free 36-page booklet called *Making a Great Master*. The booklet discusses the various analog and digital sources for master recordings, preparation and handling of the master, and mastering to CD, cassette and vinyl. You can get this and other booklets (*The Independent Musician's Survival Guide*, and *The Musician's Guide to the Web*) by calling 1-800-468-9353 or by directing your web browser to www.discmakers.com/mix).

Sharing MP3 Files:

MP3 is a lossy audio compression standard available for reducing the size of AIFF or WAV audio files on your computer. The idea is to compress the file size to about $1/10$ the size of the uncompressed audio file, so that the file can be shipped more efficiently around on the Internet. Of course, the sound quality of the audio is somewhat compromised, but that is the tradeoff for a smaller file size.

You may already have a software program on your computer that can encode an AIFF or WAV audio file into an MP3 file. For example, on my PC, MP3 conversion software was included with my SoundBlaster Audigy Platinum system. Check the software that came with the audio hardware for your PC to determine if you have anything that can convert uncompressed audio files to the MP3 format. If you don't have any MP3 encoding software, then try downloading some freeware or shareware off of the Internet for this purpose. A good place to start is www.jumbo.com. Go to that site, click on MP3, and then click on Encoders/Decoders. If you don't find what you like there, then do a search on Google for "MP3 encoder."

Once you have your songs encoded into MP3 format, you can post them to the web. Some good sites for doing this are www.mp3.com, www.yourmp3.net, www.amp3.com, www.homegrownmp3.com, www.musicbuilder.com, www.iuma.com, and www.garageband.com. For a more complete list of sites where you can post your own MP3 files, go to http://www2.bitstream.net/~weis0205/mp3.html.

Can't Sing In Tune?

One device that has really impressed me is the Antares ATR-1a Autotune Processor. This device can automatically correct the pitch of any solo vocal or instrumental track in real time, and it does so without distortion or sonic artifacts. I have one in my studio, and it works very well. You can configure the device to know what key you are (supposed to be) singing or playing in, or you can tell it specifically what off-pitch notes to correct via MIDI. A software-only version of the algorithm is available as a plug-in for various computer software applications also. You can learn more about this device at Antares' web site (http://antares-systems.com). They have also just come out with a new device called the Vocal Producer that includes the Autotune Processor along with microphone modeling and other vocal processing functions in one box. If you are into karaoke and can't sing in tune, this might be the processor to straighten out your crooning.

Shielding Your Monitors (non-invasive method):

Given the choice (and the money), it is always best to buy shielded monitors for your studio. These contain a ferromagnetic material that stops the magnetic field surrounding the magnets and voice coil in the speakers from coupling into other external equipment (such as a nearby computer CRT). Hint: don't ever store your magnetic media on top of your unshielded speakers; over time, the stray magnetic field can scramble the contents on your magnetic media. The ferromagnetic material will also prevent other external signals (such as from a nearby CRT!) from coupling into your speakers and causing an annoying hum. You can take steps to build your own ferromagnetic shield if you own unshielded speakers. Buy a sheet of ferromagnetic material (iron or steel) and cut it into a size that is slightly larger than the speaker. (You can identify a ferromagnetic material as the metal to which a magnet is attracted. Aluminum is not a ferromagnetic material.) Place the ferromagnetic material next to the speaker and in between the speaker and the offending piece of equipment (e.g., computer CRT). Grounding the ferromagnetic material may help with the shielding. You can run some 18-gauge lamp cord from the ferromagnetic shield to the center screw in your AC outlet cover. (Make sure the center screw is really grounded first!)

References:
Campbell, Gary Alan, "Questions and Answers", *Electronic Musician*, April 1994, p97.

Shielding Your Monitors (invasive method):
Another idea you can try for shielding audio monitors is to use a bucking magnet. This idea involves opening up the speaker cabinet (which will void your monitor's warranty) and installing a bucking magnet on the rear of each speaker. A bucking magnet has the opposite magnetic polarity as the magnet in the speaker that surrounds the voice coil. So, when you glue the bucking magnet to the back of the speaker, the net effect is to reduce or cancel out the free-air magnetic field from the speaker's magnet. This should not affect the speaker's ability to interact with the internal voice coil, but it will affect the externally radiated magnetic field. You can get 7.5oz bucking magnets at Parts Express (www.partsexpress.com) for about $0.69 each. Look for their part number 249-325.

Which Unit To Buy?
Can't decide which of several pieces of equipment to buy? Why not first rent each one for a week or so? Renting equipment doesn't cost very much. That way you can learn first hand the strengths and weaknesses of the units, and whether or not they should have a permanent place in your studio.

Low-cost, Lightweight Portable Recording System
This book is mainly about recording audio in your own home studio; however, there may be occasion to record audio outside your house (e.g., at a concert or club, at a lecture, at an important meeting, etc.). Here is a great idea to capture a quality recording with a lightweight, highly portable recording system. The key to this system is to find a set of extremely small yet high quality microphones. SuperCircuits (www.supercircuits.com) sells the PA3 high gain mic/preamp combination. It consists of a tiny (and I mean *tiny*) condenser mic element with a built-in mic preamplifier. The mic/preamp combination outputs a line-level signal, so you can plug it directly into a recorder without further amplification. Audio output is via a 6' cable

with a RCA phono plug on the end. The tiny amp runs on 6 to 15 VDC with a current draw of 20 mA. The bandwidth of the mic/preamp is 20 Hz to 16 kHz. The whole mic/preamp weighs less than ½ ounce. The best part is the price— $12.95. You can buy two of these mic/preamp systems for stereo recording and mount them on a pair of glasses, in a hat, in the shoulders of your jacket, or any place covert recording is required. You can run them off of a wall wart if AC power is near, or if portability is required, wire a couple of 9VDC batteries in parallel and connect them to the preamps. For a recorder, you can use anything that has line-level inputs, such as a DAT recorder or cassette recorder. My favorite for this application would be a small MiniDisc recorder. You can buy a small MiniDisc recorder such as the Sharp MD-MS702 for less than $90 (try www.half.com). For a review of the small and compact Sharp MD-MS702 MiniDisc Recorder, go to http://members.tripod.com/aerohead25/702/702.html. Of course, you won't be able to get the same quality of recording with this setup as you would with a DAT recorder or a CD-R recorder and a pair of professional condenser microphones, but this system costs at least $1/10$ the price and is much more portable.

If you don't want the lossy compression associated with MiniDisc compression, and you have a sizable wallet, you can use a small portable DAT recorder, or one of the new portable CD-R/RW recorders from Marantz Professional or Superscope. The Marantz CDR300 looks and acts like a small portable tape recorder, but it records directly to CD-R or CD-RW media. It also has low-impedance, XLR-type microphone inputs, and provides 48V phantom power for condenser microphones. It is meant for tabletop use, however, and not for over-the-shoulder mobile recording. The price is about $850. The Supersope PSD300 is a portable desktop CD-R or CD-RW recorder and duplicator. It has dual CD drives (one for recording and the other for copying). It also has low-impedance, XLR-type microphone inputs, but does not provide 48V phantom power to them. The price for the PSD300 is about $1100.

Musician's Earplugs:

If you are a musician who plays in a loud band or if you go to many concerts where your ears get blown out on a regular basis, you definitely need to invest in a pair of musician's earplugs. These earplugs are a cut above the normal foam earplugs, because they have a tailored frequency response that cuts loud noises according to the way the ear normally hears sounds. For more on the way the ear perceives sound, see the Fletcher-Munson information in the "Nature of Sound" section of this book. A good place to get these earplugs is http://www.etymotic.com. The ER-20 earplugs will set you back about $10. The ER-20s will cut the perceived sound pressure level(SPL) evenly across the audible frequencies by an average of 20 dB. Etymotic also has earplugs that cut the SPL by 9 dB, 15 dB and 25 dB.

Recording Vinyl LPs:

Many people have asked me how they can record their LPs to cassette or CD-R if they have a turntable. The problem with a turntable is that its output can't be plugged directly into the line level input of any recorder. Most turntable cartridges put out a signal on the order of just a couple of milliVolts (mV). The turntable also can't just be plugged directly into the mic inputs on a mixer or recorder, even though they are setup to handle a signal with an amplitude of only a couple of mV. The reason is that when LP vinyl records are recorded, they have a special equalization curve (called the RIAA EQ curve) applied to the signal. The RIAA is the Record Industry Association of America. This special EQ curve is used to limit low frequencies and accentuate high frequencies when the disk is made to account for the limitations of the vinyl LP medium. Then when the LP disk is played back, the opposite EQ curve is applied to flatten the signal out again (i.e., accentuate the low frequencies and reduce the high frequencies). This special EQ resides in what is known as a phono preamplifier. You will need one of these to record LPs from a stereo turntable, but many new receivers and amps do not have a phono preamp built in. The most inexpensive standalone phone preamp I have seen is the MCM Electronics P/N 40-630 for $13.50. Call them at 800-543-4330 or go to www.mcmelectronics.com. Another low-cost phono preamp is the Rolls VP29 for about $55. You can find this one at several places, including www.bswusa.com.

Adding a MIDI Retrofit to a Synthesizer:

If you own an old analog synthesizer that you would like to have controlled by MIDI, you can buy a Synhouse Midijack for about $100 and install it yourself. Synhouse (www.synhouse.com, 702-284-5233) offers one model for volt-per-octave monophonic synthesizers and another model for hertz-per-octave models. Once installed, your synthesizer can then receive MIDI Note On data and Sustain Pedal commands. You need to be comfortable with a soldering iron to install this retrofit inside the synthesizer.

Non-slip Material for Desk-top Units:

In my studio, I use a non-slip liner material called Magic Cover Extra Grip made by the Kittrich Corporation in La Mirada, CA. This non-adhesive, rubbery material comes in a 12" x 5' roll, and is easy to cut with scissors. On top of my master keyboard controller, I have a RedSound DarkStar synthesizer, an Oberheim Strummer and Cyclone, and a Kawaii MM-16 MIDI Controller. To prevent these units from sliding around on top of the keyboard, I cut the grip material to the proper size and put it under each unit. I also use it under equipment that sits on my mixing desk. You can buy this non-slip liner material (or a similar product) at many supermarkets. They sell it for lining drawers or as an underlay for rugs, but it works great in the studio. Do not use this product on a lacquered or urethane finish, or damage to the finish may result.

Figuring Out Speaker Polarities:

If you are running your speaker wires over any distance, it is easy to become confused as to which is the positive conductor and which is the negative conductor. I always color code BOTH ends of the speaker wire with a black magic marker on the negative conductor and a red magic marker on the positive conductor BEFORE I ever install the cable. There is a theory that most electrical equipment runs on smoke. Rigorously observing proper polarities is just something you learn being an electrical engineer, because once you let the smoke out of your equipment, that is the end of the line for it. If the cable is dark so that a magic marker won't work, I either use a stick-on label with the polarity written on it, or I put a tie wrap on just the positive conductor. If the speaker cable has ribs on just one of the conductors, I always use the ribbed conductor for the positive signal. Pick a convention, and then don't ever deviate from that convention!

But what if the speaker cable is already installed, and it is not marked with proper polarity? Here is a good way to identify the correct polarity without having to trace the entire wire. Connect the speaker cable to the speaker at the far end of the cable. At the audio amplifier end, disconnect the speaker cables from the amp, take a 9 VDC battery and then simultaneously touch the positive battery terminal to one speaker cable conductor and the negative battery terminal to the other speaker cable conductor. Observe the speaker cone on the woofer. If it moves outwards from the speaker, then you have identified the positive and negative conductors correctly on the speaker cable. If the speaker cone moves inwards, then you have the cables reversed. Once you have identified the correct polarities, mark the cable this time!

Long Speaker Cables:

One inexpensive way to run long extension or external speaker cables is to buy a 50' or 100' industrial 3-wire power cord from a home improvement store, and then cannibalize the power cord. The thicker the gauge of wire in the power cord the better, but don't use less than 16 gauge. Cut off the power plug and the power receptacle, but leave a little bit of a service loop with them, in case you want to use them for something else later. Strip back the insulation from the three wires and tin them (i.e., heat each one with a soldering gun and apply a thin amount of solder to each bare wire end). Now, you have a waterproof, jacketed pair of speaker wires with a black common ground wire, all in the same cable.

Figure 39: Low-cost Phone Ringer/Signaler

Telephone Ringer/Signaler:
    It is always a bummer when the phone rings right when you are in the middle of recording audio with microphones in your home studio. After many such episodes, I finally wised up and bought a ringer that could be switched to a mode where it silently flashes a light. (See Figure 39.) Using this device, I could decide whether to stop the recording or not, rather than having the phone make the decision for me. I paid $4.95 for this phone ringer/signaler, but the online company that sold it has since gone out of business. There are many such devices available on-line, however. You can order one at <u>http://</u>

www.globalmart.com/page/tl 96512.htm for under $10, or use the Google search engine to search for "phone ringer flasher".

Battery-Backed RAM Memory:

Now that much equipment available to the home recording studio is microprocessor-based with battery-backed RAM memory, you need to be aware that these back-up batteries can eventually become discharged over time. Generally, these internal batteries are Lithium batteries that can last anywhere from 5 to 10 years. They are installed onto the processor board in the equipment to preserve any presets that the user has saved to memory. These batteries come in different physical shapes and sizes. The battery itself can be held in place in a battery holder, or it can be physically soldered right to the circuit board. For the latter case, here is a generic procedure that you can follow to remove and replace a battery from your digital equipment. I assume that if the Lithium battery has died, then so too has the warranty on that piece of equipment. If the warranty is still valid on the equipment, then you should take the unit to a recognized service center instead of performing this procedure yourself.

- Back-up anything you have in the unit's user memory that you want to save. After you remove the old battery, all user data saved to memory will be lost. Of course, if the battery is dead, you will not be able to save user data to memory anyway.
- Lay a towel down on a table, and then lay the unit facedown (or top down) on the towel. Make sure you are not breaking or bending any knobs and switches on the face or top panel of the unit. If the unit is a rack-mount module, you might instead be removing the top cover to gain access to the circuitry inside.
- Use an ESD wrist strap for this procedure or ground yourself appropriately.
- Remove the appropriate cover from the unit to gain access to the internal circuitry.
- Identify the processor printed circuit board (PCB) that contains the battery.

- You may need to remove any screws and cables from that PCB in order to get access to the battery.
- Locate the Lithium battery on the component side of the PCB. The battery looks like a coin with an orange (or some other colored) plastic edge, or it might look like a coin held into a plastic holder, or it can look like a small penlight battery. Make a note of the orientation and location of the + and – terminals on the battery.
- Unsolder the old battery if it is soldered directly to the PCB. The best way to do this is to use a solder-sucker tool. Heat the solder connection until the solder is liquid, and then suck the solder up into the solder-sucker tube. You can also use solder wick for this task. Be sure not to overheat the connection, which can lift the solder pads off the circuit board.
- Replace the old battery with a new battery of the same type (or one with equivalent specifications).
- Solder that new cell into the PCB. Observe the cell polarity markings.
  - o If you can't find a Lithium cell with PC mount solder terminals, you will need to buy a separate battery mounting bracket, solder that in, then install the Lithium cell into it. Make sure you find a mounting bracket that has solder pins that are the appropriate width apart. You may have to bend the leads on the battery-mounting bracket to get it to fit into the PCB holes.
- Plug any cables you removed back into the appropriate connectors on the PCB.
- Replace all PCB screws.
- Replace bottom (or top) cover and screws.
- Power-up the unit and test it.

This procedure should give you a good handle on how to replace the memory back-up battery in any piece of equipment. In the worst case, remove the battery and it's holder, solder in some wires where the battery was, and install your own battery (same voltage and amperage) elsewhere inside the equipment chassis. You can anchor the battery with pieces of Velcro.

How do I learn more about all this Studio Stuff?
If you really want to learn about audio, making music and home studios, then you need to get yourself an ongoing subscription to at least one of these industry magazines: *Keyboard, Electronic Musician* or *Recording*. These magazines continuously give how-to instruction for home studio owners, reviews of the latest equipment and various other features such as how to sell your music and get noticed by the record companies. *Keyboard* magazine (www.keyboardmag.com) is first and foremost geared to all things keyboard, but they also do an excellent job of covering everything else involved in making music and recording audio. There are other great targeted magazines if your instrument is guitar (www.guitarplayer.com), bass (www.bassplayer.com) or dums (www.moderndrummer.com). *Electronic Musician* magazine (www.emusician.com) and *Recording* magazine (www.recordingmag.com) are excellent cover-it-all magazines. I highly recommend them. Both are very well written, and I have subscribed to them (and *Keyboard*) for many years. In recent years, I have also acquired subscriptions to *Mix* (www.mixmag.com), *Pro Audio Review* (www.proaudioreview.com), and *Tape Op* (www.tapeop.com). *Tape Op* is *free*— what are you waiting for? Other great written sources of information are *EQ* magazine (www.eqmag.com), *Home Recording* (www.homerecordingmag.com), *Pro Sound News* (www.prosoundnews.com), *Computer Music* (www.computermusic.co.uk), and *Sound On Sound* (www.sospubs.co.uk).

There are tons of sites on the Internet that are repositories of all sorts of good information on recording and studios. To start locating these resources, just type things like "recording audio", "sound recording," or "sound advice" into the Google search engine. A couple of good sites to get you started are http://www.phys.tue.nl/people/etimmerman/RecordingFAQ.html, http://www.tapeop.com/, and http://www.shure.com/support/default.htm.

FADE TO SILENCE

Hopefully, you were able to glean some useful information from this book. I tried to impart a low-cost, DIY philosophy in this book, since that is the same philosophy I have used in assembling my own homw studio over the years.

I know you want to mainly focus on making music in your studio (everyone does!), but it really is in your best interest to take the time to do some homework and discovery on your own to learn as much as you can about recording, sound and audio concepts. Buying and reading this book was a good first step; however, the learning process should be open-ended. It should be a journey and not a destination.

Good luck in your musical endeavors, and happy mixing!

Index

Symbols

A

I

J

K

L

M

R

S

T

NOTES

NOTES